An Association of the U.S. Army Book

FROM

Omaha Beach
TO
Dawson's Ridge

FROM
Omaha Beach
TO
Dawson's Ridge

The Combat Journal of Captain Joe Dawson

EDITED BY
COLE C. KINGSEED

Naval Institute Press
Annapolis, Maryland

Naval Institute Press
291 Wood Road
Annapolis, MD 21402

Library of Congress Cataloging-in-Publication Data
Dawson, Joe, 1914–1998.
From Omaha Beach to Dawsons Ridge : the combat journal of Captain Joe
Dawson / edited by Cole C. Kingseed.
  p. cm.
Includes bibliographical references and index.
  ISBN 1-59114-439-6 (alk. paper)
1. Dawson, Joe, 1914–1998—Correspondence. 2. United States. Army. Infantry
Regiment, 16th. 3. World War, 1939–1945—Campaigns—Western Front. 4.
World War, 1939–1945—Campaigns—Africa, North. 5. World War, 1939–1945—
Personal narratives, American. 6. United States. Army—Officers—Correspon-
dence. I. Kingseed, Cole C. (Cole Christian), 194 –9 II. Title.
  D769.3116th .D39 2005
940.54'1273'092—dc22

                                                                    2005013475

Printed in the United States of America on acid-free paper ∞
12 11 10 09 08 07 06 05   9 8 7 6 5 4 3 2
First printing

To Those Who Served

Contents

Preface

On the fiftieth anniversary of D-Day, journalist Tom Brokaw described those who fought in World War II as "the greatest generation any society has ever produced." Historian Stephen E. Ambrose, whose books *D-Day: The Climactic Battle* and *Citizen Soldiers* have inspired the current generation to reflect on the achievements of their parents and grandparents, concurs.

In describing America's sons and daughters of the 1940s, Ambrose notes they were mostly high school and college students when the United States entered the war. Most didn't want to fight but did so because there was a job to be done and simply no one else to do it. They were drafted or enlisted voluntarily between 1941 and 1945. Beginning June 6, 1944, they entered France as liberators, not conquerors. From June 7 to V-E Day, they remained in constant combat against the German *Wehrmacht*. When the war ended in May 1945, they gladly exchanged their uniforms for civilian attire and returned home to rebuild their lives and world.

Essential to the Allied victory in Europe were America's citizen soldiers who comprised the combat divisions that fought on the front lines against the German war machine. By early 1944, the U.S. Army plan called for ninety combat divisions—sixty-seven infantry, two cavalry, sixteen armored, and five airborne. All engaged in combat in World War II, some longer than others. Of the infantry divisions, none had a more storied heritage than the 1st Infantry Division, the Big Red One. (Throughout this book, the 1st Infantry Division is variously referred to as the Big Red One, the Fighting First, and the First Division.)

First to fight in World War I, it was one of the first divisions to deploy to England in World War II and the first division to land in North Africa. Its regiments waded ashore in Sicily in 1943, and in June 1944, it cracked the Atlantic Wall on D-Day. The Fighting First left the flower of its youth on the rising tide of Omaha Beach, in the village of Colleville beyond the Omaha escarpment, and in the hedgerows of Normandy.

Always in the forefront of the First U. S. Army, the Big Red One ruthlessly pursued the *Wehrmacht* across the Seine, into Belgium and

Germany. At Aachen, two of its companies repelled vigorous enemy counterattacks for thirty-nine days on a hilltop now known as Dawson's Ridge, named after one of the company commanders who refused to withdraw in the face of overwhelming pressure. The end of the war found the First Division in the heartland of Germany along the Elbe. The price in casualties had been high: 4,325 of the approximately 50,000 men who served in its ranks during World War II died.

Commanding one of the companies in the forefront of the Big Red One's advance was a thirty-year-old captain from Waco, Texas, by the name of Joe Dawson. Few outside the First Division will recognize his name, but he was representative of the generation that fought World War II. Born immediately before the United States entered World War I, he completed high school and enrolled in Baylor University, graduating at the height of the Great Depression. He entered the army in March 1941 and soon found himself at Officer Candidate School at Fort Benning, Georgia, the "Home of the Infantry."

Assigned to the Fighting First upon commissioning, Dawson served on the regimental staff when the troops deployed to England in August 1942. Within one hundred days, he was in North Africa as part of Operation TORCH. When that campaign ended the subsequent May, he repeatedly requested command of an infantry company for the upcoming invasion of Sicily. Though he fought with the Big Red One throughout the Sicilian campaign, Dawson did not receive troop command until August, when he assumed command of G Company, 2nd Battalion, 16th Infantry Regiment. Except for a brief respite when he was wounded in action, he retained command until he was evacuated for wounds received outside Aachen in October 1944.

As a prelude to Operation OVERLORD, the invasion of Western Europe, the First Division deployed to England and prepared to lead the invasion of France. As it was the most tested combat division in the European Theater, Lieutenant General Omar Bradley selected it for the most difficult task, an amphibious assault along a four-mile stretch of sand called Omaha Beach. Above the shore was an escarpment rising nearly two hundred feet before it leveled off to a fertile plain, repeatedly cut by the Norman *bocage*. Dawson's company hit the beach at approximately 0700 hours on D-Day. In his own words, "Utter chaos reigned," but he quickly organized his troops and led the assault on the heights above the beach.

According to historian Ambrose, Dawson's G Company was one of the first, if not *the* first company-size element, to penetrate the German defenses in the Big Red One's zone of action. Wounded on the afternoon of D-Day, Dawson returned to his company and led it in the breakout and pursuit of the retreating enemy forces during the summer.

Early autumn found him defending a ridge outside Aachen, the traditional capital of Charlemagne's empire and the first major German city to be liberated by the Allies. For the next thirty-nine days, G Company held the hill and earned the Distinguished Unit Citation for extraordinary heroism under fire. Wounded a second time, Dawson recuperated in the United States before returning to France, where he worked in the Office of Strategic Services until the end of the war. Over the course of twenty-four months overseas, Dawson earned the Distinguished Service Cross, the Silver Star, the Bronze Star, the Purple Heart with cluster, and the Combat Infantryman Badge.

I confess I was unfamiliar with Joe Dawson until I read Stephen Ambrose's *D-Day*. As an army officer and infantryman myself, I was naturally inquisitive about leadership in combat. Dawson seemed to have the potential for a good case study. Since I began my own military career with the Big Red One, I wanted to know more about this particular commander. Was Dawson representative of American leadership in combat, or did he possess a unique command style that repeatedly produced victory? It did not make any difference to me whether he was the best company commander in the regiment or if the 16th Infantry Regiment was the best regiment in the First Division. That will always be subject to interpretation, and most veterans generally have some pretty strong feelings on that issue.

Still, Dawson obviously did something right, and I wanted to know how and why. It's striking that Dawson always seemed to be in the thick of action. This seemed true when I read Ambrose's *D-Day* and *Citizen Soldiers*, which confirmed that the most successful line commanders on D-Day were still leading soldiers several months later when the fighting neared the German frontier. Wars are won at the squad through company levels, and the key to victory has always been combat leadership at the lower echelons of command. I was sure this was the case with the 1st Infantry Division, and I was determined to examine Dawson's role.

By then, I had contacted Dawson and begun a lengthy correspondence. Would he come to the Military Academy and address my military history classes on the finer points of heroism under fire and leadership in combat? Regrettably, cancer had begun exacting its toll, and he was unable to make the journey, although he was excited at the opportunity to address the future officers of the U.S. Army. Finally, in

May 1998, I decided if Joe Dawson couldn't come to West Point, I was going to Corpus Christi, where he spent the majority of his adult life. Although he was in obvious pain, he spent the better portion of two days with me, answering my questions about why some leaders succeed while others fail.

What was the quality of the army's junior leadership? Was historian S. L. A. Marshall accurate when he wrote that only a small percentage of soldiers fired their weapons in combat? What was his toughest decision in combat? What about combat fatigue? When does it set in? As a commander, how do you cope with a soldier who breaks under the pressure of constant combat? As an officer, what was his breaking point? My questions seemed endless, but he took the time to respond. What surprised me most were his repeated references to a fear that he would not measure up to his personal standards and the expectations of his men. When I finally discovered his rather voluminous letters, that trepidation of whether he would "measure up" emerged as a constant theme.

In recent years, a veritable avalanche of monographs and manuscripts has depicted virtually every aspect of the World War II experience. In addition, every military bookshelf now contains an ever-increasing number of excellent war memoirs. Why another book on World War II? *Saving Private Ryan* aside, what has been missing is an account of the war from the ground up as viewed through the eyes of an infantry company commander.

Dawson was not just any company commander, but like Ulysses S. Grant, he matured as a combat leader in the greatest crucible of all: combat. He learned his trade as a staff officer in North Africa and Sicily, and then commanded soldiers on the bloodiest beach on D-Day. As a liaison officer in North Africa and Sicily, Dawson endured danger without responsibility for the lives of fellow soldiers. From D-Day onward, he encountered danger with responsibility for the lives of soldiers entrusted to his leadership. This change of responsibility found expression in his letters. By the time Dawson led his company into Germany, he had refined his craft to the point that he was able to hold the line against repeated counterattacks for six weeks of constant combat.

This edition of Dawson's letters, set against the backdrop of war in the European Theater, is my attempt to examine leadership in combat. As with most letters written during wartime by frontline soldiers, a word of caution is in order. At times, letters provide an incomplete picture of events. Combat veterans often hesitate to include those incidents that may cause pain to their families, and, intentionally or not, inflate their own special role in events. Dawson's correspondence, however, seems to paint a more accurate picture of the war from a small unit level. A religious man, he learned to work around censors and did not pull many punches. Moreover, personal modesty and his immense pride in his company's achievements led to a more disciplined approach that tended to diminish his own role in combat.

The net result is that Dawson's correspondence provides a more complete picture of a combat commander enduring the stress of combat. Despite the number of works currently in publication, I believe firmly that World War II was so vast in its scope, so encompassing in its magnitude, and so horrific in its casualties, that there is still a story to tell.

If Dawson was forgotten by all save a few dedicated historians and veterans of the 1st Infantry Division, his nation and his community have not forgotten him. A half a century to the day that he led his men in the successful assault on the bluffs above Omaha Beach, Joe Dawson returned to Normandy. Standing at the American cemetery located on the exact site where he first reached the crest, he introduced the president of the United States to a crowd of several thousand veterans who had traveled half a world away to commemorate the fiftieth anniversary of D-Day.

Then in September 1997, fifty-three years to the week when Dawson first entrenched his company on the ridge outside Aachen, Corpus Christi paid homage to its favorite son by dedicating the Joseph T. Dawson Elementary School in his honor. The twin ceremonies were a fitting conclusion to a career marked by selfless service and devotion to the United States of America. The letters that follow make it clear why his country and his community chose to honor him in this manner.

Acknowledgments

No author endeavors to write any book without substantial assistance from a number of sponsors and contributors. This book is no exception. First and foremost, I am grateful for the generous support of the Dawson family, particularly Roslyn R. Dawson, the independent executrix of the Joseph T. Dawson estate. Captain Dawson first introduced me to his daughter following my visit to Corpus Christi, Texas, in the summer of 1998. Roslyn supported the publication of these letters and encouraged me to tell her father's story. I spent a most enjoyable afternoon with Roslyn three months after her father's demise. She not only shared her family memories but also permitted me to examine the family archives, consisting of letters, newspaper accounts, photographs, and related memorabilia from Dawson's military and civic career.

Second only to the Dawson family were the sponsorship of the Department of History, U.S. Military Academy, and the archival support of the Robert R. McCormick Research Center, 1st Infantry Division Museum, at Cantigny, near Wheaton, Illinois. At West Point, Colonel Robert A. Doughty, chairman of the Department of History, permitted me to take a yearlong sabbatical from my duties as professor of history to complete this project. Without his sponsorship, I could never have undertaken such a monumental work.

In addition, Dr. Linda Frey and Dr. Fred Kagan offered numerous suggestions to improve the quality of the text. Cataloguing and Reference Librarian Elaine McConnell provided invaluable archival support in acquiring official records from the 1st Infantry Division and other resources through interlibrary loan. Mr. Rodney Ryan, an indefatigable researcher, also examined newspaper and journal accounts that focused on the Big Red One's activities in England in 1942 and the winter of 1943–44.

At Cantigny, Colonel John Votaw, USA (Ret.), the director of the 1st Infantry Division Museum, hosted me on several occasions and put his staff at my disposal. Votaw also placed Dawson's story in the proper context and read the preliminary draft of this manuscript. Archivists Eric Gillespie and Andrew Woods in particular were helpful in uncovering the records of the 16th Infantry Regiment and the 1st Infantry Division for the period in which Joe Dawson served. I would be negligent if I did not also include Colonel William T. Bowers, USA (Ret.), who offered numerous recommendations to improve the text.

Among the many contributors of this book, several merit special mention. Lieutenant General Harold "Hal" G. Moore, USA (Ret.), re-kindled my admiration for the American warrior in a series of lectures at West Point. A fellow infantryman, Moore demonstrated a certain coolness under fire in his own battalion's victory at the Ia Drang Valley during the Vietnam War. He personified the virtues and values that I found so frequently in Joe Dawson's own correspondence. My good friends Don Higginbotham, from the University of North Carolina, and Dennis Showalter, from Colorado College, read the initial draft of this book and provided immeasurable support and editorial revisions that greatly enhanced the text.

My eternal gratitude also goes to historian Stephen Ambrose, whose own works on World War II are the *sine qua non* for any author examining the GI's perspective of the European Theater of Operations. More than any historian, Ambrose taught me to let the characters speak for themselves, and this is what I have attempted to do by letting Dawson relate his own story. Finally, Martin Blumenson, author of numerous biographies of generals George S. Patton Jr. and Mark Clark, instilled a biographer's pride and objectivity in an aspiring author.

In my research, I also met three superlative company commanders: John Howard, who commanded the British airborne company that seized Pegasus Bridge in the first action of D-Day; Joe Dawson, one of the first American officers to penetrate the German defenses on the bluffs overlooking Omaha Beach; and Dick Winters, who commanded both an airborne company on D-Day and a battalion of the 101st Airborne Division's Screamin' Eagles after Bastogne. It is to these commanders, as representatives of the coalition that defeated the German *Wehrmacht* and the Imperial Japanese Army, that this book is also dedicated.

Last, but certainly not least, my heartfelt thanks to my children, who encouraged me to write and who supported me throughout this entire endeavor. They have always been my most vocal advocates and have constantly urged that I not be satisfied with letting the World War II generation pass from the scene without paying a personal tribute to that remarkable group of men and women. My son, John, has consistently expressed a silent pride in my association with the officers and men who fought the greatest war in history. Nor could I have completed the text without the consistent urging of my daughter, Maura, who insisted that I complete this book before I retire from military service. To both John and Maura, I owe an incalculable debt.

To those mentioned above, and to all others whom I may have unintentionally omitted, I express my gratitude and thanks. I alone am responsible for any errors that appear in this narrative.

A Note on Editorial Method

The wartime correspondence of Captain Joseph T. Dawson is large. In addition to Dawson's private papers, which alone consist of 154 letters, there are citations of awards and the official records of the 1st Infantry Division. Why so many letters from a frontline commander? How did he find time to correspond so frequently? Dawson himself provides the answer. From aboard the ship that would carry him to North Africa, Dawson asked his family to keep his letters because he intended his correspondence to serve as a diary that would refresh his memory of his wartime experiences.

There was a more important reason once he witnessed combat. While he was serving on the regimental staff in Sicily, he noted, "When at long last the night comes and with it a haunting stillness pervades this valley of death, I find it difficult to calm my nerves that have been stretched to the breaking point by the strain of combat." Finding himself uttering nonsensical and empty thoughts in a subconscious effort to assuage the torment of physical and mental exhaustion, he sought "solace in writing these words and unburdening the tight skein of jumbled feelings that enmesh my being."

Most of the Dawson collection consists of correspondence between Dawson and his family from the time he entered military service in March 1941 until the eve of V-E Day. These letters eventually found themselves in cardboard boxes stuffed in the attics of Dawson's parents and siblings. Fifty years after the war, Dawson donated copies of his correspondence to the 1st Infantry Division Museum at Cantigny in Wheaton, Illinois.

It was there that I came across Dawson's private papers and decided to edit his wartime correspondence. To reproduce all this material would require more pages than most readers would care to read. Many of Dawson's observations when he was off the front line are of little significance to those outside his immediate family. Surprisingly, there is little repetition because Dawson was an extremely erudite officer who prided himself on his prose. This book focuses on his wartime correspondence as a junior officer in the U.S. Army. Of particular interest is the period between August 1943 and October 1944, when Dawson commanded G Company, 16th Infantry Regiment, 1st Infantry Division.

The rigors of leading soldiers in combat placed incredible demands on Dawson, who frequently wondered if he would measure up to the task ahead. The letters also provide insight into Dawson's personality. Joe Dawson was a deeply religious man, the son of a Baptist preacher from Waco, Texas. As with many from his generation, he viewed World War II as a moral crusade against fascism. His letters include constant references to a better world emerging from the chaos of destruction. There is also a fundamental admiration for the American fighting man, the citizen-soldier who left the comfort of his home and family to battle the forces of tyranny.

I debated whether it was prudent to include all of the letters to his family. Prior to his deployment to England in the summer of 1942, Dawson repeatedly spoke of training schedules, daily soldierly skills, and letters from home. I included only portions of this correspondence to provide a flavor of the transformation of the American army from peace to war, and to put Dawson's military career into the framework of an infantry division preparing for overseas deployment. Once in England, Dawson spent the majority of his time conducting routine staff actions and touring the countryside.

Many of these letters read more like a travel journal than those of an officer preparing to engage in combat for the first time. Consequently, I omitted much of this correspondence. I was surprised to discover that Dawson remained an active correspondent even when he was in combat. The only period when he faltered was during the breakout from Normandy, when the pace of the Allied advance prohibited even the most devoted writer from practicing his craft.

The letters are reprinted here as written, even in respect to spelling because Dawson seldom committed even the smallest grammatical error. As I noted, he prided himself on his ability to communicate in writing. Deletions of sentences or parts of sentences are indicated in the usual way by ellipses. Borrowing a page from James and Patricia McPherson's *Lamson of the Gettysburg: The Civil War Letters of Lieutenant Roswell H. Lamson, U.S. Navy,* I omitted the salutations and valedictions in all of the letters. Dawson addressed many of his letters to "My dearest family," but letters that depicted the horrors of the battlefield were addressed to a specific sibling.

To provide thematic continuity between battles and campaigns, a short introduction and an excerpt from one of Dawson's letters follow the title of each chapter. Though the letters comprise the majority of the narrative, I placed the correspondence against the backdrop of war in the European Theater of Operations. I have also purposely avoided excessive editorial revisions and have limited the annotations to the minimum necessary to identify persons, events, and places that might be unfamiliar to the general reader.

In the final analysis, however, this is Dawson's story as told in his words. I hope that these letters will inform a future generation of young leaders and will be of interest to the current generation, which owes a tremendous debt to America's heroes and heroines of World War II.

Foreword

When Germany invaded Poland on September 1, 1939, igniting World War II, the United States Army ranked seventeenth in the world and consisted of a mere 130,000 men armed with woefully obsolete weapons and equipment. By the time the United States entered the war in December 1941, a citizen army was in the process of being raised and, by 1945, totaled more than 8 million men and women. Although most were conscripted, a great many enlisted, believing it was their patriotic duty to serve their country in its hour of need.

One such ordinary young man who followed his conscience was Joe Dawson, a Texan who dreamed of searching for oil, not going to war. Dawson gave up a promising career as a geologist and instead enlisted in the army. Slightly older than the average GI at age twenty-seven, Dawson was a natural-born leader who quickly developed into an outstanding soldier. The army recognized his potential and sent him to Fort Benning, Georgia, to Officer Candidate School. Eventually, he was assigned to one of the army's legendary fighting divisions, the First Infantry, also nicknamed the "Big Red One."

Writing in the *New York Times Book Review* in 1989, Yale historian Paul Kennedy noted that, historically, "Americans have an insatiable craving for heroes." World War II produced its share of unsung heroes who served their nation in extraordinary ways. One of General George S. Patton Jr.'s maxims was that "wars may be fought with weapons, but they are won by men." He had in mind leaders with the initiative and courage that won battles. Historians, journalists, and military professionals have written about leadership more than any other subject. Clausewitz and others have tried to define it. Schools of leadership have been created, dedicated to capturing the essence of a subject as elusive as the search for the Holy Grail.

Patton once mused about leadership, noting, "I have it, but I'll be damned if I can explain it." Joe Dawson had it. Dawson would have modestly spurned the label of heroic leader, but that is exactly what he was, in the most literal definition of the word. According to *The American Heritage Dictionary of the English Language*, a leader is "a person noted for feats of courage or nobility of purpose, especially one who has risked or sacrificed his or her life."

From Omaha Beach to Dawson's Ridge is Joe Dawson's account of World War II from the time he joined the Big Red One, through the battles in North Africa and Sicily, and from the beaches of Normandy on D-Day to war-torn Germany, where he witnessed the ultimate inhumanity of the Nazi death camps. Told in his own words through his poignant and insightful letters to his family written between 1941 and 1945, this book is a testament to the truism that "war lives up to all of its terrible implications."

Dawson also wrote unsparingly of his grief and anger at those who lacked his patriotism and moral stamina: the deserters, draft dodgers, war profiteers, and others whose motives were self-serving. "I have seen cowardice displayed that hurt my heart more deeply than a knife stab. . . . Seeing it expressed in men of America cuts at one's very life," he wrote in both sorrow and anger while in England before D-Day.

Dawson was more than just a good soldier. He represented a generation of young Americans called to the colors during World War II who did their duty. In his article "The American GI" (published in the May–June 2000 issue of *USAA* magazine), General Colin Powell has said of them: "They were America. They reflected our diverse origins. They were the embodiment of the American spirit of courage and dedication. They were truly a 'people's army,' going forth on a crusade to save democracy and freedom, to defeat tyrants, to save oppressed peoples. . . . They were the Private Ryans, and they stood firm in the thin red line."

However, *From Omaha Beach to Dawson's Ridge* is far more than merely the story of a World War II hero. It is the tale of an ordinary American thrust into the horror of combat as an officer responsible for the lives of his men, a leader whose faith in the Almighty and courage in the face of death was recognized fifty years later on the same beach in France where the men of his rifle company of the Big Red One landed and fought the bloody battle of Omaha Beach on June 6, 1944.

With nearly thirty years of experience as an army officer, military historian, and West Point professor, Colonel Cole Kingseed is uniquely qualified to edit and present the riveting story of one man's journey through the hell of war. Combining a historian's knowledge of World War II and of the infantry, Kingseed has done a great service, not only to the historiography of the most devastating event in all of human history but also of bringing Joe Dawson's story of courage, leadership, and humanity to reveal a rare human being.

Carlo D'Este
author of *Patton: A Genius for War*
and *Eisenhower: A Soldier's Life*

Prologue

Joseph Turner Dawson was a product of the Texas hill country. The son of a Baptist preacher from Waco, Texas, Dawson was born in Temple, Texas, on March 20, 1914, to Joseph Martin and Willie Turner Dawson. The Reverend Dawson enjoyed a regional reputation as a prominent church leader and served as pastor of the First Baptist Church in Waco. The third of five children in what his daughter later recalled "was a family of over-achievers," Joseph Turner Dawson enjoyed the normal amenities of life, typical of his generation. Brother Leighton, also known as "Shorty" or "L. B.," followed his oldest sibling, Alice. The two youngest Dawsons were Ralph Matthew and Donna. All of the children matured into outstanding citizens who were equally adept in business and civic circles.

Reared in a deeply rooted religious environment, Dawson was particularly fond of hunting and the arts. His father later remembered that the only thrashing his son ever received as a boy was for shooting a gun within the city limits. Dawson also possessed an extraordinary, inquisitive mind. His father recalled that they talked on virtually "every issue, political, economic, religious, social, as only a son was prone to talk, always with animation, sometimes with heat, but invariably with profit."

As a young man, Dawson attended Waco public schools, and like his father and grandfather before him, graduated from Baylor University in 1933. At college, the younger Dawson acquired a love of the arts, including poetry, opera, and music. One of his first discoveries came through the teaching of Professor A. J. Armstong, an incomparable Browning scholar, whom Dawson listed as the third most important influence in his life. While he attended the university, Dawson majored in business administration, "only because you couldn't get a degree in geology back then." His goal was to be a Texas oilman, and before too long, he earned a reputation as an excellent geologist. Naturally, he drifted into the oil business and soon found a job with Humble Oil Corporation in Houston and, in 1938, with Ren-War Oil Corporation of Corpus Christi, where he was working when he enlisted in the U.S. Army in May 1941.

As with many American army officers who served in World War II, Dawson never intended to enter military service. In fact, military life was the furthest thing from his mind. His first inkling that war was on the horizon came in 1935, when he was returning from Houston to Beaumont. Along with the Houston ship handlers, he noticed several large vessels being loaded with scrap iron. Inquiring from a friend about the ship's destination, he was informed they were sailing to Japan, where the iron would be converted into guns. Dawson replied, "Wouldn't it be ironic if we'd sent a Singer sewing machine to Japan only to be transformed into a bullet" that might be fired at an American on some distant battlefield?

Dawson recalled that by the spring of 1941, "it was pretty well determined" that the United States would be drawn into war. With the draft now in its second year, Dawson reasoned that sooner or later he would be called into service. Rather than wait for his summons, he enlisted in the U.S. Army in the hopes of using his collegiate education to apply for a commission in the air or ground service through the various Officer Candidate Schools (OCSs). Though the U.S. Navy and Marine Corps were frequently considered more glamorous, Dawson selected the army because it had more military bases closer to his native Texas. Moreover, service in the army allowed for a transfer to the U.S. Army Air Corps if he was so inclined.

In the twilight of his life, Dawson reminisced about the circumstances that led him to enlist in the army. "Uncontrolled hate, hatred, evil hate can reduce rational people to beasts," Dawson reflected. "Those who live in a free society must assume the responsibility of protecting those ideals that were sacred to an ordered peaceful life." Convinced that Hitler's advancing armies threatened the very principles of civilized behavior, "I enlisted because I *knew* my country and my freedom were in peril from a force bent on destroying us." Thus began the military odyssey of Joseph Dawson.

FROM
Omaha Beach
TO
Dawson's Ridge

1
Joining the Big Red One

*Here is the cradle of defense for our entire nation, and the men
gathered here are the cream of our entire country.*

When Joe Dawson entered military service on May 8, 1941, the
U.S. Army was in the throes of rapid expansion. With mobilization plans calling for a strength of 1.4 million men by the
end of June, the army had already grown to well over a half-million
men by the spring of 1941. The soldier who entered the army in 1940–
41 began his training with a mobilization training program (MTP) that
lasted approximately thirteen weeks. Training occurred in one of
twenty-one replacement training centers established for the express
purpose of liberating tactical units from the responsibility of conducting basic training so that they could concentrate on more advanced
unit tactical training.[1] Dawson underwent his basic training at nearby
Dodd Field, adjacent to Fort Sam Houston in San Antonio, Texas. He
was delighted that the proximity of "Fort Sam" enabled him to visit
family frequently.

Following the completion of a physical examination, the recruit
then reported for initial in-processing, drawing his uniform and equipment, undergoing a series of immunizations, and attending a number
of classes on personal and field hygiene. The army next administered
an "intelligence test" to assess the soldier's potential for military life.
Mobilization training itself consisted of several weeks of individual
training, involving physical conditioning, marksmanship, and an introduction to the rudiments of military courtesy and discipline.

Pay for a private in 1941 was a mere $21 a month, a far cry from
what Dawson had previously earned with Ren-War Oil. The first
phase of military training was immediately followed by a second
phase, which introduced the soldier to his service specialty and
taught him to function as an integral part of a team. Much to his
astonishment, Dawson was assigned to the Chemical Warfare Branch,
while the vast majority of the 250 inductees who arrived with him
were transferred to Camp Leonard Wood, Missouri, an engineer training center. His specific specialty was chemical equipment maintenance, not traditional chemical warfare. What bothered the 1933

Baylor graduate most was the fact that only seventeen of the original inductees remained with him, and these were men who had achieved the lowest scores on the intelligence test.

Dawson's initial weeks in "this man's army" were hardly exhilarating. Taken as a whole, his early letters reflect the problems experienced by the U. S. Army as it mobilized for war. Dawson had joined the army to do his part in what he anticipated would be a united war effort against Japan and Germany. Having no prior military experience, he discovered that the best way to obtain an officer's commission was to enlist and go through basic training. If his qualifications were good enough, he could then apply for an officer's candidacy through the various OCSs. In the interim, he was subjected to what he considered demeaning and meaningless tasks designed merely to occupy his time.

As was common with most recruits, Dawson was convinced that the officer and noncommissioned officer corps were hopelessly unprepared to provide the leadership essential for a modern military force. The training he experienced in his first month seemed to him more designed to produce an army of morons than to prepare men for battle against Hitler. Though a significant amount of planning went into the training centers, the problem lay in the execution of the plan.

Inadequately trained cadre, coupled with the large influx of draftees, created obstacles that only time and experience would solve. Despite Dawson's increasing frustration, one highlight occurred as he completed his fourth week of training. Because of his college education, he was promoted from private first class to corporal. In the process, he became the unit "poster boy" whom his leaders would drag before visiting officials who were inspecting the progress of America's expanding military force structure. Dawson expressed his bewilderment in several letters, in which he outlined his initial month in the U.S. Army and pondered how this army could ever survive in combat against a disciplined force.

Dawson to My Dearest Family

Undated[2]

Reviewing my first days of service in the nation's army, I find that little in the way of unusual events have transpired in my existence. However, I will briefly set out my experiences. Upon induction, I was sent from the induction station at Fort Sam Houston to the reception center at Dodd Field, which adjoins Ft. Sam. Here I underwent what is termed "processing." I was given my uniform which consists of two khaki shirts, one pair of pants, three pairs of socks, one brown tie, three suits of underwear, an overseas cap, a pair of high-top service shoes, blue denim dungarees, two sheets, one pillow case, a blanket and a duffel bag. Also, they generously bestowed one bath towel, two face towels, toothbrush, comb and razor. I was issued a pack, which has a knife, fork, spoon, canteen and mess kit. I also received a pair of leggings. Thusly accoutered, I'm following a routine that is supposed to develop me into a soldier.

I arrived here at Dodd Field Thursday, May 8. Friday, I was vaccinated and given my first typhoid shot. I was shown films on sex hygiene, personal hygiene and first aid. I was then lectured by the chaplain and given the army intelligence test and classified according to my qualifications. Saturday, we were given a brief drill on the drill field, and then were relieved from duty at noon. Sunday, I was on K.P. washing dishes that occupied nearly fourteen hours.[3] I never felt so grieved at having thus to break the Sabbath day. I can well understand why Moses made it the keystone of the Ten Commandments. I only wish Uncle Sam had a bit better Biblical knowledge.

Monday, I was given my first drill, which consisted of marching ten miles. It left me a trifle sore, but no ill effects. Mainly the entire week has been devoted to drilling and exercise, interspersed with lectures on military courtesy, care of equipment, the articles of war and the learning of General Orders which govern a soldier when serving on guard duty.

The entire group of 250 men inducted with me, with the exception of seventeen mental deficients [sic] and myself, were sent to Camp Leonard Wood in Missouri on the 16th. That left a rather motley crew, and I was rather cast down at the thought of being held back because of my low intelligence test. However, with the aid of my own private "fifth column," I learned that my grade was the highest of the group of 259 who were examined with me. Please, dear ones, do not feel inflated over this for it only speaks of the very poor types who I was inducted with!

So far from the general espionage that I have been working, I feel that I may be restrained here until word from Washington is received concerning my commission. I learned yesterday, although not positively, that I would probably be sent to Fort Sam next Tuesday for training in the Chemical Warfare branch of the service. What my duties will be are not known to me, but upon reaching there I will let you know.

Thus far, I have a frank observation to make. The United States Army will not last two minutes if we have to depend upon what I've seen thus far. Everyone works harder to keep out of work than lifting a feather's weight. All the N.C.O.s thus far whom I've met are a very low average mentally and are unwilling to cooperate with each other.[4] The officers seem to be extremely anxious to get out of anything that might in any way interfere with their personal pleasures. However, things may be different when I get to my permanent post. Well, we'll see what the outcome of next week is, and maybe I'll have a better report. In the meantime, just know that all of you are much in my thoughts and even deeper in my heart.

Dawson to Dearest Mother and Dad

Undated[5]

Well, here I am in Third Chemical Company Maintenance, Ft. Sam Houston, and after two days, I am still doing very little in the way of applying my finer senses and excellent aptitudes toward the preservation of our glorious freedom. We arrived here yesterday and have brand new barracks that have been scrubbed the past twenty-four hours, but they are still filthy. You well understand how I like that. I was on guard duty last night from 6:00 p.m. to 6:00 a.m. and after walking steadily the whole night through, I have been doing an excellent job of nothing except sleeping today.

Somehow I am very much afraid that this scheme of chemical warfare does not fit my plans, and I am at a loss as to just what might be the best way to tackle the problem. I cannot understand the strange silence in Washington regarding my application for a commission. I don't know how best to attempt to transfer. I had hopes of going straight to Kelly Field, but somehow that hasn't materialized.

The reason why I'm a bit dubious of this phase is that it is elementary in its entire concept. We have a full company consisting of a hundred and twelve men with three officers and six noncommissioned officers. This comprises a permanent company, and the entire year of service will have to be spent in just training unless I can get a transfer from it. The work, although not yet begun, will consist of repairing gas masks and trench mortars and other chemical warfare equipment. Can you imagine anything more interesting?

I was interviewed at length by the commanding officer who wonders as do I, why I'm in this group. So far, we have no answer to this. The reason for my feeling that I am far and a way above this entire group of men is that there is not one man who has had any college training and [the group] is composed of over 50 percent Mexicans. I have been given a rating as p.f.c., and could probably be a sergeant within a year, but of course, my sights are a lot higher than that, and also in something that my interest will be more suited.[6]

As you know, I've always preferred being over-matched than being under-matched. I like San Antonio, but I'm afraid that unless this proves more than it appears now, I'm going to be forced to apply to F.D.R. in person so I can get somewhere that I may be able to do work of an intelligent nature. So much for my gripe.

Dear Diary

June 6, 1941
3rd phase of the moon

On this the anniversary of my first month in a field of endeavor quite new to the heretofore disordered existence that claimed to be my life, I have come to certain conclusions and also given birth to several thoughts that have the earmarks of becoming major theorems. Thus far, these theorems are not unlike a surrealistic tantrum of a demented moron. With much time for contemplation and segregated from all phases of amusement a la 20th Century, I have achieved a state of introspection that may or may not change my complete outlook on the future. To elaborate:

The U.S. of America, so F.D.R. informs me, is in a state of "unlimited emergency." Hence certain steps have been taken on the part of forces superior to the individual, to cause a group of men—known as the army—to be the wards of the nation for a prescribed period. In this diverse group, I find that my own individualism has become subordinated to the wishes of the group. Folkways and mores of the entire entourage are therefore perforce imposed upon each one of the group. Thus the strongest becomes the weakest and vice versa.

Being thrown into intimate contact with over a hundred males whose illiteracy is appalling, I am fast becoming the

5

choice object for use as the guinea pig of 3rd Chemical Company Maintenance. When a stranger comes into close view of our number, I am automatically picked as the one to pose for the snapshots, and I know that these sociologists are doubtless gloating over their success to get the photo of the loon of the lunatics. But this is "the discipline will do you good" period.

Now don't misunderstand these disjointed elaborations. I'm only trying to say that Sherman was right in more ways than one. If all the army is like unto what I have experienced, I am truthful in saying that Lindy is *not* such a fool as one would think.[7] Think of it! Four weeks—one twelfth of the period of *training!* Training? All prior letters to the contrary, I have spent, I dare say three fourths of my entire time loading *dirt,* hauling dirt, spreading dirt and watering grass. Now you say—but Joe, it's a new army. So what? I have not spent the past *eleven* years preparing for the deeply complicated job of inserting a shovel beneath four inches of soil and by a coordination of muscles, lift the shovel filled with dirt and by this locomotion cause the dirt to be propelled from the place of beginning to a truck nearby.

But Joe, you are getting exercise. Yes, dear diary, I'm exercising; I eat heartily, my back aches, my arms ache, and I'm grateful for the privilege of getting exercise and being paid for it. Such an elevation is far from my choice of exercising! The whole point I'm making is that if I stood before Mt. Everest and said, 'Ole Mountain, I'm going to run over you in ten seconds,' it would appear that my statement would be a bit unreasonable.

On with the further elaboration: Suppose I find two men in my office; one a person who sees, speaks and hears and is above the so-called average, and the other says he can talk and hear, but cannot write. Would you give the man who cannot write a job as bookkeeper? Then the other job is picking up rocks in your front yard. Of course the bright boy gets that job and the dull dolt is the bookkeeper. Well, that's the army! . . .

After three weeks in the army, I'm determined to sit *here* and utter no sound as to transfer or anything else. I talked with our Commanding Officer today at *his* request. He asked me *why* I was in this group. I answered truthfully. I *don't know!* So what are my duties for the future? I'll tell you in a devious way in this next paragraph.

In the army. there are soldiers, non-commissioned officers, and officers. The Private is the *lowest*. Then the First-class
private, then Corporal, then Sergeant; these three are the *noncoms*. Then the officers: 2nd Lieutenant, . . . 1st Lieutenant,
Captain, Major, Lieutenant Colonel, Colonel, Brigadier General, Major General, Lieutenant General, and General. We have
one *General*—George Marshall. It takes thirty-five years and
West Point to be a general.[8] It takes something like intelligence to be any of the other officers. Then come the noncommissioned officers and privates.

For the first three weeks, I was a private, "dog face," "buck"
or what have you. As of June 2, I was commissioned corporal.
This is in title and duties only. My pay will not increase until
I have been in the service four months. I will then draw $54
per month. Until then it will be $21, less laundry, haircuts,
soap, etc. (Also $1.00 for Community Chest.)

My new duties are: Arise each morning at 5:45 a.m., breakfast, then get the menu for the next day and make up a ration
list for the entire company, go to the supply station, get the
beans, cabbage, carrots and sausage and return to the camp
with some, and then sit around with a very diligent air of concentration on my duties of—doing nothing!

So, dear diary, another chapter is written. Look forward
to Chapter 2, which will appear in the July 6th issue of "How to
Become a Moron in 12 Easy Lessons."

To a casual observer, Dawson's tirade against army life dominated by what he considered "chicken shit" and ineffective leaders
might be construed as nothing more than unjustified complaints from
a chronic grumbler. That was not the case.

Corporal Dawson was an educated man whose previous lifestyle
was oriented to successful business practices and leaders comfortable with making rapid, rational, and important decisions. Such junior leaders were virtually nonexistent in the army of 1941. With National Guard divisions mobilized and increasing numbers of draftees
arriving at hastily constructed and organized training facilities, resources were stretched to the maximum. Chaos resulted when the
inexperienced and untrained cadre was unable to instantly produce
efficient and productive organizations.

Army Chief of Staff George C. Marshall also recognized the leadership problems in the expandable army on the eve of World War II.

Many junior officers lacked confidence; senior officers lacked experience in handling large units; and many Regular and National Guard officers were average or unqualified for the positions they held. That many commissioned and noncommissioned officers were unfit for combat was well known to the War Department. Ground Forces Chief General Lesley McNair lamented, "We have verified the inevitable— that inadequately trained officers cannot train troops effectively."[9]

Nor was inadequate leadership the only problem that plagued the nation's ground forces. Prior to the 1941 maneuvers in which Dawson was destined to participate, an internal memorandum from General Headquarters (GHQ) to the army-level commanders identified the most frequent subjects of complaint: waste of training time through idleness or delay; poorly planned exercises; inadequately explained maneuvers; lack of confidence in officers and of respect for noncommissioned officers who were illiterate and unintelligent; lack of opportunity for promotion; and assignment to duty not in keeping with special civilian experience.[10]

These complaints were legitimate and received increased attention by the War Department and members of Congress. Marshall forwarded these criticisms to army commanders for serious consideration, noting that they often were written as constructive comments by educated and patriotic selectees.

For Dawson, the enlisted rank structure in the American army did not facilitate an environment in which he could reach his maximum potential, hence his quest to join the commissioned officer corps as rapidly as possible. Frustrated by his first two months in the field army, he briefly flirted with a U.S. Navy program in which former college graduates could obtain a discharge from the army and then enlist in the maritime service for schools whose program of instruction began on September 1. Following four months of intensive training, he would then receive a commission as an ensign, the equivalent of a 2nd lieutenant in the army.

The program initially attracted Dawson, but he decided to defer any decision until he heard from Washington concerning his application for Officers Candidate School. Until he heard officially from the army, "like our national government, I will assume the position of watchful waiting" with respect to his commission.

In the interim, he volunteered for field training to keep himself intellectually and physically occupied. Anything was better than his current responsibility of drawing and distributing rations. On July 30, he reported that for the first time in three months, he was participating in "real soldiering," involving daily hikes with full equipment in addition to the other tasks, such as instruction in the use of weapons and chemical warfare agents.

More strenuous activity tended to relieve his mental rebellion, and he welcomed notification that his unit had been alerted to go on extended field exercises beginning August 10. The exercises were part of the GHQ maneuvers designed by Major General Lesley J. McNair.[11] As outlined by a War Department General Directive, the objective of all training for the period July 1, 1941, through June 30, 1942, was the preparation of the army of the United States for overseas combat.

Left unsaid was the public relations aspect of the maneuvers. Congress having invested increasing funds to expand and mobilize the nation's ground forces, senior military and civilian leaders within the War Department desired to project an image of progress during the highly publicized field maneuvers in order to lobby for additional congressional funding and support. To that end, McNair established GHQ at Camp Polk, Louisiana, and served as the exercise director. A full team of exercise umpires, congressmen, and correspondents soon gathered at Camp Polk in mid-August, just as military units began to arrive.

For the U.S. Army, the GHQ maneuvers provided a splendid opportunity to conduct training on a large scale, unseen in the army's previous two decades. GHQ operated as the field headquarters for both opposing armies, providing intelligence and operational guidance to the senior commanders. Artificial constraints were kept at a minimum, though lack of financial and training resources produced some comical simulations. With no chemical munitions and little equipment in the inventory, the personnel in Dawson's chemical maintenance company had to serve as exercise controllers instead of having an actual tactical unit participate in the maneuvers. As with most field exercises, then and now, the Texas-Louisiana maneuvers produced moments of comic relief. Dawson wrote that many of his soldiers were reduced to sneaking up on units and tossing gas grenades or to simulating chemical shells. Following one episode, Corporal Dawson mused: "We will be chemical shells, thus can't be captured or even exist theoretically for we will be inanimate objects. Won't it be funny for me to run up to a general or a colonel and instead of saluting him, cackle gleefully and look him in the eye and say, 'Ha Ha! You can't catch me, because I'm not me; I'm a shell!' Doubtless, I'll be overpowered and sent to the nearest psychopathic ward for observation."

Dawson also later reported that GHQ decided that chemical simulations were not prudent because, "With the number of newspapers represented in the war and reporters 'about as thick as soldiers,' some reporter would wire a story about it to his paper in Possum Trot with headlines about the poor home town boy being gassed down in the swamps of Louisiana by his own kith and kin. Also didn't wish to run the hazard of giving Hitler and the 'boys' any ideas. So I guess we will drill a bit and hike a bit and get in the way a bit and in general do nothing."

Such unrealistic training practices only increased Dawson's conviction that he needed to become an officer and that the entire U.S. Army needed a quick kick in the backside and a group of first-class commanders who would "make a bunch of punks do something besides allow their men either nothing to do or some task so basic and simple that no one after the second time he has done it cares to waste his time [doing it again]."

As to his newly arrived platoon leader, he wrote that the men had fallen heir to another "pimply faced youngster fresh out of A&M today who had become one of our officers. I really do not wish to leave the impression that I have a superior attitude, but sometimes it becomes quite irksome to kow-tow to morons and hoity-toities [sic] who couldn't make a good supervisor for fourth grade school children." He concluded his letter by stating that this was the army of '41 with "JTD active participant." Other correspondence outlined his unit's participation in the autumn maneuvers.

Dawson to Dearest Mother and Dad

August 16, 1941
Camp Polk, Louisiana

Well, here I am in Louisiana! Our camp was already prepared, so we had nothing to do but move in. Aside from the mosquitoes and ticks, it was quite a pleasant location. . . . Camp Polk is situated about seven miles east of Leesville and approximately 80,000 men are here. Driving today from Lake Charles [to] here was really a most interesting matter. Innumerable camps dotted the way, and the magnitude of it all was the most impressive sight I have seen since my advent into military life. Doubtless, after several weeks of intensive war games, I shall have an altered conception of the situation. Even now, I am finding a lot more respect for the army. Maybe the whole thing will make sense after seeing action of some sort.

Dawson to Dearest Mother and Dad

September 7, 1941

All in all, it [field maneuvers] was interesting and really more enjoyable than anything we have done thus far in Louisiana. It assumes true realism when you are stealthily walking through dark
forests at night and come upon a machine-gun squad or an artillery setup and men all clothed in the raiment of war. Again too,
hearing the roar of tanks as they charge, the answering of the
seventy-five millimeter guns, the drone of the planes overhead,
and the boom of the big guns plus the rat-a-tat of the machine
guns.

Aside from the fact that it was simulated warfare and the bullets were blanks, everything else was just as it is in actual combat. . . . Although I do not intend to remain in [this] particular
company, I have had a good opportunity to witness a broader
view of all operations than it would have been possible had I been
in some actual combat unit.

From news accounts and editorials, I gather that the United
States will probably be drawn into the actual conflict sometime
next year. . . . As far as our army is concerned, it seems to me that
there is much yet to be done before we will be in any shape to
wage any war on such a force as the Germans.

There is one thing, however, that has come about since my
advent into Louisiana, and that is an increased understanding of
our army. I have been laboring [under the illusion] ever since my
induction that all the men should be men of high character and
noble bearing in mind, as well as intelligent and educated. Upon
close contact with some 200,000 of them, it seems that in order to
make a good soldier, all it takes is a strong constitution and a weak
mind. Moreover, this is true of 98 percent of the men in our army,
and therefore, I find that this sojourn has given me an opportunity
to realize how much alike this company I am in is to the others.

Of course, there are certain branches of the army that have a
higher [quality] personnel than ours, and to these branches I hope
to ultimately go, either the signal corps, the air corps, or the coast
artillery. I have found that these seem to possess the best groups
of men . . . [whereas in the] infantry, they are not particularly
concerned with the mental quotient of their men. . . .

I further learn that it will be in January before I am in any
position to qualify for an Officers' Training School, so I will start

out upon my return to San Antonio to see just what I can find out about all these above mentioned groups.

As with Dawson, the public perception of the army changed for the better as a result of the 1941 maneuvers season. All along, General Marshall had hoped that the maneuvers might provide an opportunity for observing the morale of the army, which by the summer of 1941 was causing anxiety to the public and becoming a serious problem to higher commands.

Initially, Marshall feared a public backlash against the army as a result of maneuver damage and financial expenditures. Coverage of the maneuvers, however, was uniformly positive.[12] The process weeded out substandard commanders and gave rise to the officers who would later dominate the war in Europe, men like Dwight D. Eisenhower, George S. Patton Jr., Omar Bradley, Terry de la Mesa Allen, Leonard T. Gerow, and William Simpson.

With the world already convulsed in conflict, the public accepted the field maneuvers as a political and military necessity. Within two months, the United States entered the war when the Imperial Japanese Navy attacked Pearl Harbor. President Franklin Roosevelt convened a special session of Congress the next day and requested a declaration of war. For Dawson, the unprovoked attack on the United States confirmed his belief that the forces of fascism and totalitarianism jeopardized the very existence of American liberty.

For Dawson, the conclusion of the maneuvers also brought welcome news—the War Department had finally approved his appointment for officer training. The school to which Dawson reported the final week in December was the brainchild of Army Chief of Staff Marshall, who conceived the project over the strenuous objections of his staff and the chiefs of the respective service branches.

Implementation of the infantry course became the responsibility of Brigadier General Courtney H. Hodges, the chief of infantry, whose headquarters was located at Fort Benning. When he passed his command colors to Brigadier General Omar N. Bradley in March 1941, the training concept took hold, and Fort Benning began filling the officer ranks of America's rapidly expanding army. With Marshall's unwavering support, Bradley developed a rigorous course designed to train junior officers recruited from the existing enlisted ranks or from the ranks of draftees with six months of basic training.[13] These OCSs concentrated on attracting elite draftees or volunteers and graduates from the nation's civilian universities.

The six men who accompanied Dawson to the traditional "Home of the Infantry" were fairly indicative of the initial classes of candidate students. The War Department delegated the authority to select men to attend OCSs to certain designated commanding generals who had been allotted quotas for several schools. No formal educational requirement was ever specified for OCS application, but many applicants possessed baccalaureate degrees. By far the most important requirement for selection was demonstrated leadership ability.[14]

Mostly in their late twenties, the men in Dawson's cohort came from a myriad of backgrounds. One candidate was a chemist, formerly with Proctor & Gamble, another a banker from Pittsburgh, a third a worker with International Harvester from New York. All were college men, from such prestigious universities as Cornell, Penn State, Notre Dame, Columbia, Chicago, and Ohio State. Dawson was excited that "all had at least heard of Baylor." Concurrently, he realized that his association with these men would prove a real test "for they all are really fine looking and intelligent, aggressive men who are here for the same purpose that I am." For the first time, he expressed reservations about whether or not he would measure up to the competition.

Dawson to My Dear Mother and Dad and Family

December 31, 1941
Fort Benning, Ga.

The old year of 1941 is now in its last hour here, and soon, the new year will enter our world with all the hopes and fears wrapped up in it. . . . I have found this to be a most challenging experience. The duties and requirements are greater than I've ever known before, and it assumes stern reality to us all when we face the issue frankly. Here is the cradle of defense for our entire nation and the men gathered here are the *cream* of our entire country. These men are neither political favorites nor privileged appointees, but men with intelligence, ability, initiative and moral and physical stamina. How in contrast is it to that which I have seen the past seven months! I truly suffer a slight case of buck fever, something I've never before experienced in civilian life, for here, the men are *all* leaders, and I feel humble in the realization of my many shortcomings. I only pray that I shall be able to measure up to them.

How unlike it is from the men I've seen in camp, who were my officers! Every man here is hand-picked and the prime requisite is *leadership.* This is stressed every moment, and indeed we are in a wonderful place to be indoctrinated with this phase of life for the officers and instructors are *peerless.* They are known throughout the entire world for their ability, and never have I seen such marvelous teachers. . . . They are inspiring, devoted to their duties, and with personalities that simply superimpose on those with whom they contact a sense or feeling of the tremendous responsibilities that are ours and a deep seated urge to merit them.

To make the point clearer, it can be said quite frankly that we sit in class for two hour stretches for a total of eight hours each day, and we come away filled with all sorts of pertinent information and still feel that it was all too short a time! There is a desire on the part of everyone to exert every effort in their power to make the most of these days.

Our commander told us today that they just received word from Washington to increase this school eighteen times or to prepare to handle 3,600 men per quarter, or a total of 14,400 men per year. The tremendous urgency will doubtless cut our time short, and it may be that we will not be here for the entire three months. . . . The seriousness of our nation's position cannot be too greatly stressed, and our whole lives must be dedicated to the responsibility of protecting our homes and our noble heritage. We must have courage to meet this, and I can tell you that nowhere on earth have I felt such an impelling sense of duty as I have the past week. I know that we all will meet the challenge with every ounce of strength, both moral and physical, at our command.

Dawson to Dearest Mother and Dad

January 3, 1942

The fall of Manila, though expected and accepted long before its surrender, definitely brought home the very serious point that we are in a pretty tough spot. This cold realization is not tending toward jitters or hysteria in our circles, but it is serving as a distinct sobering effect and is creating a deadly purposeful attitude on the part of all concerned.

The situation [has] evolved into one where our whole country will soon feel the impact of this because it is now fast approaching a point where the complete mobilization will take place in fact instead of theory. Indeed, the way things are taking place, I really anticipate the events of the next six months will bring forth such changes that the things we envision now are mere fancies. But I guess I am beginning to grow up somewhat, for in retrospect, I begin to see that the only way to live now is daily and hope the future will work itself out.

Dawson to Dearest Mother and Dad

January 11, 1942

Relaxing a bit from the rigorous past week, I find the day being well spent in being at ease. . . . The day is somewhat warmer as yesterday the cold spell hit its peak, dipping to 11 degrees with a biting wind accompanying it. This morning it was quite cold, but it has warmed up quite a bit this afternoon, so I hope that it won't be as disagreeable next week.

We are now sophomores as a new class started today, making a total of four in operation at this time. Now if I can manage to graduate, I shall feel quite up and coming. After interviewing several men who have already gained their commissions, I find that the best I can hope for is a rapid promotion. However, I guess I shall have to learn to walk before I start running.

The main difficulty experienced is the high cost of living and the low income.[15] Maybe I will be stationed in some remote spot where the cost won't be too high and manage to get along. You see the initial outlay for uniforms involves about $300, so from there on it will necessitate drastic steps to make ends meet on the $125 which is the stipend per month. But of course, I will wait for this hurdle before attempting to solve it.

Dawson to Dearest Mother and Dad

February 10, 1942

Monday morning our activities began. All day long was spent in instructing us in how to cut barbed wire entanglements, defend ourselves against the enemy. and how to fight as a squad. Then that night we were given the opportunity to witness and to participate ourselves in scouting and patrolling. This activity lasted 'til midnight and although heavy clothes were worn and much physical energy applied, I found it quite bitter cold.

Wearily, we arose the following morning at the regular time and spent that day in applying our knowledge to the map reading course and taking a written test on it. I found this to be very satisfactory and have no fear over the result. Then that night, we rode out a few miles from camp and were given directions from a given point and told to strike out and try to get to the destination which was called for. I'm sorry to relate that this little simple task became a very complex one due to an error in judgment on the part of the squad leader and instead of walking about three miles, we walked eleven and a half before we finally arrived. Needless to say, we covered every direction except the right one!

Quite wearily, we again reached our bunks at midnight only to arise Wednesday morning and spend the day in the further instruction on how to be an officer, etc. On Wednesday night, we formed into small units of six men each and spent the night scouting on a simulated battlefield. With guns firing, shells bursting, planes overhead and all the attendant disorder, we had a full-fledged maneuver. My group was successful in its mission of locating two enemy machine-guns and one rifle squad, and we technically disposed of them. Again we returned home at midnight.

Thursday, we had a full day in the field with the afternoon being spent in lectures and demonstration of the infantry company in combat. We were joined by a group of officers who comprise another officers training class here. The place was [also] full of colonels, lieutenant colonels, and an occasional lieutenant. There were three brigadier generals also there. All these officers are taking the same course we are. Upon completion of their work, they will go out to form new divisions in this ever-expanding army.[16]

Then Thursday night, we were taken afield with no equipment except our compasses and were given three compass readings and the distance to go on each reading. If I do say so, we did quite well on this venture and succeeded in getting to our destination before anyone else. . . . Friday was spent afield in the practical application of firing the rifle under combat conditions. It was a thoroughly disagreeable day due to the rain, cold and very high wind that reached tornadic [sic] proportions only a few miles from us and did considerable damage throughout the state. When we got to camp that night, we were quite busy all evening cleaning our rifles and equipment. Quite a tedious task!

OCS was the most demanding and difficult time in Dawson's life as he was "transformed from a free-thinking civilian into a member of the army of the United States." Reflecting fifty years after arriving at Fort Benning, he remembered the transformation "as some jump." Clearly, this was the U.S. Army he hoped to experience when he had enlisted the previous spring.

Training was exceptionally rigorous and oriented to producing combat leaders at the rifle platoon level. The OCS mission reflected the theory that every officer was qualified to be a combat leader. Thus the mission was defined accordingly: "To produce platoon commanders for units of the field forces."[17] The emphasis on orienteering, small unit tactics, communications, and artillery coordination were the bare essentials necessary to survive in a combat environment. The course's major contribution to his professional development, however, was the focus placed on decision making in a fast-moving tactical environment.

Dawson reasoned that OCS was patterned after the West Point program, "where 80 percent of the class passed and the remaining 20 percent automatically failed" if they didn't meet the standards. He wasn't too far off the mark. Graduation rates of enlisted personnel for Infantry OCS in January 1942 were 86.9 percent, and by July, the percentage declined to 84.6 percent. Six months later, the success rate was only 79.2 percent. The principal causes for failure were academic deficiency, specifically insufficient preparation and inadequate application, and general lack of leadership.[18]

Nor was graduation the only incentive for superior performance over the twelve weeks of instruction. The top 10 percent of the class also had a leg up on obtaining the best assignments upon commissioning. Dawson eventually fell into this category. Fully one-third of the previous graduating class remained at Fort Benning in the capacity of instructors because of the tremendous increase in the numbers enlisted in the U.S. Army since the War Department directed that OCS be increased at the rate of 39,400 officers per year. The remaining graduates would probably be assigned to Louisiana, Florida, and North Carolina for service in combat units.

Dawson hoped to return to Fort Sam Houston, where "rumor-mongers" had told him that a new division was forming. Overriding all his personal preferences, however, was the price of the war, where "death and destruction will exceed all comprehension." In his mind, the only way to survive was to envision the future by which "steadfastness of purpose and a hope" would produce a peace that would endure. He could not know his destiny, but felt that from the conflict would come "something that would induce future generations to adopt the fundamental concepts of Christianity and abide closer to them."

On a sadder personal note, he received word that his former girlfriend had decided to marry and not wait for him to return to Texas. He accepted the nuptial announcement philosophically, but then tempered his next missive with a reflective assessment of his past mistakes and a renewed commitment to excel in life.

Dawson to Dearest Mother and Dad

February 25, 1942

The day has been somewhat of a low one for me as I have reviewed events of the past and also the present with a consequent mental letdown. This perhaps can be attributed to several things, but I frankly admit that an item in the Corpus paper served to debilitate in a large measure my normal good frame of mind.

The announcement of her marriage brought to mind the bitter loneliness that has always remained, though there has been quite some time since the crisis occurred in our relations. Reviewing the situation, I find it has never ceased to be the greatest disappointment I've ever had, and I've tried to analyze the matter to somehow find a reason for it, but I can't. It is too deep a hurt to dismiss lightly for it occasions too many past events that left lasting marks, but I feel that it will never again return to bother me so greatly. It will doubtless prove to be the best in the long road ahead.

Seems funny that the one thing I've wanted more than anything else was denied. I've had in measure everything else that any person could have. I've had money, yet when I found it was impossible to have Crystal, too, I lost it through gross mismanagement. I've had independence, love from everyone I've ever known well, only to somehow end up in the army with a totally new identity, but this time, I have the future to build, and am backed by the dearest and most devoted family a boy ever had. There will probably be many times in the future when I will fail to measure up, but I am determined to somehow make this redeem in part that many portions of the years that were misspent!

Dawson to Dearest Mother and Dad

March 18, 1942

Well, the school is rapidly nearing an end and indeed it is none too soon as the past few days have begun to drag pretty badly. The material has not been very interesting, and the weather has been quite inclement. Too there has been no word concerning our fates [as of] yet, which has created a very bad nervous tension in all of us. Each day we have thought would bring the matter to a head, but it is being constantly put off. Of course, the time is now so short that a few more days won't mean too much added strain, but everyone will feel much better when a decision is announced.

Incidentally, the transfer of MacArthur to Australia will doubtless mean that we are going to make some sort of stand there. If Japan hasn't stretched her lines of supply and communication too far, I am afraid our stand there will prove quite courageous, but futile. We are all hoping that he can again perform a miracle and so delay them that we can muster an army that will be able to defeat them. However, it is frankly a dreary picture. How the thing will develop is beyond any conjecture on my part, but I believe our only chance is to delay the Japs long enough to *rebuild* our Navy and send enough troops to really do some good.

Joe Dawson graduated from OCS on March 28, 1942, and accepted a commission as 2nd lieutenant in the infantry. The graduation was somewhat bittersweet because 10 percent of the class failed to succeed; they returned to the enlisted ranks of the field army, much as he had predicted the previous month.

The rumors concerning future assignments proved prophetic. Fort Benning grabbed the majority of the graduating class, with the remnants being distributed across the country. Because of his ranking in the top 10 percent, several school committees were only too eager to obtain Dawson's services, but he had had enough of classes and requested a combat unit.

Although an officer's personal preferences have rarely interfered with his assignment, the War Department made an exception in Dawson's case. Other lieutenants were available to fill Fort Benning's allocations. Second Lieutenant Dawson requested and received assignment to the 1st Infantry Division, the fabled Big Red One of World War I fame.[19] The alternative postings were two training commands, one located in Arkansas, the other in Alabama.

Only the 1st Division promised the immediate prospect of combat, and Dawson sought combat as the natural evolution of his training, as well as the fulfillment of his destiny. Again, he pondered if he would measure up as a platoon leader, but understood that "the cold reality of this war" meant that it would take years before the United States "could effectively defeat its foe." He also ribbed his father that he would never go through the OCS experience again, and if he were born again, he wanted the Reverend Dawson to send him to Texas A&M, where a young man could obtain a commission "without working for it."[20]

Dawson to My Dearest Family

March 22, 1942

All of you are perhaps interested in the prospective outlook of your representative "in the uniform" and herewith I report all current facts. The past few days have been a bit hectic due to the fact that events of far reaching significance have taken place here at Fort Benning. This weekend has been quite eventful for it not only disclosed the outcome of all the members of Officers Candidate Class No. 6, but also gave those who are practically assured of graduation their assignments.

Friday, noon, the big purge was effected wherein some twenty-four men were summarily told that they would not qualify and thus would return to some other duty. Then yesterday, we who remained were given our assignments and also told that we would not get *any* furlough at all. The growing intensity of the war is such that it seems the army is utilizing every minute, so the pleasant days of relaxation are not to be enjoyed.

The class has been assigned to four different places. Fort Benning received priority over everything else as the demand for instructors for the ever-increasing enrollment here requires a greatly enlarged staff. I was interviewed earlier in the week by one of the committees, but I plainly expressed my feelings regarding staying here in this capacity. So Wednesday night, the class was given preference of three camps in accordance with their age, efficiency rating and scholastic standing. This was further limited by allowing only the men with the necessary qualifications between the ages of twenty-six and thirty to choose Camp Blanding, Florida. I was fortunate to have this opportunity and chose it of the three.

The other two were Fort McClellan at Anniston, Ala., and Camp Robinson, near Little Rock, Ark. These latter two are training centers wherein all the men will be rare rookies and who will receive thirteen weeks of training then sent to some combat post. This will doubtless be the case with Camp Blanding insofar as combat is concerned, as it is composed of the 1st Division, which is regarded as the crack outfit in our army. Time will only tell, however.

The coming week will be a rounding out of the lesser items of our instruction, and Friday at 11:00 a.m., the graduation exercises will take place. Tomorrow, we have our physical examinations. I received my uniform yesterday and I'll go to town tomorrow to have a few alterations made after I finish with the physical.

Dawson to Dear Dad

Saturday, March 28, 1942

After three months of combined torture and trials, I find that instead of wearing my rank on my sleeves, I now have bars on my shoulders. Of course, this is a sign of some progress in my military career and though it is still the bottom of the ladder, it nevertheless opens the way to the sky of flying eagles and silver stars that signify the upper reaches of the military scale of rank.

All in all it has been quite an experience, this OCS, and one that I will long remember. If I had it to go through again, I don't know just what my decision would be for it cannot fully be expressed in words the rigors that one is subjected to, and I can well assure you that I earned these bars the hard way. Next time I get born into this world, I expect you to see to it that I am sent to Texas A&M where one can get his commission without working for it!

The graduation exercises were brief but to the point. A battle-scarred colonel who holds more medals than MacArthur delivered the address. Terse, crisp and thoroughly military, he conveyed to us the tremendous task that confronts us, and the necessity of every man dedicating his everything to the ends of victory. This was no oratorical high-flown bit of verbal expression, but a simple-worded, straight from the shoulder command. I only pray that I will be able to carry out the missions that will bring about success and victory.

It is well to keep in our minds the cold reality of this war and to understand that the struggle has only begun and it will require years before we can effectively defeat the foe. It will require constant reinforcement of courage and will on the part of everyone as these will be our sole elements for a while. Only when we have the weapons can we finish the job, and these will come only after months of manufacture . . .

I left Fort Benning yesterday afternoon in company with three other fellows and drove here arriving around midnight. We will go on to Blanding in a little while and report for duty this afternoon. There will be no leaves granted, so it will be impossible to go anywhere for a brief vacation. Due to this, we have to report within twenty-four hours, so we will be assuming our new duties without any delay.

Now a full-fledged second lieutenant, Dawson reported to Camp Blanding, Florida, where the 1st Infantry Division had just concluded a rigorous training program. As the War Department was fairly convinced that the initial action by the American army would begin with an amphibious operation, it had directed the 1st Infantry Division to report to Cape Henry, Virginia, for amphibious training in January 1942. There, the Big Red One concentrated on delivering the landing craft to the correct landing beaches, improving air and naval gunfire support, and emphasizing the necessity of employing tanks in the leading waves of the assault, since their firepower and shock action would provide "immeasurable assistance" in securing the beach.[21]

Also at Camp Blanding was Major General Terry de la Mesa Allen, commanding general of the 36th Infantry Division, whom General Marshall would shortly reward with command of the 1st Infantry Division in May. Reporting on March 28, Dawson regretted that he did not have time for a family reunion in Texas, but the exigencies of the situation dictated that the Big Red One be filled to its full complement of officers in view of its probable overseas deployment by late summer. His first day in a combat division was uneventful, and he took what free time he had to tour nearby Saint Augustine and Jacksonville. The next day, he was assigned to A (for able) Company, 1st Battalion, 16th Infantry Regiment, but the unit was in the field, and he assumed the duties of range officer. In that capacity, he noted his primary responsibility "was to ensure no one was killed."

The following day, Lieutenant Dawson also met his company commander, who was a "fair-haired boy from Cornell and seemed to be a *bit* hard to know." Assigned the 1st Platoon, he took over his duties the latter part of the week, when the platoon returned from range firing. For the 1st Infantry Division, extensive field training exercises consumed all available time as the command prepared for deployment to England.

April was spent almost entirely in the field; Dawson practiced his craft and applied the troop leading principles that had been drilled into his head at Fort Benning. The company returned to their barracks the last week in April and prepared to receive Army Chief of Staff Marshall, who was inspecting a number of division-level commands. The next day, Dawson wrote his first letter in a month since joining the Big Red One.

Dawson to Dearest Family

May 1, 1942

Tomorrow is a truly eventful day here for General Marshall arrived yesterday, and we are honoring him with a division review. How I wish you could be on hand to witness the occasion. Last weekend, we had a regimental review, and believe me, it was a sight to see. You cannot know how stirring such a sight can be until you see this division on parade. They are superb! No wonder they are called the finest, for it matters not whether they are on parade or in the field, they function letter perfect. It truly affords one a sense of security knowing they are behind you! I can say truthfully that this division will never fail in any task [to which] it is ever committed.

Watch the newsreels there and contact the theater manager for possible newsreels of the parade. I'm sure they will be here to record the event, and perhaps I might be identified as I will be in the front of the 1st Battalion that will be the leading element of the 16th Infantry. So I may be identified if you look close.

Training intensified as the troops polished specialized training, principally close support artillery fire and air-ground support. Late spring also witnessed the first joint air-ground exercises ever held by the United States Army at various locations, including Camp Jackson, South Carolina, and Fort Benning. There, joint maneuvers were conducted under the eyes of Marshall, Winston Churchill, and an entourage of British officers, including Sir John Dill.[22]

Dawson vividly remembered the exercise because they "used live ammunition, firing overhead, giving [him his] first real experience of what might be expected in war." At the same time, the Big Red One received a new commanding general. Terry de la Mesa Allen was born an army brat at Fort Douglas, Utah, on April 1, 1889. He matriculated to West Point in 1907, but departed two years later with an undistinguished academic record. He entered Catholic University of America the next year, graduated with a B.A. degree, won a competitive army examination, and was commissioned a 2nd lieutenant on November 30, 1912. He saw service on the Mexican border and deployed to France in 1918. Now a temporary major, he earned the Silver Star "for distinguished and exceptional gallantry."

During the interwar period, Allen befriended fellow cavalryman George Patton and graduated in the same Leavenworth class as Major Dwight D. Eisenhower. Eisenhower graduated first, Allen 221st of 241 members. Promoted by Marshall from lieutenant colonel to brigadier general over nine hundred men on the promotion list, Allen earned his first star in 1940, the first member of his former West Point class to reach star rank. At Marshall's urging, Congress promoted Allen to major general effective June 19, 1942, one month after Allen assumed command of the 1st Infantry Division

Simultaneously, the War Department directed the 1st Infantry Division to move to Indiantown Gap, outside Hershey, Pennsylvania, in anticipation of overseas deployment. In the words of their commanding general, the command had made "remarkable strides in discipline, in rifle marksmanship, in the use of infantry weapons, and in the teamwork and combat firing of all infantry and artillery units."

Thanking the army chief for "the very fair allotment of ammunition and other training facilities" that he had received, commanding general Allen assured Marshall that the 1st Division was in excellent shape and ready for combat. Though the men seemed very young, Allen believed that "they are fit and hard and ready to go, and I sincerely trust that the 1st Division will live up to your expectations."[23] Dawson also praised the command for its combat readiness as he summarized his current activities in two letters to his family.

Dawson to My Dear Family

June 5, 1942
Georgia

As I have stated in the past, the rumors in an army camp defy comparison, hence the news is sometimes slow in being verified. Tonight, however, we learned our next destination and as this is definite, we at least are that far along in knowing where we are to be. Our orders call for Indiantown Gap, Penn., which is near Harrisburg, I believe. This will be our address and "permanent change of address" as it is facetiously called. How long we remain there or where we go from there is of course a guarded secret. I am only confident, however, that we will be in the middle of things ere long.

Dawson to My Dearest Dad

July 5, 1942

As it is impossible to know what the next day will bring forth, I am taking this opportunity to write tonight as I fear I may not have another chance to do so ere I depart. You will understand I am sure if you do not have any further word from me. . . .

There is little that can be said in the way of what I shall be doing these next few months for I know not. All I can say, however, is that I shall be putting forth every effort to fulfill the tasks at hand. The serious state of world affairs cannot be overemphasized, and we are all too prone to look at it from a distance rather than fully realizing its absolute inclusiveness of our own personalities. The wheres and whys of the past no longer merit our attention, for it demands our full thought and energy to thwarting the forces that are now more than threatening our existence. The strategy and the plans of the high command are beginning to be expressed, and it is incumbent that we discharge our duties to the very best of our ability.

Just know, dear father, that I shall try and justify the faith and confidence entrusted in me. I know you are constantly intervening in my behalf with Him and will do my utmost to bring it to pass. I cannot, nor will not, dwell on the physical side of the picture, for one finds little to comfort those who are dear by describing such a picture. But know that it is the supreme test of one's character and moral fortitude and I pray that I shall have the strength to meet it.

I cannot speak too highly of this division, Dad, for it is truly an excellent fighting unit. It has had perhaps more training than nearly any unit in the country and is in fine shape. We are being refitted so that when the time comes, we will be in good shape to deliver the goods. I have not yet met our commanding general, Major General Terry de la Mesa Allen, but I understand from Mother that he is a Texan . . . and a close friend of Arthur Mitchell, there in Waco.

FROM OMAHA BEACH TO DAWSON'S RIDGE

Since arriving here, the regiment has undergone a drastic shakeup, and the officers have been shifted around a great deal in order to effect a more strongly knit organization. As a result of this, I now find myself with Headquarters Company in the capacity of Reconnaissance Officer and Assistant S-2 or Intelligence Officer. This is somewhat of a promotion and a step toward the higher status.

As yet, I have not received confirmation of my promotion, but I have been assured that it is forthcoming having been okayed from regiment, as well as division. This is tantamount to assurance, but it goes to Washington, where it takes a bit of time to go through the War Department. I am hoping that it arrives this week, but should it not, I won't feel badly as I am assured of it as soon as we embark.

This about brings things down to date as to events and happenings here. . . . I urge you to make no reference to my departure to anyone and to keep all activity of mine to a minimum of informed persons. This, of course, you will understand.

Should I not get another chance to write for a while, Dad, just remember that a heart full of tenderest love is going with me and its strength is found in you.

The arrival of General Allen and Brigadier General Theodore Roosevelt Jr.[24] began what became known as the "Terry-Teddy" era of the 1st Infantry Division. Both officers had served in the Big Red One with distinction in World War I, and their assignment by General Marshall was not happenstance.

Allen in particular was a favorite of the army chief of staff, who admired his swashbuckling style and his fondness for battle. While at Benning, Allen had produced a paper on weapons instruction that then-Lieutenant Colonel Marshall liked, and from that day forward, Allen's name entered Marshall's famed black book of officers destined for higher command in the event of war. So impressed was Marshall at Allen's performance that he rated him excellent in nine of ten categories on his 1932 efficiency report, the sole satisfactory remark being in the category of "dignity of demeanor."[25] Though Marshall abhorred Allen's profanity and habit of consuming alcohol in the daytime, he entrusted him with command of the infantry division nearest to his own heart, as Marshall himself had served with the Big Red One when it deployed to France in 1917.

As for Roosevelt, Marshall admired the 1st Division's assistant commander as an "A-No. 1 fighting man with rare courage and what is rarer, unlimited fortitude."[26] Nevertheless, Marshall feared that two officers so much of the same type might not get along too well, or in his words, Roosevelt probably might "get in Allen's hair." Still, the army chief was willing to take a chance on both officers and repeatedly sided with Allen when "certain allegations" by the inspector general's office at Headquarters of the Army Ground Forces indicated that improprieties involving the relief of a regimental commander in Allen's division reached Marshall's office in mid-July.

At the same time, Marshall warned Allen not to bother him with the internal operation of the division, nor to take the inspector general's report personally, since such a course "would about disqualify you for continuing your command."[27] Needless to say, Allen heeded his chief's advice.

Within the 1st Division, however, both Allen and Roosevelt quickly imprinted their personalities upon their command. As both were charismatic and flamboyant, they possessed a leadership style certain to endear themselves to their subordinates and personal staff. In the impression of the division chief of staff, Allen and Roosevelt "got along" with each other with sufficient harmony, mutual confidence, respect, dependence, and loyalty. Both also made a favorable impression on, and a sizable contribution to, the overall prestige of the 1st Infantry Division.[28]

Dawson, in particular, admired both officers, and the feeling was reciprocated. In the "shake-up" Dawson described, he was elevated to serve on 1st Division staff, which brought him into daily contact with the commanding general. This window of opportunity opened as a result of a training exercise within Dawson's first weeks in command of a rifle platoon.

Shortly after joining the division, he noticed that the field manuals did not cover the subject of sniping. A proficient squirrel hunter as a boy, Dawson realized that the secret of success was camouflage. Subsequently, he wrote a short article on the subject that stressed the imperative of snipers blending into the background of nature in order to become effective. The article drew the attention of the Division G-3, which immediately requested Dawson's services on his staff as a training officer.[29] He remained on division staff until he rejoined the 16th Regiment at the conclusion of the campaign in Sicily.

The two months that the 1st Division was stationed at Indiantown Gap passed quickly. Dawson took a short leave when his mother visited, but warned his family that any future leave will "be for such time as will be available in accordance with the urgency of the situation."

Nor would he have time for leisurely activities, and the Dawson family would have to be content with Joe's promise that on arrival "at my destination, I shall exert all means to send word to you as to my state of being."

By June 23 the division had completed its movement to Indiantown Gap Military Reservation, and on that date the commanding general of the New York Port of Embarkation assumed command of the division for the purpose of preparing the Big Red One for embarkation. In the meantime, the War Department's Adjutant General's Office established the 1st Infantry Division's strength at 16,224 officers and men.[30]

Activities after the 1st Division arrived in the Staging Area included preparation and delivery of unit rosters, emergency addressee cards, individual and unit reports of change, and service records updating. The Big Red One's advance detachments sailed on July 1 from Pier 90, North River, aboard the *Malojoa* and the *Duchess of Bedford*.

Preparations for deployment were completed in late July as the 1st Division, spearheaded by the 16th Infantry Regiment, proceeded to New York and boarded the *Queen Mary*.[31] With Dawson and the entire regiment aboard ship, the *Queen Mary* silently slipped out of New York Harbor on the evening of August 1–2 without convoy and set sail for Scotland, where trains awaited the command to take them to their temporary home in England.[32] On July 31, the eve of his own deployment, Dawson telegraphed his parents.

Western Union Telegram—Dawson to Dr. and Mrs. J. M. Dawson

The road may be long and the traveling hard, but within my heart is the strength gained through faith ever [to] carry on. May God keep you one and all and know that your son has drawn his strength and courage from the most precious father and mother in all the world. I have a date with destiny, and some day, we will be rejoined in glorious peace. My heart [is] full of tenderest love.

Joe Dawson was going to war. He would not return home for another two years, but in the interim, he would carve his name in the history of the 1st Infantry Division and of his country.

2

Overseas

Do not worry about me. . . . Someday this mess that keeps us apart will end, and then what a glorious time will be had!

Unlike its history in World War I, the Big Red One was not the first division to deploy overseas. That honor belonged to the 34th Division, which had arrived in Northern Ireland in January 1942. The 1st Armored Division joined the 34th Division in June, followed by the Fighting First in August. Still, the Big Red One could proudly claim to be the best-trained and best-led division in the U.S. Army, partly because it contained a higher percentage of Regular Army officers at all levels, low personnel turnover, and disciplined training as it prepared for combat.[1]

Whereas on the eve of the Normandy invasion 2,876,439 Allied officers and men were assigned to the Allied Expeditionary Force in land, sea, and air forces, the United States had only just begun the vast process of mobilization in the summer of 1942.[2] Although some headquarters were being established, on the whole, an American GI on pass in London was not a common occurrence as late as July. The arrival of the Big Red One on the outskirts of London changed that situation as the advanced party settled in at Tidworth Barracks, a British army cavalry post located near Salisbury, approximately fifty miles southwest of London.

On August 7, the *Queen Mary* docked at Glasgow in the Lanarkshire of Scotland, where General Terry de la Mesa Allen immediately established 1st Division Headquarters. Two days later, the Big Red One, with Lieutenant Joe Dawson "in tow," boarded trucks and trains and traveled to Tidworth Barracks, the division's new home for the next three months.

The proximity to the British capital facilitated coordination with Eisenhower's headquarters, as well as with an increasing number of American units arriving in England.[3] Over the next several weeks, the 1st Division established its base camp, conducted field marches, and began a rigorous training program aimed at preparing the command for the invasion of Europe. As assistant G-3 on Allen's staff, Dawson's duties at HQ were such "that I get a big picture of things that would ordinarily be impossible to see. It's great, and I enjoy it immensely."

Unbeknownst to all but the senior members of Eisenhower's command, the target was not to be Europe, but the northwest coast of Africa. On July 25, President Franklin Roosevelt approved the execution of Operation TORCH, and the next day, General George C. Marshall informed Eisenhower that he would command the operation. As the plan evolved over the following month, Ike tentatively assigned the task of capturing Oran to the 1st Division, less one regimental combat team, with certain British reinforcements. The remaining combat team would participate with the 34th Division in an assault on Algiers.

As Ike informed Marshall, the capture of Oran was vital to the development of air strength along the Mediterranean coast, as well as important in providing badly needed additional port facilities.[4] Allen received his preliminary instructions on September 4 and immediately devised a training plan to support the Oran landings. In addition, he established an advance command post at Norfolk House, London, to plan the operation in conjunction with the Royal Navy, II Corps, and Allied Force Headquarters.[5] Unfortunately, most of the essential equipment for his division did not arrive in England until late August, causing a great deal of consternation, but logistics have always proved the sinews of war.

When he assumed command of the Big Red One in May, Allen inherited a training schedule largely determined by the War Department. Now in England, he firmly imprinted his personal mark on the 1st Division with command inspections and a rigorous training schedule. Because unit training for an amphibious assault in North Africa now received his personal attention, he could direct his efforts to perfecting this capability.

Since the combined Anglo-American staff in London focused primarily on shipping and naval support, the intricate planning became the responsibility of division level commanders. In Allen's case, his intimate knowledge of the 1st Division's personnel and its capabilities ensured that the command was as prepared as possible for the impending assault. Still, with so few officers with combat experience, Allen was forced to concentrate on basic troop-leading procedures for the junior officer corps when he would have preferred to focus on platoon- to battalion-level field exercises.

For Lieutenant Dawson, the first month in the United Kingdom read like a page from a travel log. As an officer on the operational staff, his duties necessitated continuous travel to coordinate the command's dispersed units. Such responsibilities provided an unparalleled opportunity to visit cities and towns about which he had previously read—London, Bath, Manchester, Salisbury, and Leeds.

He found Westminster Abbey inspirational, but noted that the ravages of war were apparent in every corner of the English countryside and urban areas. A quick visit to Scotland to coordinate the shipment of the 1st Division's equipment and to inspect potential training areas particularly delighted him. Moreover, the presence of a six-foot-two inch Texan with a Southern drawl made Dawson the darling of many an impromptu gathering in local pubs and restaurants. He found the local inhabitants warm and entertaining, not characterized by "the typical British aloofness" which he had expected.

As for his letters, fear of censorship prohibited him from "relating in detail all the things I know you would like to hear about." He conspicuously dated all his correspondence "somewhere in England" to escape the censor's knife and avoided all mention of military activities except in the broadest sense. Rather, he concentrated on his travels and his interaction with the people in the countryside.

Dawson to Dearest Family

August 9, 1942

The loveliness of this country has been written in every form of literature, and I honestly confess that everything said thus far has been an understatement. Thus far, I have experienced a most happy time, and the people of England are indeed most gracious. We had a most enjoyable trip over and since our arrival, the only item that could be said against the place is that the weather is a bit chilly and in quite a contrast to that which we would be having at home. . . . I plan to go to London the first chance I get and see the famous old town.

Be sure and write as often as possible, and I shall keep you informed as best I can. Above all, have no worry about me as I am with the Winner, therefore, cannot come to harm. My heart [is] full of tenderest (sic) love for each of you. I cannot tell you how much I miss you all.

In case you have a chance to do any knitting, I can assure you that mittens and sweaters and such are to be most appreciated. Also candy and cigarettes. Take good care of yourselves and above all, know that yours truly is well and happy.

Dawson to My Dear Family

August 12, 1942

What with the pleasant surroundings and the interesting work, I find life quite agreeable these days. Of course we have many things that are new and different from that which we have been experiencing at home, but it never ceases to be a source of great interest. My only regret is that I am unable to relate in detail all the various items that I know you would like to hear about.

Inasmuch as this is the case, it does not allow for much latitude in making a very comprehensive analysis of my daily activities. The daily shower, plus the cold weather, has upset me a little and I have a rather disagreeable sore throat and cold, but not serious enough to warrant more than casual comment. Otherwise, my health is tops. It is really amazing to me how well I have been since I have been in the army, and doubtless, the time spent will add many years to my life. . . .

I still find myself overjoyed at this country. It is absolutely the most beautiful spot I have ever seen. You can take North Carolina, East Texas, and Pennsylvania and roll them all together and they still would not approach this scene of loveliness. If I stay here long enough, I think I shall be tempted to spend the rest of my life here. Truthfully, one cannot help but understand why the colonials felt nostalgic for the Mother Country. The one striking thing about it is the fact that though there are forty million people in this country, there seems to be no more thickly populated than our own state [of Texas].

The typical British aloofness, or shall I say restraint, is not at all apparent and on the contrary, they seem to be quite the opposite. In fact I would say that though they differ in speech or idioms a bit from the Texas drawl, I still can understand them better than I could the Brooklynites [sic].[6]

Dawson to Dearest Mother and Dad

September 1, 1942

There is little opportunity these days to write much, but I am taking this chance to let you know that everything is going well and that I am in quite good health. The main thing that has been necessary here is the necessity to acclimate oneself to the constant rain. However, when the sun does shine, it really is a sight to see. . . .

Incidentally, I hope to call you by telephone one of these days as it is possible to do so in London. I was there this last weekend for the day and managed to see a bit of the town. Truly it is a most interesting city and one that I hope I shall be able to spend some time in and really get to see the many interesting things there. It has been most exciting so far, and the outstanding events are doubtless reflected in the news accounts. Naturally, we are unable to say anything in letters as to our doings, but I can assure you that there is never a dull moment. . . .

From the appearance of things, it seems that Texas is well represented in this man's war, as I am constantly running into people from the old home state. Several Wacoans are here, as are many Dallasites and San Antonio men. Incidentally, there are a number of charming nurses, some forty of them from Texas who afford much consolation for us, though to date I have found the British girls quite attractive.

I have visited several places since I have been here, among them being Bristol, London, Bath, Oxford, Manchester, Salisbury, and Leeds. All of them are quite interesting, as well as educational for each of them so fit into the stories and literature that has been our reading throughout the years. I went to Westminster Abbey last Sunday and indeed it is perhaps the most inspiring place I have ever been. One just cannot help but feel that it is a place apart though the ravages of war are evident throughout the city. . . .

I never worked harder, but it has been most exciting and interesting. I meet many people of all types and my work is such that I get out into the countryside most all the time and have had many chances to really see England. Incidentally, I have been to Scotland, and one learns a new appreciation for the Scots, and also there is no more beautiful country in the world. If I don't watch out, I am going to fall in love with this island and never come home. But that is another story and I shall promise a long letter just as soon as I can get it off to you.

Dawson to My Dearest Family

September 8, 1942
Somewhere in England

Life here in England has been truly delightful this past month as we have had really unusual weather. The rain of course is a bit unpleasant at times, but when the sun does shine, it makes this look like the Garden of Eden. Never have I seen such gorgeous flowers, and the well-tended fauna all around makes one feel that you are in a magnificent estate. Also, I have been privileged to meet several most interesting people, and they have treated me most royally.

This past weekend I spent in London, where I met a young Canadian captain, who had one of the most intensely interesting stories I have ever heard. He was on the Dieppe raid, so you can imagine what we spent the better part of the night talking about.[7] He is from Saskatchewan. . . .

Though there is no doubt in one's mind that there is a war going on, and we are very much in it, the people of London have the most wonderful spirit one can possibly imagine. Truly, it makes one feel a bit sheepish about our complacency before Pearl Harbor. But it seems that that is all past history and we are now 100 percent behind the effort.

[Recently] I met an English major who has a lovely place about halfway between Bath and Bournemouth. We spent the night with him, and he has asked me down to his home next month for the annual pheasant shoot. You will be interested to know how that is conducted. You dress in your very best clothes and sally forth with your trusty fowling piece to a shooting box, which is nothing more than a cozy little grandstand with room enough for four people. There you sit while the beaters and gamekeepers round up the birds for you to shoot. It is hunting deluxe and calls for absolutely no effort on one's part. It is the event of the year, and I can assure you the smart set of Waco can never raise their eyebrows to me after such a wonderful invitation. . . .

In England, Dawson's favorite city was undoubtedly London, a city that was a "never-ending source of things that recall books and characters in the literature I have read in the past." American servicemen on leave in the British capital had at their disposal various agencies where they could obtain free tickets to most theatrical performances. Tickets were available at the newly opened Information Center of the English-Speaking Union, the Special Service Section of the headquarters command, and the Queensberry All-Services Club.

Because of his personal affluence and the fact that he was better off than most American officers in London at the time, Dawson frequently made his own accommodation arrangements. While in London, he usually stayed in the Savoy Hotel, an upper-class hotel frequented by visiting dignitaries, correspondents, and performers from the USO troupes. It was a hotel that offered the "good life."

One incident proved as unfortunate as it was entertaining. It seems that Dawson and two friends, a captain from Boston and a Canadian captain from Saskatchewan, planned a dinner party to impress three English ladies. It fell to Dawson to coordinate the evening's menu. He asked the maitre d'hôtel for the best menu available and the man suggested some soup, hors d'oeuvres, fish, pheasant, rolls, red wine, and coffee, with the dessert being plum pudding. All that sounded better than the "porridge and other horrible concoctions" that comprised Dawson's normal diet.

The guests arrived late in the afternoon, and after two hours of enjoying the piano in the suite, the sextet sat down for dinner. Dawson noted that the first three courses went off quite well. When the eagerly awaited breast of pheasant entered the room, Dawson "noticed a most rank odor entered with it. Then when the plates were served, I could hardly refrain from capitulating then and there. Honestly, it was the foulest bird that I ever had the misfortune to smell."

When he recovered from the gas attack, Dawson immediately called the waiter to the side and attempted to find out what had gone wrong. Taken aback, the waiter informed Dawson "quite stiffly" that "the bird was *high* and in the best condition to eat." Though the ladies attacked the pheasant and thought it was fine, Dawson added "we three colonials asked to be excused, and immediately retired to the bathroom, where we promptly lost our lunches."

The next day, Dawson and his friends inquired about the preparation of pheasants and were surprised to find that "these people let a bird hang until he is almost rotten, then they cook it." Dawson confessed that his sense of taste was pretty good considering some of the places he had lived and eaten, "but this was really just too much for old Joe."

Still, London offered a pleasant distraction from the routine of military life, and Joe Dawson took every opportunity to tour England's most famous city. At the Savoy, he met actress Vivien Leigh, whom he characterized as "quite a gal!!" Often in residence were many news correspondents whom he had previously met when they were touring the military camps in search of stories to report to the home front. This "limelight of the news business" included freelance journalist H. R. Knickerbocker of the *Chicago Sun* Foreign Service, Jack Thompson of the *Chicago Tribune,* and Kenneth Downs, who before the fall of France had been in charge of the International News Service in Paris. He particularly enjoyed the company of Quentin Reynolds, whose *Only the Stars Are Neutral* was popular in 1942 London. Other staff duties included escorting the increasing number of VIPs whenever they arrived at 1st Division headquarters.

Dawson to My Dearest Family

September 14, 1942
Somewhere in England

This past weekend has been quite interesting for me as I have been in company with a group of entertainers who have been here for the benefit of the troops. One of the USO shows has been here throughout the weekend doing their bit for the men. The cast consisted of Al Jolson, Merle Oberon, Patricia Morrison, Allen Jenkins, and Frank McHugh. They were all quite nice and really went to extreme lengths to try and make things happy for the men. . . . The show went over with a bang, and the boys really appreciated it no end.

Mrs. Roosevelt is in charge of the American Red Cross Chapter here.[8] She, by the way, has five sons who are serving throughout the world, besides her famous husband, who is our brigadier. And incidentally, she is not quite as well off as you are, Mother, for she doesn't know where any of her boys are.

Yesterday, I escorted several foreign correspondents around camp in an effort to get them something to write about. Billingham, who is with Reuters, Arthur Kluckholm of the *New York Times,* and Jack Thompson of the *Chicago Tribune* were the men, and they seemed to get a big kick out of what is going on. They seemed to be quite amused to find a lone Texan among so many Easterners, but when I told them the number of important Texans within the unit, they then changed their tune somewhat. Oh well, I guess we will never cease to be a bit snobbish or superior, though really it is not a manner intended to offend.

The other night, I went to a party given by a group of R.A.F. men at one of their fields.[9] It was one of the most interesting evenings I have ever spent in all my life for the place happened to be the oldest school that they have in England and has perhaps the same hallowed background that is found at Kelly Field at home. It dates back to 1911 and the place is filled with mementos and relics of persons and heroes who have made history for this great land. . . . One has only to talk with these men and be with them a while to realize the tremendous power vested within the R.A.F. And when the story of this war is written, it will be found that the world will have them to thank for its salvation more than any other force.[10]

I have learned several things since my arrival here that may be worth repeating for your benefit. The first is regarding mail. The V-mail comes at regular intervals, but one must so time their correspondence that it will catch the transcription of that particular week else it will not be sent until the next week.[11] Thus far, the Air Mail seems to be the most efficient as it has taken only an average of nine days for a letter to come from you, so as long as this is the case, I suggest you keep to this method. I am quite anxious to know just how long it takes for my letters to reach you and in what form is it most rapid.

Then there is the matter of censorship. I attempt to refrain from mentioning anything that would be of a nature that would require censoring and therefore, do my own insofar as this country is concerned. I do not know if there is another censor at that end of the line and would like to know if my letters are being held up there.

Another thing that is brought to my attention is with regard to packages. I am told that one may expect a package anytime within two to three months after being mailed, so if you expect to send me a cake for Christmas, I would suggest that it be hermetically sealed or in such a manner that it would keep for an indefinite period.

And speaking of Xmas, I can think of nothing that would suit me more than a Presidential order that would allow me to come home for that day, but as that is quite out of the question, I would settle for a letter a week from each of you for the duration. But as that too is probably not to be expected, I will settle for just the fact that you are thinking about me a little bit on an occasional date.

Dawson to My Dearest Family

September 21, 1942
Somewhere in England

I promised to relate in my next letter a trip recently to see a lovely country place situated in southern England near the town of Salisbury. It was Cholderton House, the home of Lady Hamilton and Lord Nelson many years ago, and is also the birthplace of General Sir Archibald Wavell.[12] His family secured it from the Nelson family, and it is now owned by Sir Stevens, who controls the ink and dye industry in England. It is not an unusually large place, but is ample enough to house quite a sizable family along with a large number of servants. It was built in 1690 and is of Queen Anne style, though there have been numerous additions to the house since it was originally built.

The walls in the main portion of the house are quite lovely, all being of wood paneling, and the fixtures, such as the fireplaces and so forth, are as they were several hundred years ago. Indeed, they are perfectly beautiful. The house is of brick and stone, with a tile roof and the reinforcements are all old hand-hewn English oak beams with the curves and joints shaped to fit each other as a jigsaw puzzle—really a most substantial place. . . .

But like most English places, the grounds are the main attraction, and this place is no exception. In the front yard, is a perfect geometric star composed of all different colored flowers and is kept in excellent condition. The center has the famous sundial, and each flower-bed is bordered with some lovely greenery that is about four inches high. Of course, most of the family, with the exception of Dad and myself, can name all these various botanical children, but I won't even attempt it. . . .

Over in the northwest corner of the garden is the summer house with a cozy bench for two, and one cannot help but feel that the great Nelson must have whispered sweet nothings in the attentive ear of M'Lady. Perhaps I am somewhat of a romantic anyhow, but as I have met Vivian Leigh recently and had a very interesting evening with her charming company, I have felt that she did a pretty good job of bringing back the past in her characterization of "That Hamilton Woman."

This is merely a note, and as I have spent the remainder of the light of this day in writing this to you and as there is a blackout every night, which means that I must stop. To be sure the blackout over here means just that and completely so. Do write when you find time, and give my fondest love to all the family.

Military duties focused on coordinating the division's various combat teams for movement between Tidworth Barracks and Glasgow, Scotland, for amphibious training. These kept Dawson busy throughout late September and early October. Constantly on the move, he noted that when one considered the relatively short distances in England, it was sometimes most amazing to a "Texas-reared long distance hopper" like himself. As a result, the impact of what was occurring and the fact that only a very few miles separated the adversaries in the struggle made him realize that home was really a "fur piece away."

In his somewhat restrained manner, he attempted to convey an incident that occurred on September 24 that he thought might prove interesting to his family and friends in Texas. Couching his letter in a manner that would not divulge items of a military nature that might prove valuable to the enemy, he described what was the highlight of his sojourn in England.

In early September, Dawson had been fortunate enough to meet several officers in the Royal Air Force (RAF), and through them, had formed a very high estimate of their martial abilities. In his estimation, no group of men exceeded the pilots in courage, fortitude, perseverance, and valor. They were indeed the backbone of England's armed forces. To his great surprise, one of the pilots asked Dawson to the air base that morning to take a little trip. He accepted without the slightest hesitation and without seeking permission from the 1st Division's Operations Officer, Lieutenant Colonel S. B. Mason, or asking just where he would be going.

Arriving at the RAF base, he met his friend and joined the RAF pilots in the squadron mess for morning tea. "Now a cup of tea," Dawson wrote, "is truly sacred to an Englishman, and no matter whether he is about to go into battle or spend his nuptial bliss with his lovely bride, he must fortify himself with a cup of tea!" Only then did he discover he was going on a reconnaissance flight 'over there,' meaning the Continent. To the pilots, such flights were merely routine, but for the American officer, this spelled as exciting an adventure as one could expect, "particularly a doughboy."

Suited up in a flight suit, he donned a parachute and looked "more like a man from Mars than a regular native of this planet." He then had thrust under his nose a little piece of paper to sign, which he did automatically. When he asked what it was that he had signed, his colleague informed him that it was merely a formality known as a blood chit. Should the enemy down the aircraft, the RAF would be absolved from any claim on the part of his dependents.

"Remembering the Alamo and other historical examples of Texas courage," Dawson merely shrugged his shoulders and "assumed an attitude of casualness that would do justice to a New Yorker visiting Chicago." Having received last-minute instructions on how to bail out in the event of an emergency, the crew of the small formation of three aircraft then taxied toward the runway and, on receiving the blue signal from the dispatcher, swiftly took off for XX.[13]

Once the aircraft had gained altitude, Dawson took over the controls and spent the next quarter hour quite busy keeping on course because the weather had become rather bumpy. The feeling for the Texas infantryman was exhilarating as Dawson "played hide and seek as the clouds would scatter briefly then suddenly close" over them.

Checking out the map, he noticed they were over land, then water, then land; then clouds with rain that quickly turned to ice. At times, he was lost in thought, letting his mind unconsciously dwell on things far remote from his immediate surroundings. Finally, his friend grabbed his mouthpiece and yelled in his ear that there was something very interesting below. Instantly focusing his attention in the direction in which his finger was pointing and with the aid of field glasses, he could distinguish a rather large city stretched beneath them. By referring to the map, he immediately knew they were over their destination.

On preliminary observation, Dawson reported that the city looked like Dallas, but it wasn't Dallas, for no sooner had this thought occurred than the flight commander waggled his wings and motioned for the pilots to look below. What they saw were "more birds flying up toward us that bore a very odd looking mark clearly distinguishable to us and from the manner in which they were approaching. It seemed that we were in the wrong barnyard and the roosters didn't like the intrusion." As the RAF was not interested in engaging them since this was a reconnaissance mission, they "wheeled about and started for home as fast as we could, and believe me that is fast."

Traveling at 350 miles an hour was a new experience for Dawson, but he confessed he did not have too much time to think about it as "Jerry" had a fairly fast plane himself, and they were playing for keeps. Suddenly, he realized that "life was a pretty precious thing and discretion was often better than vainglorious valor." Still, it was his first experience at war other than an occasional German plane that dropped a few bombs in England.

The experience was all Dawson hoped it would be, even as he observed "puffs of smoke coming from their wings, and brother, that smoke wasn't coming from a tobacco pipe!" Thus ended the flight, and when they returned to the base in time for afternoon tea, Dawson concluded that it had been quite a sensation, "particularly when you know that somewhere not too far from you is a guy that is looking for you with murder in his eye."

The remainder of September was spent in casual activities. As with most GIs, Dawson requested the usual assortment of goods not available in England: fur-lined gloves, sweets, cigarettes, a camera, and film. He also spoke of English hospitality, which he felt was superior to any that he had ever experienced. The English really knew how to throw a party, and American officers were always invited and placed in the seats of honor.

His good friend in the RAF outdid himself on one occasion by assuring one and all that Dawson was a "terrific Texan" who enjoyed himself in such gatherings. Social functions were always a highlight, but there was a serious side to the war too.

Early October found Dawson in Scotland, where the 1st Division was preparing to conduct final amphibious rehearsals for the impending invasion of North Africa. His letter encapsulated all his previous experiences since arriving in England the prior August—the picturesque countryside, British hospitality, and his military duties that brought him into daily contact with the common people who had weathered the storm of war for three years.

Lieutenant Dawson was now assistant G-3 in charge of training, a promotion from what he termed "assistant-assistant G-3." As usual, he expressed his bewilderment at Scotland's natural beauty, particularly the lochs, which were more beautiful than he could conceive. Writing his final letter on board the HMS *Reina del Pacifico*, a transport that would convey 1st Division Headquarters to North Africa, Dawson encouraged his family to write and not to worry because when the war was finally over, there would be ample time to celebrate. In the interim, he would do the best he could.

Dawson to My Dearest Family

October 4, 1942
Glasgow, Scotland

Having spent the entire past week traveling the length of this island of Great Britain, I can now sit back for a few minutes and
indite [sic] a little report to the headquarters there. The early part
of last week, I journeyed to London on business and spent the day
there. My duties prevented me from doing anything in the nature
of visiting or seeing the city again as I had hoped, but I had a very
interesting time nevertheless as old London town is truly the hub
of the Allied war effort these days. From it, one can see that the
whole world is engaged in this war for one sees every type of
uniform and also every nationality. . . .

I got back to my station late that evening, and on arriving,
learned that we were returning various courtesies to some of our
RAF friends by giving them a party. The committee in charge really outdid themselves to make everything nice and the highlight
of the whole affair was the presence of chili con carne, which we
served for dinner. We had recruited three Mexican boys in the
division to cook this for us, and they did a masterful job. All agreed
that it was excellent.

Early Wednesday, I started out for Glasgow and as I have been
stationed in the southern part of the island, our journey was truly
the longest I have had since I arrived here. I drove through the
country, so I must try and give you a description of the trip so that
you can in part enjoy it with me as it was the most wonderful trip
I have ever taken. Though the mileage from the tip of the island
on the south to the tip on the north is about the same as from
Corpus [Christi] to Dallas, it is much different over here, and one
takes considerably more time to make the jaunt than would be
the case for the same distance there at home. As it was left entirely up to me as to the route to follow, I decided to come by way
of Liverpool, then up through the Lake district and into Scotland
by way of Carlisle. This perhaps was as short as any other way,
and as it is regarded as the loveliest drive in the whole island, I
naturally took it.

Throughout the first day's drive, the weather was truly beautiful and not unlike a golden October day at home. The gorgeous
fields and rolling country made one recall the road from Dallas to
Waco along about this time of the year, when all the harvest is

being reaped, and the grain fields of gold and brown contrasting with the yet still green cotton fields. Over here, the trees are carefully cultivated and grown very close together in what is called belts. They are planted so that there is just enough room between them to allow them to reach toward the sky, and then when the green foliage begins, they become as one. Consequently, it seems that they are a solid mass.

I think these are the English fir trees as they are not over two feet in thickness and have the greenery much alike to our cedar or Oregon firs. One can readily imagine them at Christmas time, gracing the homes of the charming country and all alit. But I won't think too much on that vein now for fear of inducing homesickness (a disease I am most susceptible to).

I stopped for a bite to eat in the lovely city of Hereford, and there enjoyed myself immensely by stretching my legs a bit and wandering about the cobblestone streets that are most abrupt as the village is built on the steep hillsides. The thatched roofs and the typical English style architecture are prevailing in this city and in my feeble estimation, there is nothing more beautiful or charming.

From this city, the panorama changed to the even lovelier, and it seems that the entire distance into Shrewesbury [sic] was one magnificent estate, for all along the roadside the hedges abounded and were broken only by an occasional bridge or giant oak that must have looked down on six hundred years of travel along this road . . . the little brooks and streams winding their ways over the rocks made me recall the Rito de los Frijoles along the Santa Fe Valley.

And the forests created visions of Robin Hood and his merry band of followers. Truly, it made one feel as if in a wonderland. . . . Just as night descended, we reached Shrewesbury [sic] and as I was a total stranger to the town, I decided to go to the police station to inquire about accommodations for the night. The officer in charge was most helpful and sent along a charming young lady to act as guide to the hotel.

Our rooms were very nice; in fact, there is a homely atmosphere about the little English hotels that make them seem like private dwellings. Ray Leeds, the American Red Cross representative, was with me, and we got ensconced into a nice little apartment that only lacked a bath to complete the place into a home. Our meals were served in our drawing room, and after a supper of roast chicken, mashed potatoes, English peas and real coffee, we felt that the war was something that happened many years ago and we were back home. The charming old couple that ran the place outdid themselves to make us feel at home, and I can assure you they succeeded. . . .

We journeyed all morning over the winding road that continued much like the evening before, though as we began to approach Liverpool, the little villages became more numerous, and activity along the road increased. We passed through Liverpool by means of the underpass or tunnel that surpasses anything I have ever seen at home. It is simply marvelous and is much longer and larger than our Holland Tunnel in New York. I do not know the extent of it, but I would guess it to be over six miles in length, and as it is quite wide and high, it seemed that we were in some gigantic labyrinth [because] on three occasions, we passed points where it branched off in other directions. . . . After emerging from it, we found that though we had missed much of the city, we still had a lot to go through.

The north side is not at all pretty nor particularly interesting, as it is row on row of tenements and cheap living quarters and dirty factories. . . . We lunched at a little roadhouse just outside of town and had a nice meal of roast beef, the first I had found in some time. The innkeeper was a very nice chap and while we lunched, he sat and talked with us and plotted our route to Carlisle, giving us the names of the cities and villages along the way . . .

Already we have done a lot over here towards helping the little children here in England by 'adopting' them. Two of us, Paul Gale and myself, have adopted a charming little girl of three and have agreed to keep her for five years. . . . It costs us $80 or 20 pounds per year to take care of the little one, and should I manage to increase my income by promotion, I hope to be able to [sponsor] one all to myself.

From Preston to Carlisle is perhaps the most beautiful country in all the world—at least it seemed so to me. This is known as the Lake District, and I feel that James Hilton had it in mind when he wrote of Shangri-La. It is quite high, the hills rising almost perpendicular to heights of over 1,000 feet, and all throughout the area are rock fences that cross and criss-cross the countryside. . . . We were most fortunate in having a day that was an artist's dream, for the clouds were the cumulus puff balls hanging in a sky of purple blue. I honestly believe I would give a thousand dollars for a color movie camera, so I could send the film back home to you.

The very heart of the country is at Kendal, and one feels from seeing the inhabitants there that they are living in as near a heavenly atmosphere as is on this earth. I learned from a friend . . . that this country was the home of very rich lords who devoted their full time to fighting tribes that sought to come into this country. [This] made me reflect that after all is said and done, we cannot enjoy the heavens on earth without fighting for it. These knights of old are reincarnated in the present generation that is now doing the self-same thing and in talking with them. I found that the people living at Kendal feel the impact of this war as much if not more than any I have come in contact with for truly they have a segment of earth that is as near perfect in natural beauty as any I have ever seen. . . .

We reached Carlisle at about six o'clock and decided to spend the night there for we could not have made our destination of Glasgow that night, especially as we did not know the road. We were fortunate to find a hotel room and after freshening up a bit, set forth to find food. . . .

We arose at eight, and after getting our little group together (four trucks), we set forth towards Glasgow. We encountered little difficulty in getting out of town, for by this time I had mastered the most used phrase in all England, 'stairate awn, you cawn't miss it,' though straight on is comparable to a roller coaster trip at Coney Island. . . . Our ride through Glasgow was perhaps the most amazing I have ever taken as the streets are very crowded and the people pay absolutely no attention to automobiles and trucks and seem to resent their presence on the streets.

I was quite uneasy and nervous, as I had to keep the trucks close together for fear we would lose them in the heavy traffic. And traffic here is something I have never before experienced. Trucks of all sizes rumble alongside of wagons drawn by the huge gray horses predominant here, while thousands of people rush to catch the double-decker trolleys and buses that pass every minute. . . .

Throughout the afternoon, I spent the hours in going to various places in the city on several duties . . . I stayed at the American Red Cross, which has taken over Grand Hotel and made of it a haven for the soldiers and sailors and officers of our nation. The work they do here is really something that requires a little elaboration. . . .

This is perhaps the largest canteen in the world for military and naval men, and in it, one sees soldiers and sailors from all over the world. [It includes] lads who have seen action and suffered many trials, for here, one finds the boys who have not only been on the battlefronts, but who have also been members of crews of the ships that have been sunk. Their stories are merely the recapitulation of the headlines of the past three years, but here are the men who actually made the record.

The Red Cross charges forty cents a meal to officers and fifty cents per night for a cot. For these men, the charge is twenty cents per meal and thirty cents for a cot. Here, a man can get not only good food and a place to sleep, but also can take a bath and get a shave and haircut. It is in truth a Godsend for no other place I know of in all of England can offer these things to the men twenty-four hours a day. . . .

As today has been Sunday, my thoughts have been about much of you at home. To be sure, I have spent the better part of the day in jotting these lines to you, and it has been the best way I believe I could have spent it. Duty required my presence, though there has been no other demand. . . . Well, dear ones, I had best close now for the hour is late. . . . I have not had any mail in a little over two weeks, but hope springs eternal over here and someday I may be surprised to find a letter. Take good care of yourselves and remember that though the miles separate me from you, my heart ever remains there encompassed in the little spot called HOME.

Dawson to My Dearest Family

October 20, 1942

Now that a month has gone by, and no word from the other side of the big pond, I am assuming that all communications are being sent by mental telepathy. But as my wavelength has always been a bit screwy anyway, I find it difficult to tune in as I would like to do. But every night now before I go to sleep, I mesmerize a bit and conjure up a real bit of conversation with you, though my friends and comrades are beginning to feel sure that I have definitely lost my mind. Albeit I live in the hopes that things will become readjusted so that I shall have a word from you ere too many years go by.

By way of resume, I will admit my own shortcomings as far as writing the past two weeks. Due to the press of travel and duties, I have really been at a loss to do anything of a personal nature. To a large degree, my time was spent in travel over the island from Scotland to London and back to Glasgow, so by now I believe I know every turn in the whole journey. And I can assure you that the trip is quite a lengthy one as the distance is around 400 miles. From this, you can surmise how long it takes to make the trip, and after one goes four times, you can see how the days have gone by. . . .

I left last weekend and journeyed quite some distance away and boarded ship, where I am now situated and from which this letter is being written. The journey was uneventful other than another eye filling spectacle that made me think I was in wonderland . . . so now a word about the ship.

I have comfortable quarters and am well fixed as regards personal comforts. My duties are now assistant G-3, whereas before now, I was merely assistant assistant G-3. The ship is really a nice one, though not as large or as commodious as the one we came across in. It is not nearly as crowded, though as we do quite well. It has quite a pretty lounge, being done in green and gold and the dining room is paneled in South African stinkwood.

And to add to the charm and comfort of the place, we have very good food. In fact, the food is better than any we have had. Added luxury consists of a private bath, so really I have begun to feel that life as a staff officer has its compensations.

We have been going through maneuvers in a setting of scenic beauty that is almost too perfect. The lochs of Scotland are really something that must be seen to be appreciated, but I can now see why someone with the means would put sailing on the lochs in Scotland in first priority. For sheer grandeur and loveliness, I cannot conceive of any place more beautiful. The jagged hills rise abruptly from the very waters edge and tower to an altitude of over three thousand feet. Incidentally, the depth of these waters reaches a thousand feet. The hills are of a color that is an artist's dream. The brown and reddish gold of the scotch heather that covers the entire surface and the silver bands of the little streams trickling down the sides toward the sea is just too much for this poor soul. I can assure you that I shall have to come back here someday. . . .

So ends this chapter in my reports to the loved ones. I hope that all the others have reached you and as I am relying on these letters to serve as a sort of diary, I hope you are keeping them for me to read later in the years to come. Though there are many things left unsaid due to the restrictions, I still believe I have covered all the things worth noting and which will recall to my mind later on the many wonderful sights I have seen.

My parting word is that you do not worry about me for I am doing well and am happy. Things may prevent us being together, but my thoughts are so much of you these days and I would that word would reach me that you are well and happy. I cannot say too much about the fact that letters are ever becoming dearer to me, and I hope that in the future there will not be such long waits. . . . Above all, know that whatever may happen, I find my heart filled with tenderest thoughts of you, and someday, this mess that keeps us apart will end and then what a glorious time will be had! I only wish that time would allow me to write everyone, but believe me when I say it, I am a busy man!

Please take care of yourselves and know that I shall be doing the best I can.

These maneuvers were the final field exercises conducted by the 1st Division prior to embarkation. The exercise, MOSSTROOPER, was held in Scotland on October 18, after which all troops, staffs, and commanders began final embarkation.

Eisenhower was on hand and found the exercises both encouraging and discouraging. Returning from "a rather difficult inspection trip" in Scotland, where he witnessed an amphibious exercise carried out by the 1st Division during abominable weather, he informed Marshall that he was impressed that the "men looked fine and, without exception, were earnestly trying to do the right thing." Speaking to scores of them in the dead of night, Ike also determined "that their greatest weakness is uncertainty! Most did not know exactly what was expected of them. This extended all the way from the method of challenging to actions in tactical moves."

These problems, of course, were a reflection of the junior officers at the platoon and company levels, areas at which, Ike reported, "we have our most glaring weakness." In short, the 1st Infantry Division was short on experience and trained leadership below the battalion commander.[14] Even the commanding general realized that corrective action was beyond the capacity of any division commander or any colonel to cure hurriedly. Time was essential, and time was one thing that the Big Red One did not have.

Several days after Ike cabled his assessment, the 1st Infantry Division departed the United Kingdom under Royal Navy escort for operations in North Africa. The division embarked on eleven personnel ships and nine cargo vessels. The voyage itself was without incident, and the convoy remained in the Atlantic Ocean until November 6, when it quietly passed through the Straits of Gibraltar after dark. On the high seas, the largest armada ever assembled experienced what the division history labeled typical 1st Division weather. On land it was rain and mud; in the air it was overcast, operational for enemy planes, but not their own; on the seas, it was rough water provoking its usual discomforts.

Not until November 1 were the soldiers briefed as to their ultimate destination. By that time, the armada was cruising toward its rendezvous with destiny, and once again, the soldiers of the Big Red One sought to engage the enemy on a hostile shore.

3
North Africa

It now boils down to the big show, when Rommel gets here and the big fight begins.

When American GIs waded through the surf in northwest Africa in the predawn hours of November 8, 1942, they represented the initial contingent of more than 1 million Americans to see service in the Mediterranean area during World War II.[1] What brought them to Africa's northwest coast was a compromise between President Franklin Roosevelt and British Prime Minister Winston Churchill regarding the timing and location of the first coordinated Anglo-American offensive against Nazi Germany.

Under the direction of the Combined Chiefs of Staff, Operation TORCH called for three distinct landings in French North Africa: one on the Atlantic coast of Morocco, and two on the Mediterranean shores of western and central Algeria. Once ashore, the three task forces were directed to consolidate near Casablanca, Oran, and Algiers before driving eastward to trap Erwin Rommel's *Afrika Korps* in a vise with General Bernard L. Montgomery's British Eighth Army. The strategic purposes of TORCH included occupying French North Africa, opening the Mediterranean Sea lines of communication, relieving the pressure against the Soviet Union by creating another front against Germany, and destroying Axis forces in North Africa.

In overall command of TORCH was Lieutenant General Dwight David Eisenhower, whose official command was designated to be that of Commander in Chief, Allied Expeditionary Force. For security reasons, he altered the title to Commander in Chief, Allied Force. Major General George S. Patton commanded the Western Task Force; Major General Lloyd R. Fredendall, the II Corps commander, led the Central Task Force, to which the 1st Infantry Division was assigned.

Fredendall's Central Task Force was assigned to capture Oran in an attack that included a double envelopment by the 1st Infantry Division and a wide encirclement from the southeast by Combat Command B of the 1st Armored Division. In the plan of attack for the 1st Infantry Division, the "Y" Force drove on Oran from the west and the

"Z" Force attacked from the east. H-Hour—when the military operation began for the Oran landings—was 0100 hours on November 8.

Assistant division commander Brigadier General Theodore Roosevelt led the "Y" Force as it attacked in the area adjacent to Les Andelouses, fourteen miles west of Oran, while the vast majority of the Central Task Force landed in the vicinity of the Gulf of Arzew, or over "Z" beaches, extending eastward from the town of Arzew. In overall command of these landings was Terry Allen, commanding general of the Big Red One.

Accompanying the task force was H. R. Knickerbocker, a correspondent who later contributed to a history of the 1st Infantry Division during World War II. Years after the war ended, Knickerbocker asked Allen what had been the high point of the war for him. Allen smiled and responded, "The landing at Oran. Yes, nothing has ever equaled that night. There was something about it that never was repeated. It was the first time. That's what made it [special]."[2]

The 1st Division's initial assault on a hostile shore in World War II was virtually uncontested—what Dawson described as a "brisk action"—though he noted that the Big Red One's opposition was the highly trained French Foreign Legion. Allen immediately consolidated his forces and continued the attack to seize Oran. Calling a staff conference on the evening of November 9, Allen directed that the final assault on Oran commence the next day at 0715 hours.

At this time Colonel Norman Cota, the division chief of staff, suggested that a written order be prepared for distribution to all 1st Division units. Allen then dictated to Cota the initial order of the 1st Division on enemy soil in World War II. After specific directives had been received for each of the major subordinate commands, Cota asked Allen for "any general instructions" for all units, whereupon Allen dictated, "Nothing in Hell must stop the 1st Division."[3] Oran capitulated on November 10 after a brief struggle.

As training officer for the G-3 Operations section, Dawson served as a liaison officer (LNO) to division headquarters. In essence, he was the commanding general's eyes and ears. His first mission was to establish a forward command post (CP) for the division headquarters, which he did in a tiny native schoolhouse. Other duties involved repeated trips to the front to ascertain troop dispositions and the status of current operations, then shuffling back to division headquarters to report to Allen.

Not surprisingly, Dawson found the units were somewhat disorganized. For example, during the initial attack against St. Cloud, the major obstacle on the road to Oran, the Division's 18th Infantry Regiment suffered a severe setback. Conducting an immediate after-action assessment, the regimental commander then fixed the enemy with one battalion, then bypassed St. Cloud under cover of darkness and continued the attack on Oran. The garrison of St. Cloud subsequently surrendered the next day, but the night maneuver foreshadowed many boldly executed night attacks in subsequent campaigns.

Dawson's personal assessment was that at times, commanders "had to throw away the book" and develop a concept of "cohesive action, which was the only effective method in which you could conduct a battle."[4] By the time the soldiers reached the outskirts of Oran, the commanders had settled down and operated as a collective group.

The opportunity to work closely with Allen thrilled Dawson, who spoke of his chief's charismatic leadership and his own fascination with battle in his first letter, which he wrote eight days after Oran's capture. As with most of the soldiers, this was the first time that Dawson was exposed to enemy fire. The experience of hearing "the whine of bullets around one's head" produced a healthy respect for the enemy, as well as a yearning for more action. The low casualty rate had only fueled his enthusiasm to engage and destroy the enemy. Additional combat and the loss of beloved comrades would change this attitude of course, but Dawson would have undoubtedly agreed with his commander that 1st Division's amphibious assault in World War II "was something special" that he would always remember.

What the young officer really desired was command of a rifle company on the front line, but at present, he had to be content with service on the 1st Division staff. He then included his analysis of combat, as well as his initial impressions of Africa and its inhabitants, in several letters to his family in mid-November.

Dawson to My Dear Family

November 18, 1942
Somewhere in Africa

The events of the past several days have doubtless proven to be most exciting throughout the world, and as I have been in the thick of the whole thing, I find that it has been quite an experience. To be actually amid the din and fire of battle is something that is a bit different from the staid maneuvers of peacetime training. And to have the lead whining about the old ears makes one think of a lot of things that have lain dormant in the old head.

However, I have been most fortunate and have had no mishaps thus far.

I have written several very lengthy epistles and am hoping that some of them have reached you, though I have heard rumors that the last boat that I was on had been sunk. I am afraid that there is little hope of the last few letters reaching you as they were on the boat going to a point where they could be transferred to the airmail. . . .

[Africa] is indeed a land of unreality, and when one thinks about the fact that here in 1942, I am over in Africa trying to protect the USA, it makes things seem quite strange indeed. Though it was no great surprise to me when I learned where we were going, I was nonetheless quite interested when I learned the exact place in which our actions would take place, and just how we were going to affect our efforts.

Though there were casualties and the resistance was bitter for a time, the good old 1st Division made their objective within the appointed time and acquitted themselves nobly.[5] I had an opportunity to see about everything that took place and I got into the fray on more than one occasion. The intimate details will have to be reserved for a future date, but I can say that the business of war today is really something that defies description.

Incidentally, H. R. Knickerbocker is along with us and he doubtless will have sent many stories of our actions back home, and his comments will doubtless give the story to you. I find that time for writing is a bit limited and that I have not the means available to send as much of the story back to you as I would like. Just know though that I shall give you a full resume as soon as I possibly can. . . . My tenderest thoughts go with this little message and will convey in part the fact that there is never a moment that I do not think of you.

Dawson to My Dear Family

November 21, 1942
Africa

Again, I sit down and try to compose a letter and I fervently hope that this time, I shall be successful, as the other attempts have proven of no avail. Since the moment I first set foot on the soil of this continent some two weeks ago, life has been a progression of history-making events. I have found little time to do much about reporting on my actions, as they have been so many and varied, that time has not been a factor that would enable my thoughts to be set forth in any orderly manner.

As I was at sea for several weeks and therefore incommunicado with the outside world . . . fortunately, I can say that thus far, the war has left no scars, and I am safe and sound. The brisk action that developed when we took this country was indeed a foretaste of the demands expected of us, and it is truly an awesome feeling. I cannot quite express just how it feels to hear the whine of bullets around one's head, and the mental reaction one has when he knows that this time, it is directed at you with a deadly purpose. For the magnitude of the operation and scope of the battle, we were indeed fortunate in receiving so few casualties.

During the three days of the battle, I had the job of liaison officer, and as a consequence, spent most of the time on the front line seeing just what was going on and then dashing back to headquarters when the opportunity presented itself. All I can say is that all of us developed a healthy respect for the French, and I am quite glad that they are now fighting on our side. Since the end of the battle, they have come by the score to join with us, and I feel that the next few weeks will see them almost 100 percent with us.

As a large portion of them in this theater are natives, one cannot help but reflect on the stories of Kipling and the description of them that he gives. They fight like the devil and are as good shots as you can find anywhere. Their snipers are the best in the world, and they took a deadly toll before they finally gave up. Our men fought bravely and did a wonderful job. Everything was accomplished that we set out to do and it was all done on the schedule set.

Truly the most remarkable thing about the whole operation to me was the masterful job the British navy did in bringing the largest convoy in history to the exact spot on the exact time. I marvel at them, and the result of their seamanship afforded us a chance to obtain complete surprise over the opponents.

The night was perfect for our mission as we slid quietly into the harbor. The ships slid through the water with almost absolute silence. When we reached our appointed rendezvous, the assault boats were silently filled with troops and guns and lowered into the water. It was uncanny the way in which quietness was achieved, and one could only make out the silhouettes of the little boats by straining one's eyes. They all got off and started for the beach in perfect order.

The first objective was reached almost on the exact second that had been set, and everyone got ashore in the first assault wave without losing a single man. Just as dawn began to limn the eastern sky, the guns began to fire and soon, it seemed as all hell had broken loose. As it approached the shore, my little boat was the object of machine-gun fire, and I really was happy that the steel sides prevented them from penetrating to us.

One thing that served to inspire everyone was the General [Allen], who refused to crouch like the rest of us, but instead elected to stand in the prow of the boat with the bullets flying around him like a bunch of angry hornets. All who saw him felt the same sense of gladness that we had such a wonderful, courageous leader. I can assure you that I am proud of having the opportunity of being as near him as I have been these past few months.

For the next three days and nights, there was no cessation of the gunfire, and life was lived most dangerously. Though one assumed a healthy respect for the opposition, I can honestly say that I did not find myself afraid, though the last day of the battle was one that brought me into the fray very intimately. I am more than ever convinced that my spot in this affair is with the men instead of behind the lines. Should I be fortunate enough to get a command next month, I think I will be much happier.[6]

Since the time that actual fighting ceased, we have been very busy getting all the administrative matters cleared up and setting up the plans for the future. We are ensconced fairly comfortably, and the only bad feature is the presence of millions of flies. The country is perfectly beautiful and is just like a page from a picture book.

The natives are predominantly Arabian and their costumes are unusual to say the least. They are about the dirtiest people I ever saw, though, and their clothes seem to be a mass of tattered rags. The land appears to be most fertile and the whole of it is in cultivation—the crops being vegetables and huge vineyards of grapevines and olive trees and date alms. This is one of the greatest wine centers in the world, and the land is owned by rich French wine merchants who have built most impressive homes in the traditional Moorish architecture . . . the general landscape is not unlike that of west Texas, with broad valleys and gently rolling hills that merge in the distance with majestic mountains.

These mountains afford a barrier between this strip of land along the Mediterranean and the Sahara Desert. Their presence enables the climate to be quite agreeable, and the temperature is very welcome to me . . . the sky is almost unbelievably blue, and the nights are a poet's dream. The stars shine in a manner that makes each one clearly visible.

No sooner had the 1st Division regrouped and reorganized, when as an emergency measure, various units were hastily assigned to Tunisia to bolster Allied defenses against the rapid German buildup on the Eastern front. As division commander, Allen bitterly contested the fracturing of his command, but military expediency overrode his personal desires.

With headquarters still in Oran at the end of the year, Allen received a communiqué from a frustrated George Patton who, like Allen, was waiting to be sent to the front to kill Germans. Patton inquired, "Why in the hell don't you get into the war! Maybe if you would get up there and get in enough trouble, they would let me go up and get you out. In any case, we would have a better time than sitting around."[7]

Allen would not have long to wait. On January 18, 1943, the remainder of the 1st Infantry Division received orders to deploy to central Tunisia and constitute a general reserve. Two weeks later, the division took over a combined American-French sector in the Ousseltia Valley.

As for Dawson, he spent his first Thanksgiving overseas, prompting him to ponder the history-making events of which he was a part. If anyone would have told him years earlier that he would be spending his twenty-ninth year in northern Africa, he "would have thought him a candidate for the eighth ward."[8] Still serving as LNO, Lieutenant Dawson worked closely with the French, against whom he felt no personal animosity although they had opposed the 1st Division's landings in early November. Now that they had joined the Allied cause, he hoped that together "from now on, we will ultimately achieve the universal peace" that he felt was not too far away.

December 8 found Dawson in a hospital "somewhere in Africa," suffering from a severe case of hives that would trouble him for the next two months. He regretted that three letters and all of the Christmas gifts he had purchased were now at the bottom of the Atlantic, thanks to an accurate hit by a German submarine, but he promised to write more frequently. Returned to duty at division headquarters, he received a camera from his brother Leighton, which he immediately put to good use.

With General Allen visiting the front, Teddy Roosevelt granted the junior officers permission to use the general's villa for a New Year's celebration. Dawson found himself seated at the piano as the "gala affair" went well into the morning. He noted, "good old Teddy stepped aside and let us have the dining room of the chateau for a party." He sent several photographs home, and urgently requested mail and more film, which was a scarce commodity in North Africa. Correspondent Ernie Pyle concurred with Dawson in listing a soldier's fundamental needs. "They say," noted Pyle, that a soldier's three primary needs are "(1) good mail service, (2) movies, radios and phonographs, and (3) cigarettes and candy."

Pride in the 1st Division's achievements also emerged as a constant theme in Dawson's correspondence. Somewhat angered that the newspapers did not credit the Big Red One for the decisive role they played in the TORCH landings, Dawson wanted to set the record straight. Yes, the Rangers and the paratroopers had participated in the operation, but the 1st Division had "carried the ball."

Additionally, he discussed the increasing reports of casualties from the front. War lived up to "all its terrible implications," he informed his family. Henceforth, his letters would serve as a reflection of the actual heartaches and grief that result when men die for their country. Having witnessed combat for two months, Dawson now assumed a "sort of fatalistic attitude as a result of seeing the war at first glance." He reflected this new sense of fatalism in his correspondence.

Dawson to My Dearest Family

January 11, 1943

This being the first time in over four weeks that I have had a spare moment, I shall indite [sic] this little resume of my activities to you and trust that you will forgive my being so delinquent in my correspondence. With a war going on and we being active participants therein, I find that time relegated to personal pleasures is somewhat limited. I have truly been busy and the situation has evolved little in the way of news that could be transmitted homeward.

Ever since we arrived here, some of our troops have been in actual combat, and as a result, I can assure you that war lives up to all of its terrible implications. Though we on the staff have not been subjected to too many hardships, the life of the troops has been most trying. I can assure you, however, that they have acquitted themselves most valiantly, though there have been many that have paid the price of their life in service to the cause.

From now on 'til the end of the war, the tenor of all these communiqués will doubtless be a reflection of the actual heartaches and grief that result when men die for their country. One assumes a sort of fatalistic attitude as a result of seeing the war at first glance, but then when the thought comes to mind of why it all is so vitally necessary, the big picture begins to make sense. I, for one, feel that the whole thing is so big and so well worth the maximum effort we can put forth, that I do not feel that one's personal comfort of livelihood is too important so long as the best effort is being expended. . . .

Dawson to Dear Family

January 11, 1943

It has been cold and rainy here, and things are beginning to hum around here. We are in for some tough times and the impact of the war is hitting us pretty hard now. . . . I find after reading the newspapers that are now arriving from the States with the accounts of the occupation of North Africa that there is a tendency on the part of the news hawks to alter the truth in many instances and not tell the story as it actually occurred.

Though the air corps, the Rangers and the paratroops played important parts in the action, they are not to be regarded as the primary units that did this job. In reality, they were in the minority and did very little until the war was almost over. Johnny Doughboy did the job and he did it alone. Our division was the key to the whole action, and we had the toughest fight and highest casualties. It was no picnic and ever since then, it has been fighting.

One does not begin to realize how terrific this battle is until the reports come in and bring out the pertinent details.

I will write again just as soon as I get the chance. Meantime, know that I am well, and though the hives continue to cause discomfort, I am in good health.

In mid-January, Dawson joined division headquarters as the Big Red One deployed to Tunisia for the inevitable clash with Rommel. Spirits, including his own, were high. The deployment was not conducted without mishap, however, as Dawson described in his next missive. The stark realization that the 1st Division was now opposed by a very disciplined German force, and not the French and Italians who had previously contested Allen's command in the vicinity of Oran, was not lost on Dawson. Upon arrival in Tunisia he took time to summarize his first three months in a combat theater of operations. Somewhat careless in listing exact locations of friendly troops, he was not surprised when army censors deleted specific towns around which the 1st Division settled.

The problem, as always, was that the units of the 1st Infantry Division were scattered across a wide front under British, French, and American command in northern, central, and southern Tunisia. Because they were so dispersed, the 1st Division was unable to stem the Axis attack that struck Faid Pass in late January. On January 30, German troops attacked and defeated the small French garrison at Faid Pass, guarding an opening through the mountain range known as the Eastern Dorsale. Though no one knew it at the time, this engagement was the opening round that would develop into the battle of Kasserine Pass. Writing in the immediate aftermath of the German breakthrough, Dawson summarized recent activities and prepared his family for the upcoming engagement.

Dawson to My Dearest Mother and Dad

February 6, 1943
On the Tunisian Front

I will devote this to a resume of what has taken place these past few months that have not been covered before. As I spent most of my time in and around (censored) . . . since arriving in North Africa, you will know that I got into the big show from the very start. It was our group and unit that took Oran, and I can assure you our mission was the toughest of the lot. Unfortunately, the papers did not mention the large part that was played by the General and this particular division for there were some political aspects that seemed to prevent this from being properly aired. However, I will relate when I return the full story, and you can be assured that it is most interesting.

Looking back over the months of November and December, there were many happy days there as well as days that were not so good. The highlight of the whole thing was the fact that I had a nice place to stay, and it was really a wonderful experience. Major Gaskell and I rented a very comfortable farmhouse that was situated a couple of miles from the headquarters.[9]

Here, we were able to enjoy a warm bed and also have a bath and a fire occasionally. We also had a nice larder that we supplemented the normal ration with, thus allowing a pretty nice menu. The Germans and Italians had done a very thorough job of denuding this country before we arrived, and there is a shortage of many things, such as cattle and livestock, but we didn't have much trouble in getting an occasional pig and a chicken or so.

By so doing, we were able to entertain nearly all the staff and most of the nursing corps in North Africa at one time or another. In fact, it provided a very nice place to relax, as there is absolutely no place in this country that has any recreational facilities. The nearest approach, therefore, was to have guests to a special dinner, such as real fresh meat and fresh vegetables. . . . Also, the General came over for the Christmas party, and we all had great fun in singing songs and listening to the radio as news came about midnight from the States direct, thus making us all a bit homesick, but nevertheless happy in the thought that everyone there was safe and sound. . . .

Finally, orders came to move the division to the front, and for a period of several days, my duties carried me near and far in coordinating the movement east. One night shortly before I left, it was my responsibility to fetch a battalion from their bivouac to the train station. They were ensconced in the shelter of the large mountain near . . . (censored). . . . Of course, all movements have to be accomplished in utter darkness and with as little fuss as possible.

All the trucks were loaded, when suddenly, the air was filled with the sound of a number of airplanes coming over our heads. It was easy to tell that they were enemy planes for the German planes have a very distinct sound, and once one has come in contact with them, it is not easily forgotten. I had some bad moments at this time, for it really would have been a catastrophe had they seen us. They sped on to Oran and did some slight damage, but were not too successful for the air was soon filled with anti-aircraft fire. I can assure you that we all breathed easier when the men were safe in their train, which was well camouflaged and hidden.

I will briefly describe the trip through North Africa through Algeria and into Tunis. In and around Oran, the terrain is largely dominated by a broad, fertile valley with a mountain chain on the seacoast and one inland about twenty-five miles. It was a lovely sight when we left, for all the valley was green with the growing wheat, and the orchards were all beginning to blossom. The orange and tangerine trees were heavily laden with fruit, and it seemed to be the land of peace and plenty, though only a short three months before, it was anything but a Valhalla.

From this valley, one enters the mountains, and for the most part, from Orleansville to Tunis, the whole terrain is dominated by very rugged and rough mountains. The roads are quite serpentine and indeed it is a marvelous bit of engineering to see the manner in which this road has been built. I can assure you that one does well to make a couple of hundred miles a day over such roads. . . . We spent the night near Algiers, but did not go into the city as there was nothing to see there after dark as the town closes at 7 p.m. by order of the military authorities.

The next day, we continued our journey eastward, and it was a continuation of the same sort of country that we had traversed the evening before—perceptible turns and steep grades all day long as we climbed the various ranges of mountains. Soon after lunch, we struck rain, and the wind was biting cold. Traveling without a top and the windshield flush with the radiator, there was absolutely nothing to break the force of either of the elements. By the time we reached (censored). . . . I was about frozen, as were all of us.

The next evening, we rolled into Tunisia and to our destination. I spent the entire night working with some of our elements that were going forward to the front. Between the rain and cold, plus the lack of sleep, I was a very tired young fellow when I finally got into bed the next morning at seven. Early the next morning, I left this spot and came on to the front where I have been ever since. The first few days here were wet and extremely cold, and as my duties have been many, I seldom found much time to do anything about my personal comfort. It seems I am continually cold, which is the main thing that annoys me. . . .

Life on the front has been quite interesting as well as exciting, and I have come to know the true significance of the thing. In this sector, every type of weapon from the heavy bomber and the huge fifty-two-ton tanks to the smallest pistol are being employed in an effort to gain a decision, and though the battle so far has been one of a defensive nature, there have been a great deal of minor engagements that have been fierce and deadly. I witnessed one recently that took the life of a very good friend of mine and also a number of others. It is no picnic, and the enemy is not only strong, but a cunning and artful fighter. We have accounted for ourselves in a most creditable manner, and to date, have managed to uphold the traditions with good account.

This task is a bit greater than most people realize. We have all lived under a false impression as to the enemy's capabilities, and believe me, they are many. One thing that disturbs me is the fact that so much of the news is devoted to our deeds and accomplishments, when in reality, we are still a long way from the ultimate goal. . . .

This about sums up the news from here for now. Aside from the fact that we have a constant noise of artillery being exploded and an occasional air raid, things are a bit slow right now. I predict, though, that there will be more occurring in the near future, as Rommel is getting close now, and the time for a showdown is not too far off. Ironically enough, von Arnim is commanding the Northern Army.[10] Woe betide him or his satellites, as I can assure you there will be a personal attention directed at him by me.

Unbeknownst to the Americans, Rommel and Hans-Juergen von Arnim were far closer to the American front than most Allied commanders realized. Fresh from the their victory at Faid Pass, German General von Arnim launched a strong counterattack against French and American troops in Tunisia on February 14. Von Arnim's attack drove the Allied forces westward in confusion, and Rommel immediately reinforced that success.

With Rommel now personally directing operations, the Germans attacked again on February 19 and drove the American 1st Armored Division through Kasserine Pass the following day. It was a humiliating defeat in the U.S. Army's first pitched battle against the German Wehrmacht.[11]

The battle continued for four days before Rommel decided that the Allied forces in the region were too strong. By then, the 1st Infantry Division had been bloodied badly, with several of its units retreating in panic. On February 22, Rommel called off the offensive and returned his men to southern Tunisia to strengthen the Mareth Line in the wake of Montgomery's approach. The breakdown in the Allied high command soon resulted in Lloyd Fredendall's relief and his replacement by Patton as commander of II U.S. Corps.[12]

For Dawson, the events of the first half of February were bittersweet. To his immense satisfaction, his promotion to captain was finally approved, and he instructed his family to direct all future correspondence to Captain Dawson. Division commander Allen, who remained quite fond of Dawson, enjoyed a joke at his liaison officer's expense, stating that he wasn't even aware that Dawson was up for promotion, but now that he had pinned on his captain's bars, he owed his commanding general 10 percent of his raise as "his cut." Allen also remarked that "like generals, captains are now getting to be a dime a dozen."

What Dawson enjoyed most was the opportunity to serve as the general's junior aide for two weeks. Duties included inspecting front lines, talking to the GIs in the forward foxholes, and trying to keep Allen from taking unnecessary risks. The irrepressible Allen continued to make a strong impression on officers and men of the 1st Division, and Dawson was not alone in describing the general's charismatic leadership style.

Both officers felt at home with the infantry on the front line, as evident in Dawson's description of the courage of "John Doughboy" and the impact Allen's visits had on morale. On a side note, Dawson also took the opportunity to discuss a dogfight between eighteen British Spitfires and six German *Messerschmidts*. The courage of pilots, however, in no way diminished his admiration of the infantry soldier.

Accompanying Allen on the front, Dawson repeatedly witnessed acts of courage that made a profound impression on him and reinforced his desire for command of a rifle company. Writing in late February, he described a young man from Georgia who rescued a young lieutenant whose leg had been blown off while he was leading a bold counterattack. Then all hell broke loose, and the rescued officer's platoon fell back upon seeing their leader struck down. Amid heavy fire, this soldier suddenly turned around and started back toward the lieutenant. He dropped his rifle and as "calmly as if he were in the garden of some quiet secluded spot," he carefully lifted the lieutenant in his arms and started walking very slowly and carefully toward safety. It was simply the bravest thing Dawson had ever seen.

The soldier brought his platoon leader back to the lines and laid him down gently in a protected spot. When Dawson and his party went over to him and asked why he had done it, the soldier replied, "Seems like he needed a little help, so I thought I best fetch him back!" As Dawson concluded the story, that night "found our lads still in position." General Allen presented the GI with a Silver Star and recommended him for the Distinguished Service Cross.

Though his schedule was extraordinarily hectic, Dawson found time to update his journal and to inform his family of his activities.

Dawson to My Dear Family

February 15, 1943
On the Tunisian Front

The days pass in a series of connected hours that leave little time for one's personal thoughts to be expressed, as life on a modern warfront is such that one has practically no time to call his own. You cannot imagine just how this dominates the situation, I am sure, so believe me when I say this and know that I am not shirking my correspondence intentionally. . . .

Our unit continues to do wonderful work despite great odds and handicaps. Truly the magnificent spirit of the American doughboy makes one feel a deep sense of humility towards them. The other day, I accompanied the General on a tour of the front lines. The tales of heroism and bravery are so numerous that it would take a book to properly justify them all. The men fight and do their duty one and all.

So far, we have had comparatively light casualties and have accounted for ourselves in a manner that cannot be discounted, and I can only reiterate the fact that I am grateful to be with such a wonderful outfit. And I also can say that nothing is more inspiring than to be with and intimately associated with such a wonderful man as Terry [Allen].

Now, for the past two weeks, Terry has been without a junior aide, so it has been my good luck to be with him a great deal. The other day, when we visited the front lines, we went to every unit on the whole sector and the General personally spoke to nearly every man up there. We also visited the observation posts that were often well forward of the front lines themselves.

There is nothing that is more inspiring than to have a general walking about the front lines when the bullets are flying, talking with the men and looking around with the same air one would assume walking down Austin Avenue. He doesn't know what the word fear is and he is just like a hypodermic to the men of his command.

Yesterday, about four-thirty, we had a most spectacular air battle over our heads between eighteen of our planes and six of the Germans'. Our Spitfires were returning from a reconnaissance mission when the six German planes swooped down on them from out of the clouds, catching our planes unawares. The whole action lasted only about three minutes, but it was the most dramatic three minutes I have lived through in a long time.

To begin with, the air has been dominated by the enemy over here and our constant question has been, 'Where are those 50,000 planes we are supposed to have?' This is usually the case, though, for one always sees more enemy over our lines than our own planes. . . .

Though we outnumbered the Jerries three to one, they had the advantage because they were above our planes when they attacked. The air became untenable, for much steel was flying about as they sought to single each other out. In fact, two of our men here on the ground were injured by flying shrapnel. In the initial attack, one of our planes was mortally hit and plummeted to the ground in flames. Then, in a few seconds, two of the enemy seemed to disintegrate as our lads struck back. The bulk of the planes then tucked tail . . . the action then devolved upon two of the planes in a dogfight that was the most thrilling thing I ever saw . . . as one of our Spitfires and one of the German *Messerschmidts* fought it out between themselves. The German came out victorious, as he was able to put a cannon shot into the Spitfire and knock it out.

So it goes, with the battle slowly shaping up for the final showdown. So far, the activity has been a sort of sparring battle with neither side assuming too much initiative or attacking too strenuously. We have been able to hold our own, and the myth that the German Army is invincible is rapidly being exploded. I can assure you that we have given much more than we have received. It now boils down to the big show when Rommel gets here, and the big fight begins. We are ready for him, and it is only a matter of time when the end of his sojourn in Africa will end. . . .

Give my love to all there, and as soon as I get a chance, I shall try to catch up and write all the friends that were so nice to remember me on Christmas. Incidentally, all future correspondence is to be addressed to Captain Joseph T. Dawson.

Dawson to Dear Shorty[13]

February 21, 1943

Ever since I arrived in North Africa, I have had a most disagreeable case of the hives that has made life almost unbearable because of the intense itching it causes. I stood it as long as I could, and early in December, I spent about four days in the hospital at Oran in an attempt to get some relief. However, they had no facilities at the time for skin diseases, so I decided to try and worry along somehow and hoped that sooner or later, it would go away. Unfortunately, it has persisted.

As life on the front line is tough and uncomfortable under the most ideal conditions, you can readily see that with this constant torment, I found my foxhole anything but a happy home. Though on two occasions when the *Boche* came over and strafed us, it assumed a very satisfactory appearance. To add further, the water supply is a bit short, and as yet we have not been able to take time out from actual fighting long enough to build any stream bathhouses or showers. In fact, the only stream we have here is from the water jacket of the 30-cal. heavy machine guns. As a result of incessant scratching and irritation of the skin, I finally have accrued about 497 sores and boils, and the inability to get a bath in over *forty* days!

When I first came to North Africa, I was nauseated by the sight of the terrible filth that existed amongst the Arabs. I thought it was some religious superstition to cause them to never bathe. Too, I had read in any number of encyclopedias and reports that stated rain was something that came only once every year or so. Instead, I have seen about the same number of sunshiny days in North Africa as I did in England! (There, we had four days complete with sunshine).

But back to my Arabs and sans bathing. I just couldn't understand 'til I learned that this has been a year of unusual weather, which naturally changes the picture a bit. Then some days ago, I got to the front and there I learned that things are quite different. As we are high in the mountains, it has been extremely cold and one seldom has an opportunity to remove more than two layers of clothes. . . . As you keep three layers on below the two outer ones, you see how it makes it impossible to see your skin more than once a week. Thus, you can see that one learns many things in the army!

What with the heavy snows of the past three weeks, I decided Iceland would be a veritable paradise, and had thought of transferring there to get warm. But alas—my condition became so intolerable that I was forced to seek the hospital far back of the front and try to get rehabilitated for the Spring push. Here, I get a hot bath anytime I want, and my body is beginning to look like a human anatomy should, instead of that of a Mexican hairless dog with the mange. Though I haven't yet had a cure affected, I am definitely improving and hope that another three or four weeks will see me back at the old stand. The only regrettable thing is there are no medals given for the itch. Frankly, I want you to urge Congress to have one struck and award it, because I can assure you it is well earned.

But to more serious things! The Germans are playing for keeps, and I can assure you that they are not only tough, but crafty as well as smart. After six weeks of fighting them, I have come to many realizations, and from bitter lessons, we are learning what it means to face them. They know how to utilize their weapons, but pay little heed to losses. So far, we have given about as much as we have taken, and that has been plenty. It is no military secret that the battle is gaining momentum, and ere too long, the showdown will come. I do not fear the outcome, for I have come to see things that make me completely convinced of our superiority as to the capabilities of our men.

As I said before, we have taken lessons from the Germans, and from these bitter pills, we are molding a force that will soon bring victory. The tales of individual heroism and bravery make one realize just what stuff America is made of, and though the majority will remain unsung, the essence of the mold will yield the finest fighting outfit in the world.

You can assure each and every one that the American Doughboy is still the best man this world has produced. Take your glamour boys in the Air Corps and paratroops and all the rest, but as for me, give me John Doughboy. The guy that walks everywhere, sleeps on the ground, eats occasionally, faces every device Hell ever conceived, is seldom comfortable, constantly harassed, but always is on the spot for whatever task he is called upon to do. He does it without the plaudits and the aid of the picture magazines, and with it all, gives his heart and soul to his God and his country! Yes, these are the boys that mean everything to me.

There are others who I wish to say are doing a grand job, namely the British and the French. Candidly speaking, I find the whole American army praising the British Tommy. He and our boys have been fighting right alongside each other, and many are the words of praise for his courage and staunchness [sic]. The sneering snob who sat complacently these past three years, while England has fought for the whole shebang, should come to some quiet little village like Medjez el Bab, Sbeitla or Tripoli and see some of the things that are going on. They will change their tune, I can assure you.

Then the French. Ah! These Goumies (we call them the Goons) are really terrific. They are native Moroccan troops, and are the scourge of the Italians and Germans. They are given 200 francs for every enemy ear that they can bring back. For instance, the other day, they brought back 175 ears, and I understand that due to a heavy artillery concentration, they were unable to collect several more that had gone to sleep, due to their convincing sleep talk.

I was with them several days ago when the Germans tried to take their position. They took all the Germans could throw at them for two hours, then decided it was time they went to work. So instead of holding or retreating, as was expected by the enemy, they counter-attacked! *Mein Kampf* doesn't have a page on what to do in this event, so the *Boche* just couldn't understand such action. They had been laboring under the false impression that when they attacked with dive bombers, artillery, tanks and infantry, the French were supposed to retreat. One prisoner frankly admitted that they had played dirty football because his coach had assured him that the game that day was against a weak team! Honestly, he just couldn't understand such actions!

Over here, we are somewhat divorced from histrionics and movies or collegiate pep talks. The General doesn't say, "Now boys, go out there and give 'em hell" or such stuff. John Doughboy is a smart boy now, and his college days are over. Instead, the General may say to his officers, who in turn will tell the men, "Well, boys, this is our sector—we will fight in place." That simple sentence tells the greatest story I've found yet, for it means just what it says, IN PLACE; *no retreat, no strategic withdrawal no surrender*—just plain IN PLACE!

Well brother, that about winds up the journal for now. . . . Do write soon, and if possible, send me some film. Next step—MAJOR.

With Patton now in command of II Corps and Omar Bradley serving as his deputy commander, the Allied forces prepared for a final offensive to destroy Rommel's presence in North Africa. Again, the Big Red One played an important role in the impending offensive. Patton's immediate task was to rehabilitate II Corps in the wake of the Kasserine debacle, and to cooperate with British General Harold Alexander, who now directed Allied ground operations.[14]

Patton's corps had a threefold task: to draw off reserves from the enemy forces facing Montgomery; to gain control of forward airfields in order to assist the British Eighth Army; and to establish a forward maintenance center from which the Eighth Army could draw supplies to maintain their expected advance against the Mareth Line.[15] In what was essentially a British show, Patton's response was to attack and seize Gafsa, then to seize a pass through the Eastern Dorsale, thereby threatening Gabes from the flank and weakening the German defenses in front of Montgomery.

On March 16, the 1st Infantry Division spearheaded the attack on Gafsa. The next day, Gafsa fell and the 1st Ranger Battalion, operating under Allen's command, advanced and occupied a forward covering position, east of El Guettar, about twelve miles southeast of Gafsa. The remainder of the Big Red One followed on March 21 and secured all objectives against weakened Italian resistance.

So rapidly did the Americans move that Allen mused, "It's all going like maneuvers. It can't be right."[16] Not surprisingly, the enemy counterattacked with brute force. The Germans, now under von Arnim, reacted swiftly and launched a major counterattack two days later.[17] The major effort was directed up the valley of the Gabes Road, with medium and heavy tanks preceding the infantry. By noon, the German attack had temporarily stalled, but by 1645 hours, they attacked again and were decisively repulsed, taking heavy casualties.[18]

Having access to the German codes ordering the second attack, Allen recklessly broadcasted to the enemy that the 1st Division was ready. Allen's breach of signal security prompted Patton to admonish him to take the war more seriously. With the Germans now showing signs of abandoning the Mareth Line, Patton immediately counterattacked, and the 1st Division seized all its objectives in the vicinity of El Guettar. The next day, American armored elements broke through to the east and linked up with the British Eighth Army.

For the Big Red One, the battle of El Guettar held special significance. In Allen's official report, he noted that during the critical early days of the battle, "The 'Fighting First,' alone and unassisted, had stood 'toe-to-toe' with the *10th Panzer Division* (the pride of the German *Afrika Korps*), and had 'slugged it out,' to a well earned decision. Thereafter, the First Division had a battle confidence, and a belief in itself, second to none."[19]

News correspondent Ernie Pyle agreed. He had previously described the Kasserine predicament as "damned humiliating." Two months later, he noted that battle experience had hardened the GIs to the point that "the 1st Infantry Division is an example of what our American units can be after they have gone through the mill of experience. Those boys did themselves proud in the semifinals [the cleaning up of central Tunisia]. Everybody speaks about it. [Their] casualties included few taken prisoners. All the other casualties were wounded or died fighting."[20]

Other accolades quickly followed. For his cool direction of the division's recent battle, Teddy Roosevelt received the Distinguished Service Cross. Eisenhower predicted, "the Hun will soon learn to dislike that outfit [1st Division]." The final word was found in an unfinished letter of one of the division's combat infantryman: "Well, folks, we stopped the best they had."[21]

Dawson, fresh from several days in the hospital, concurred with the army's high command and outlined the specifics of the battle that, in his mind, wiped out the disgrace of Kasserine Pass.

Dawson to My Dearest Family

March 26, 1943
Tunisia

As the battle assumes its crescendo, I find that time has been filled with a multiplicity of duties that have left little in the way of personal pleasures, so my correspondence has been neglected. . . .

No sooner had I been released from the hospital than things started humming in these parts. I had thought this would be the case, so I arranged to get back in time for the whole show. Though I continue to scratch, I am much better than before. I flew back about two weeks ago, stopping off in Algiers for one night then on east the following day, and through a great stroke of luck, succeeded in getting a ride in one of our vehicles from the airport to headquarters. Immediately, I fell into the duties at hand, and since that date, have hardly had a moment to call my own. . . . As all of this is past history, it is probably safe to assume that it will be passed by the censors so I will try and hit the high spots in the resume.

Returning to this front, I found the weather still quite cool, and rain continued to fall where we were located. All the first few days were spent in the gathering together of the various elements of our force and putting everything in shape for the assault. Our mission was to take Gafsa, which has been necessary to the strategic situation in that it has afforded a base of supply for our operations. So it was several days ago that we started rolling toward this objective.

We had anticipated a rather tough time there and came prepared to launch an all out assault. . . . Early in the morning, the enemy started forth with several tanks and attempted to shell us with artillery, however, our artillery began to go to work on them, and ere long, the tanks had vanished and their guns ceased firing. Then our air corps came over and pasted them with a tremendous load of bombs that took all the fight out of them. Our troops marched into the town in record time, and we didn't have a single casualty.

The enemy withdrew to the region of El Guettar about ten miles east of the town and there took up positions. We spent the next few days in organizing the city and preparing ourselves for the next step, which meant the continuing of the attack. . . . The resistance stiffened around El Guettar, and only after brief but fierce fighting, were we able to take this little town and the range of low-lying hills about three miles east of the city. However, we succeeded without too much trouble, and at the end of the day, secured our position and had taken over 1,000 prisoners, all Italian. It was interesting to note how quickly they gave up and how glad they seemed to be to surrender. . . .

However, during the night, the Germans came in, and by dawn, they had thrown in a terrific amount of strength, including 100 tanks and armored cars. Then we really went to work. All day long, the battle raged fiercely, and again I was fortunate enough to have a spot from which I could observe the entire battle. . . . I shall never forget it and though I have had many experiences since I have been in the army, I shall always remember this for it was warfare on a grand scale.

Every weapon at the command of either side was fully used that day, and it was an awesome sight. The fierce tank battle wherein all our armored forces and theirs locked in a death struggle defies description. Accompanied by bombers and fighters, the battle roared all morning long, and by noon, both of the armored elements retired to the protection of their lines. The plain, however, was a mass of tangled wreckage of tanks and guns that had been knocked out. The enemy was in clear view all day long, and throughout the afternoon, our artillery shelled them unmercifully.

Then promptly at four o'clock, it seemed that the jaws of Hell opened up as they launched their final assault. First came the artillery barrage that encompassed us and caused me to nestle into Mother Earth as I have never nestled in anything. Believe me, we learned the value of a foxhole that day! For an hour this continued, and just as the final round exploded, the *stukas* came over and did their dirty business.

Now that I have experienced all the various weapons being shot at me, I can conclude that there is nothing quite as terrifying as a dive bomber. They come in like giant vultures and drop their bombs with deadly accuracy, and the thing that adds to their terror is these bombs that are equipped with some mechanism that creates the most appalling noise I ever heard. It's like the approach of death, and one feels it more from a psychological standpoint than any other . . . then came the fighters and strafed us with blazing machine-guns.

After this, we shook ourselves a bit and stood up to see what else was coming. Then began the most amazing sight I ever witnessed in all my life . . . from out of nowhere over 200 Germans rose out of the ground before us on the very same ground that had been fought over by the tanks all morning long and in plain sight of all of us. How they had gotten there is a mystery to me, but sure enough there they were.

Without the slightest hesitation, they arose as one and started toward us, with their tanks behind them in three groups of ten each. It looked like a great team in football formation coming toward the goal line. I have come to learn that this is their method and one that has been used in all theaters of war. Nothing in all history can quite compare to this for it is the most audacious thing ever seen.

Then our artillery went to work on them with sky bursts that exploded shrapnel shells over their heads and literally cut them to pieces. It was murderous and deadly. In the space of five minutes, the whole force was reduced to a small handful. It was a terrible sight to witness, and of the 200 who started the attack, I dare say there were less than ten who survived . . . so ended that encounter, and night found each side regrouping and sending in fresh men to take the place of those who had fought all day long.

Yesterday, the climax came as Jerry started his final thrust and attacked on all sides. I was in the midst of one heavy battle far to the front and am frank to confess that it was a miraculous incident that saved my life. Artillery started falling out of nowhere on us, just as a battalion commander and myself started over a small hill together. I noticed a small, eroded gully about twenty yards in front of me. And as the shells began to fall pretty close, I started to run for this gully. I heard the swish of a shell coming and instinctively dropped where I was rather than try to reach the gully. Sure enough, the darn thing landed squarely in the spot where I was headed for. You can imagine how I felt!

Now that the Mareth line has been cracked, and [Rommel] is on the move backwards, I guess this phase has about ended and ere long, we should see the final act to this North African drama. It has been a terrible conflict and one that will ever live in my memory, but when the final chapter is written, it will be well to remember that the far-reaching significance of this battle will mean much to the completion of this war. The lives that have been given here are many, but the issue has been settled for the best, and they have not died in vain.

With the penetration of the Mareth Line, the ultimate defeat for the Axis powers in North Africa was only a matter of time. After the battle of El Guettar, the 1st Infantry Division took a brief period to rest and refit in preparation for further combat operations. Following two weeks of constant combat, Dawson was only too ready to relate news from the front and to inquire about events at home. Constant themes of his missives included complaints about food, fear of mines, and fatalism that always permeated the ranks of soldiers on the front line.

The respite from action on the front was short-lived. On April 16, the 1st Division joined the remainder of II Corps, now under Bradley, in the vicinity of Beja in northern Tunisia.[22] Together with the 34th Infantry Division, the Big Red One was to clear the way for a subsequent breakthrough by the 1st Armored Division to Mateur. The 34th Division was to neutralize the enemy on Hill 609 and protect the 1st Division's left flank. The width of the division's zone necessitated an attack with three infantry regiments abreast across a valley checkered with enemy defensive positions, each of which had to be reduced by fire and maneuver. It was attrition warfare at its worst, with frontline units suffering staggering casualties.

The 1st Division crossed the line of departure on the night of April 22–23 and attacked against stiffening resistance. Following the loss of their forward positions, the Germans then conducted a general withdrawal under enemy pressure in preparation for occupying a second defensive line about five miles to the northeast. II Corps immediately continued the attack, and by May 1, the enemy faced a critical situation. On May 5, II Corps attacked again, with the 1st Division seizing the crossing sites of the Tine River. With their northern flank in disarray, the German defenses crumbled. And with Allied armies advancing on all fronts, von Arnim surrendered unconditionally on May 13. The campaign in North Africa was over.

Casualties within the Big Red One had been high, particularly in the final seventeen days of the campaign. Allen counted 2,030 battle casualties, with the infantry bearing a disproportionate number.[23] Severe casualties reduced infantry companies to little more than reinforced platoons, prompting Dawson to decline a rifle company when Allen initially offered him a field command.

In a later letter, Dawson elaborated on his declination of command. Casualties had been excessive in the North African campaign, especially among the officers. The company to which Allen intended to assign Dawson had been reduced to a single officer and eight men. Though reinforcements and liberated prisoners later raised the company to full strength, such attrition was natural among American front-line units.

Rather, Dawson was assigned duty to the 16th Infantry Regiment, which provided him the opportunity to sharpen his combat skills before taking command of a forward unit. In assessing the campaign in northwest Africa, he characterized the battle as "grim and terrible with fierce and intense fighting on all sides." So horrendous were the casualties in the Big Red One that Dawson compared losses in the infantry battalions to the World War I poem "In Flanders Fields":[24]

> In Flanders field the poppies blow
> Between the crosses, row on row,
> That mark our place; and in the sky
> The larks, still bravely singing, fly
> Scarce heard amid the guns below.

His letters home again reflected pride in the 1st Division, coupled with an increasing concern for his personal well-being. He took time to describe his own near fatal encounter with the Germans, as well as his profound respect for the chaplains and other combat service support troops who afforded a small degree of comfort to the GIs in the forward battle areas.

Through it all, nothing fascinated the young officer as much as the behavior of the American citizen-soldier. Even during the thick of battle, Dawson found enough "humaneness in their being to think first of helping" the enemy rather than killing him. Such "a complexity of human emotions" was sufficient to convince him of the righteousness of the American cause and the humanity of a soldier of democracy.

Dawson to My Dearest Family

April 3, 1943
Tunisian Front

Tonight, the wind is blowing a gale, and a dust storm is raging. All of which makes us quite happy and enables us to relax for the first time in many nights. This is accomplished because the elements are keeping the *Luftwaffe* on the ground tonight, thus preventing them from harassing us all night long with bombing attacks. Nothing is more disconcerting to one's rest than wave after wave of bombers flying low over your head and dropping his load of bombs.

I am frank to confess that this form of amusement is not at all conducive to sleep and sweet dreams. Last night, his attentiveness lasted from nine o'clock to five this morning without a minute free from his nefarious presence. And though it is quite terrifying, particularly when one hits rather close to your foxhole, it also produces a cold anger so intense that one spends the best part of the night expressing both mentally and orally his hopes and wishes to the effect that the devils may soon be in the innermost *sanctum sanctorum* of hell, bathing in liquid fire and brimstone, and having a sandpaper towel to use after the bath. All of which is a somewhat verbose way of saying that the *Luftwaffe* is not very popular.

I feel sure that by the time this letter will reach you, the battle of Tunisia will have ended, and the intruders will have been overcome completely. However, one is forced to admit that he is a tenacious foe. Today marks the fourteenth day of this battle, and its intensity has never let down the whole time. The terrain over which we have been fighting is as tough as one could possibly imagine. Sharp, jagged hills deeply cut with innumerable crevices, and ravines require strenuous effort and arduous fighting against such a determined foe.

And though the bright boys who jauntily skip up here and get as close to the front line as fifteen miles, then sneak back a couple of hundred miles to safety and a bottle of cognac to write their literary masterpieces of pure poppycock, may leave the impression that our army is a raw and untrained group of men, I feel sure that the enemy will not agree. I can assure you that the opposition is paying a terrific price and is learning that we can bite with a vengeance.

Never have I been quite so incensed as I was when I read some of the accounts of the fighting over here and the opinion voiced by many correspondents that inexperience and the like was the cause for the breakthrough by the Germans last February.[25] Though losses were heavy, it is also true that the enemy paid dearly for that little sortie, and the only reason he broke through was because he had a superior number concentrated at that point. We readily admit that each day teaches us new things, and we also admit that he is a very tough and formidable foe, but we also KNOW that we are tougher than he is and a darn sight smarter! Each mistake we make can be acknowledged, but never have these mistakes assumed the stature of a blunder. . . .

This has been pecked during the hours of one and four in the morning, and as I stated earlier, the night is filled with a very high wind, which has reduced the enemy from harassing us too much. Now, it is time for me to catch a couple of hours of sleep, as tomorrow will be a busy day. God bless you one and all, and never forget that my every thought is of each one of you.

Dawson to Precious Loved Ones

April 4, 1943

The telegram of some weeks vintage came yesterday, which was most timely, even though it had been sent some time ago. Now that the battle we are in passes the fifteenth day, I find that we have really done a wonderful job. I will spare you the details, but you can know that it has been a bitter and terrible conflict. Yesterday, the highlight was the great victory we had over their diabolical *stukas*. Our air force destroyed fourteen out of fourteen of the devils, and I can assure you that we appreciated it no end. They have been quite active over us, and I assure you they are a bit upsetting to one's nerves.

The weather continues cold, and I am beginning to wonder when it will begin to get warm. The Sirocco winds are now beginning to blow, and the dust is very disagreeable. Soon I know, however, that I shall be bathing once more in the Mediterranean! Which makes me realize that it is now almost a month since my last bath. But I'm feeling fine, and my hives are about all gone. Right now, I have no time to think about personal discomforts, so I don't notice such things.

Dawson to My Dear Family

April 6, 1943

The good part of being on duty during the wee small hours of the night is that I am able to write a few letters and thus keep you abreast of my current activities. Insofar as action on the front is not great during this period, it allows time to sort of catch up with such duties. . . .

Now that spring is about here, I am beginning to thaw out a little and ere too long, I hope to be able to shed my winter case. . . . Yesterday was highlighted by a little trip to a nearby village, where the most wonderful water in all the world flows naturally from the ground at a temperature of about ninety degrees. It is an ancient Roman bath which has served this section for countless ages, and I can assure you that it has been put to great use by the American army. When we took it from the enemy, it was a bit run down and quite dirty from the abuse suffered at the hands of the Germans and Italians, but it is now restored by our engineers and enjoyed by all who can find time to get to it. As it had been twenty-eight days since I last had a bath, its enjoyment by me cannot be overemphasized. I stayed in almost an hour and managed to dissolve a good deal of the crust of dirt that had accumulated. . . .

Yesterday was further highlighted by the fact that it was the first day in over fifteen that I did not go to the battle front, so my day was truly quiet and peaceful and without the blood-tingling noise of whining shells or sodden brr-ump of the bombs. All of which left one with a sort of let down feeling and somewhat on edge, for after being subjected to gunfire daily, one learns to adapt his nervous system to it, and when it absents itself, the old nerves begin to perk up and wonder what it is all about.

Only the deep throated booms in the distance from the artillery and the whistle of the Spitfires as they came over were the expressions of what was going on at the front. Such it is in the battle as it is being waged, and a day of comparative quiet is usually a prelude to bigger things. I feel sure that there will be a showdown in the very near future, and this mess over here will be finished up.

One thing I wanted to mention concerns one of our men who was on a lonely outpost the other day, far out in the front of our lines on an observation mission. Jerry had thrown everything in his basket at us, and this trooper has received a lot of attention from a mortar that had located him perched high on a mountain. He spotted a German soldier wandering around about 200 yards in front of him and seemingly alone. He decided he would try to capture him, so he slipped away from his post and crept up on the guy and surprised him.

Our lad was so excited over his conquest that instead of disarming the guy or shooting him, he drew from his pack a can of C-rations and gave it to him, extending a lighted cigarette at the same time. Such it is this strange person, the American doughboy who fights like a tiger, gets shot at and hit in a lot of instances, [gets] subjected to innumerable pains and discomforts at the hands of these wretches that started this affair, but [he] still has enough humaneness in [his] being to think first of helping the fellow who is doing the dirt to them.

So it is with many of them. A complexity of human emotions. and I can assure you they are fit subjects for the boys to try to fathom in the circles of science of human behaviorism.

So ends this little story. I am well, and know that I think of you always.

Dawson to My Beloved Family

April 26, 1943

It is now early morning (4 a.m.), and the dawn barrage is beginning. The solid boom of the big guns bangs out the doom of the *boche* as we slowly close in on him. Every day brings forth a little more advance on our part, and ere too long, we should have this battle won. . . .

Over these ridges and peaks, the bloody battle is being waged and every inch of the controlling ground is being gained from the defenders by dint of blood and sweat. One becomes somewhat apathetic toward death here, for the issue provides little time for personal feelings, and it devolves on one to build a wall of steel around his soul in order to fully devote his energies and strength to the task at hand.

Yes, it is a deadly task that confronts us all over here, and the sooner we get it over, the happier we, and this world, will be.

One finds it hard to neutralize their feelings for this is too great a moral issue to equivocate upon now. It demands that one's entire being be concentrated in force and get the task done. One has only to reflect, however, on the misery, pain, suffering and tragedy that the enemy has inflicted upon this world to clarify their conscience.

To see men die, to hear the whine of shrapnel or the dull thump of a bomb or the sharp clatter of a machine-gun, only adds to one's resolve to exterminate the devils that brought this mess to us. And I speak whereof I know. One does not go to war any longer for the glory (and it is a false glory) but rather to meet a necessity imposed upon them to do away with a group who threaten a life worse than death. . . .

Yesterday was Easter Sunday. Having been up late the night before, I slept till eight o'clock and awakened only when the artillery started laying down a solid barrage. But it was a beautiful day, and the sun was bright and warm with just enough of the latter to remind me of a nice spring day at home. Instead of donning my new spring suit, complete with colorful shirt and tie, and driving myself to the church, I merely laced up my shoes, put on my leggings, buttoned my pistol belt, rubbed the sleep out of my eyes, and made my way to the kitchen truck.

There, I humbly paid my best wishes upon the cook (nicknamed Hitler) and asked in my most solicitous manner for a cup of coffee. As you know, the cook is the number one general in this man's army, and one always uses discretion when addressing him. It pays real dividends to stay on the right side of him, and I go to great lengths to sell him on the idea that I am OK.

By turning the full throttle of my personality and charms upon him, I was able to get a wonderful bit of the outside of roast pig— crisp and brown with all the sealed-in delicious flavor and juiciness that makes my mouth water even now for more. . . . We often wonder if all the hogs in America have been turned into Spam and all the cows into corned beef. The devil sure took charge of the situation when these two items were concocted because I am sure the Lord would have no part of either of them if He had to eat them as often as we do.

When this war is over and big day of judgment comes to the perpetrators of this mess, I think the order of the docket should be Hitler, Tojo, the guy who invented Spam, and Mussolini.[26] Mussolini is just another misguided rat who thought the cheese was better in the rat-trap than it was in the cupboard, whereas the other three were sold on the idea of inventing and imposing new methods of torture and misery on a gullible world. I hope I am on the jury for I think I can mete out some excellent methods of punishment.

Duties required me taking a tour of the battlefront during the afternoon, and it turned out to be a little more exciting than I really care for as a steady diet. Our units had displaced forward from the previous day's fighting and were in the process of establishing our newly won positions. As the *boche* uses mines to a very great extent, it makes it a bit dangerous to run around the front lines in a jeep until the roads and trails have been cleared. Then too, the terrain is always different when you get on it than it appeared from a distance, so it is easy to take the wrong turn in the road or trail.

Sure enough, I landed squarely in front of our front line in such a manner yesterday afternoon. I did it quite unknowingly, for though one is an expert at reading a map and with full knowledge of the disposition of friendly troops, it is quite easy to get off the beaten path in these hills.

I won't elaborate too much on this point, but will merely mention that the biggest hazard is from mines and booby traps. One exercises greatest caution, and though the jeep might not blow up, the element of its likelihood gives one an uneasy feeling somewhat akin to such small physical items as nervous prostration. After doing this a number of times, however, you sort of adopt the same fatalistic feeling that you get after dodging artillery shells or machine-gun fire—it's either your time or it isn't. If one worried about such things, he would be a nervous wreck inside of two hours. . . .

Well, anyhow I doubled back behind our lines just in time to be greeted by a deluge of high velocity 75s that started raining all around my poor little jeep just like raindrops. They really were acting personal about the whole thing because I was the only thing within a half-mile to shoot at.

After a few incidents like this, I have come to sense the fire pretty well, and it has become second nature to either hit the ground or give her the gun and run like the wind between barrages. So the only injury I suffered was a scraping of the knees as I hit the ground. Now all of this could have been avoided as it developed later that the destination which I sought was not where I had been told it would be, which is another thing that sometimes happens in the best-regulated armies.

After three hours of wandering around under such conditions, I spotted a soldier on top of a hill and made my way to him. It developed that it was a chaplain from the unit which I was seeking and whom I knew quite well. He was engaged in the task of clearing the battlefield of the dead—another of his many duties—and preparing them for burial.

I talked with him for about ten minutes, though time was precious as I had not completed my mission. I could not help it, however, for the circumstances were a bit significant and struck me rather forcefully. He is a young chap, about twenty-five years old, though he looks considerably older than his years. There on a hilltop covered with beauty and horror alike, he was seeing to it that friend and foe alike were given a Christian burial. . . .

Amid such natural beauty were the remnants of the defenses that they [Germans] had constructed and the wreckage of their equipment. It seemed as though some hand of destiny had struck the place with devastating force. It struck home the fact that righteousness can be terrible sometimes. We who know the instruments of death can understand the thing and appreciate the impact of it all. We all realize keenly our shortcomings, and it takes these influences to bolster and strengthen us both morally and spiritually.

'Tis not a far cry in this war to the pagan days and the sharp focus that it brought through these representatives are far deeper than words can express. All of us thank God for them [the clergy], and I am proud that my father is one of them.

So it goes. We toil here as do you back there at home. Know that my constant thoughts and prayers are of you.

Dawson to Dearest Family

May 6, 1943

You can readily understand from the news accounts that I have been busy the past several weeks, and as a result, I have not written in several days. However, I am still doing business at the same old stand and I hope that long before this letter reaches you, the Tunisian campaign will have passed into history, and I shall be enjoying a well-earned rest.

These last phases of the battle have been hard and long for all concerned, and now that the end is just a matter of days, we are all looking forward to a little rest. That does not mean a return home or any such miracle as that, we are looking to a little relaxation before we start the next chapter.

This African campaign has not about seen the final touches, and anything from now on is more or less anti-climatic. I hope that I shall have a chance to get to a place where the days will not be filled with the incessant noise of the various implements of war and find time to write a summary of some of this that has taken place. . . .

Well, my mind is not so sharp tonight as I have other things to do besides write letters. We are now attacking, and ere the day ends, we should see the *boche* about whipped. Between us and the British, we are now pounding him at Bizerte and almost to Tunis, and by the time the day is over, I expect we shall be on the outskirts of Tunis.

He is getting noticeably weaker and it shouldn't be long now. After fighting him from one end of this country to the other, I have come to the conclusion that the dose we are now giving him is really too good for him. Though sometimes one thinks a bit callously about war, I have come to the conclusion that all the misery this bunch of guys have inflicted on me personally, gives me plenty of latitude in my regards to him. We are hoping that there will be enough of them left to sorta [sic] even things up for Dunkirk and a few other little jobs he has done in the past.

With the fighting finally over, Dawson's principal duty became coordinating the redeployment of the 1st Division to its base in Oran in anticipation for the next operation. For Dawson, the duty was rather mundane since he had performed similar functions in England and upon arrival in North Africa.

He visited subordinate headquarters and arranged transportation assets to convoy the battalions several hundred miles westward until they reached their encampments from the previous November. The first combat team arrived on May 26, and the last closed two days later. During the deployment, the combat teams traveled in column one day apart.

Immediately upon arrival, Dawson reflected on the six months of continuous fighting the Big Red One had endured. He wrote with the air of a veteran who had withstood the test of combat. His correspondence also reflected a resurgence of patriotism as Dawson acknowledged that the American doughboy was merely "serving one's country the best he can."

Yet, always present were the stench of death and the fear of injury. Such fear was common among all soldiers who had experience with combat, and Dawson was hardly an exception. He had declined a command, but hoped he would receive another opportunity. Most importantly, he had survived the initial campaign against the Germans. He remained unsure how well he would fare in the future.

Dawson to Dearest Family

May 20, 1943

Now that the battle is over here in North Africa, I am enjoying a brief rest and beginning to feel the comforts of a bath and real steaks and other delicacies. Yes, I'm fit as a fiddle and can now look back on the past five months with the air of a veteran. The battle was indeed fierce, and I can assure you we felt the brunt of their power, but were able to defeat them in a most convincing manner.

I haven't time at the moment to give you one of my full recitations on things as I am going to take off in a day or so and give it the time necessary. Meantime, know that it is so nice to hear of Dad being back in harness and feeling fit once more. Give everyone my fondest love and be assured of my good health and well-being.

Dawson to My Dearest Family

May 22, 1943
Back "home"[27]

May is in full bloom over here, and indeed this is a beautiful place. The verdant growth of wild flowers and ripening grain fields give a picture that truly is lovely. Of course, the flies and mosquitoes abound in swarms, and one is constantly working on them. Still, all in all, it is really a place that seems far, far removed from the nether world we experienced a few short weeks ago. It is somewhat akin in feeling to having lived in a state of mental suspension only to finally awaken on a soft down bed and find reality once again. Yes, the feelings and thoughts one has in combat are far away from those one normally has when life returns to semblance of security and peace.

Over here, the men of this division have been in battle for almost six continuous months, and it gives them cause to wonder where the mighty legions are and what they are doing. Never since the Civil War has any one American unit been employed in actual battle for that length of time without a measure of rest. Even Bataan was only five months. So you see, the mental attitude of many needed a little jolting to prevent too much self-commiseration. That is something we all must guard against, for it is easy to get into the mental attitude that you are doing something big when everyone is singing your praises to the sky, but in reality it is nothing more than anyone else is doing now—namely serving one's country as best he can.

The last days of the battle of Tunisia were grim and terrible with fierce and intense fighting on all sides. We were in the thick of it up to the very last and played a major part in the final out-come, though the actual finale was not participated in by us. We created the breakthrough that brought about the eventual defeat, but ere the final shot was fired, we had departed from there to come here for a well-earned rest. I journeyed back by jeep and when I reached here, I was really snowed under for the first week, getting everything arranged for the troops. . . .

From the tenor of this letter, you can see that I am well, happy and contented. Though as yet my majority has not been approved, I have hopes that I shall get it before the year is out. No longer do I aspire to high rank, but shall be most happy with a major's rank—if and when. Now don't go shouting that I'm a major be-cause I am not as yet. I'm only in the process! Let me assure you again that I'm counting on you to temper your enthusiasm as regards eulogizing your son!

Dawson to My Dearest Ones

June 1, 1943
North Africa

By the way, I will mention that during the heavy fighting on May 3, on the now famous hill 532, the entire battalion was almost wiped out completely. At the time, Alex was in command of the headquarters company of the 1st Battalion, and at the end of the day's fighting, there were only five officers and forty-eight men left—the rest of the number either killed, wounded or cap-tured, including the battalion commander.[28] *Time* magazine noted it in the May 10 issue, when they condescended to pay us a left-handed compliment to somewhat salve our feelings after previous expressions on their part that were not true and also very much out of place.

Anyhow, I was offered command of A Company, which at the time consisted of eight men and one officer. I declined the offer, and as it turned out, I think it was the wiser thing to do inasmuch as the company commander had been captured, and when the fall of Tunis took place, we were able to get over 200 men and officers back who had been captured on that day. So the company is once more up to full strength.

I can assure you that I will not return to the regiment to command a company, but when the opportunity presents itself, I hope to have a shot at a battalion command, and maybe I will get it. Not that I feel snooty about it, but to give you an idea of the thing, there have been four company commanders of A Company in the space of six months, whereas the turnover in battalion commanders in the space of six months has not been but about 50 percent.

I am quite frank in my assertion that one figures odds in a case like this, and all I ask is a 50-50 chance, and in a front line fighting outfit like this one, you begin to give these things some thought after six long months of fighting. Be that as it may, I am here to do the job as best I can and get back home, so wherever that niche may be, I will try to fill it. . . .

Know that things are well with me, and though the year will doubtless see many more terrible conflicts, that I shall be looking forward to the final day when the thing is completely finished. Until that time, don't look for me to come home.

Upon the 1st Division's return to Algeria, planning for the subsequent invasion of Sicily intensified at higher headquarters. For the average soldier in the ranks, however, it was a time to relax and to enjoy recreational activities. Members of the 16th Regiment watched Jimmy Cagny in George M. Cohan's "Yankee Doodle Dandy," a motion picture that was "enough to shake any doubting Thomas into a roaring, flaming patriot." Even the French people "went wild during the show, and many tears were shed in visual evidence of the way the show touched everyone." For Dawson and his fellow soldiers, the picture was a tremendous morale boost.

Unfortunately, the Big Red One also acquired a reputation as a "party division" during their final stint in North Africa. Dawson attributed this to the fact that once the 1st Division returned to Algeria, they came in contact with the rear echelon troops. Having already experienced combat, the frontline GIs "felt a bit different than the boys" who had been back. Dawson related one incident that helped establish the command's reputation.

A young private was walking down the street, and he had a little too much wine "to inspire him." When he passed an officer, he looked at him and then proceeded on his way. The officer, being a man who was attached to one of the rear echelon units, stopped the young soldier and inquired, "Don't you salute officers?" Whereupon the man replied, "We sure do. We only salute First Division officers."

Division chief of staff Colonel Stanhope Brasfield Mason credited Teddy Roosevelt Jr. with telling the soldiers they did not need to salute any but Big Red One officers. Mason thought that though Roosevelt might have said it, he doubted seriously that the man believed it or meant it to be anything other than a boast and show of pride in being a member of the 1st Division.[29]

On more than one occasion, Patton had chastised Allen for the division's haughty attitude. Even Eisenhower observed that discipline was lax in the 1st Division. One of Ike's inspectors noted, "The [1st] Division has been babied too much. They have been told so often that they are the best in the world, [but] as far as real discipline is concerned, they have become one of the poorest. They look dirty and they never salute an officer if they can help it."[30] Dawson later confessed that this arrogance was the attitude of many GIs in Terry Allen's outfit. They acted "rather unconventionally." In Sicily, that same unconventionality would cost Allen his command.[31]

Other commanders in the 1st Division concurred with Dawson. By the time the final combat team reached Oran, it was evident to lower-unit commanders that the general outlook of the GI sounded something like this: We have heard all kinds of rumors about the lush living by "rear-area Joes in Algiers and Oran while we were winning the war single-handedly in Tunisian mud. We have now won that war, now we are going to have some of that lush living, come hell or high water. And no rear-area Joe is going to say no."

At least one battalion commander, on arrival at Oran, suggested that troops be retained in bivouac areas for a few days so that reorientation could be accomplished and definite control be reestablished before the "flesh-pots" of Oran were laid bare to the embrace of 15,000 "conquering heroes."[32] This suggestion came to naught as troops flocked into Oran as rapidly as they arrived in the vicinity.

The respite from the fighting also gave the Fighting First time to reflect on lessons learned from its first six months of combat. Commanders conducted after-action reviews at every level. With respect to the German counterattack at El Guettar, which senior officers classified as the first real test for the 1st Division, the principal lesson was that tanks could be stopped and driven back as long as the defensive position was organized in depth, including combined arms teams of infantry, artillery, and antitank weapons. Major General E. N. Harmon, who commanded one of the American armored divisions that had worked closely with the 1st Division, urged the coordination of tanks and infantry in the attack and defense. He also noted that there existed very little close support by air for ground troops during the entire campaign. On more than one occasion, Dawson himself had been on the receiving end of German air strikes and he had witnessed the cool efficiency of air-ground operations in conjunction with a German assault.

Harmon urged the development of close air support by reconnaissance, strafing, and bombing in support of the ground components. Such cooperation required special communication equipment, special liaison teams to be established, and intensive training in map reading, orientation, knowledge of ground vehicles and weapons, and their principles of operation.[33]

Other observations centered on the nationality of the opponent. Whereas Italian units were repeatedly unnerved by artillery fire, German adversaries were far more disciplined. On the whole, the 1st Infantry Division credited their German opponents with being a tenacious group of fighters who organized small islands of resistance, which included machine guns and machine pistols. They were always supported by artillery and mortar concentrations, and were exceptionally competent in utilizing terrain to their advantage. In the defense, Germans were formidable under all conditions. These lessons proved invaluable in the subsequent fighting in Sicily and Northwest Europe.[34]

Dawson's final letters from North Africa reflected his improving physical and mental condition. With several weeks' rest, he noted that "the strain of the past few weeks has begun to lighten a bit, and now I am much more rested than I was last week when the hectic turmoil of duties were so great that I feared I would not be able to stand it much longer. Now, with a little rest, I am once more regaining a peace of mind and renewed vigor."

He was happy to report he "was now fit as a fiddle" and could look back upon the previous five months "with an air of a veteran." Moreover, the steady diet of steak and eggs was a welcome respite from the GI's scourge of spam and corned beef. With the approach of July, Dawson would have but one week to enjoy the amenities of life, for within five days, the 16th Infantry Regiment was once again at sea, preparing for its second amphibious landing on a hostile shore.

4

Sicily

*Though the battle grows in intensity, I feel confident that one
more milestone is being passed toward final victory.*

The decision to invade Sicily represented a compromise between
American and British strategic planners during the Casablanca
conference in 1943. In the session on January 18, General George
C. Marshall and the Combined Chiefs of Staff (CCS) agreed to invade
the Mediterranean island off Sicily following the completion of the
Tunisian campaign. America's Roosevelt and Great Britain's Churchill
made that decision at the highest level, but implementation of the plan
belonged to the CCS.

The CCS considered several alternative scenarios, and Sicily was
the compromise, though Marshall voiced his concern that the Allies
"not become committed to interminable operations in the Mediterranean." Considering the vast number of troops available in that region's
theater of operations, the invasion made perfect sense, as any cross-
channel assault would in all probability be delayed for the better part
of 1943 if the Germans defended North Africa as tenaciously as expected.

The objectives of Operation HUSKY—as the invasion was code-
named—were threefold: to secure sea lanes in the Mediterranean; to
divert pressure from the Russian front; and to intensify pressure on
Italy.[1] Thus the Allied High Command deemed Sicily a lucrative target
that also provided the U.S. Army with additional combat experience
before the cross-channel attack.

Sicily is a triangular island encompassing 10,000 square miles. It
is located 90 miles across the Sicilian Channel, from the tip of Africa
at Cape Bon, and a mere 2 miles from the Italian mainland. Off the
southwest tip of the Italian peninsula, the Strait of Messina separates
it from the rest of Italy. The north side of the island measures some
180 miles; the southwestern side is approximately 170 miles; and the
eastern edge is considerably shorter, roughly 125 miles.

The center of the island is extremely mountainous, with coastal
roads offering the best transportation routes. In the interior, the roads
at the time were poorly surfaced and narrow, with sharp curves and

steep grades. The major ports were Messina near the northeastern tip, Catania and Syracuse on the eastern side, and Palermo near the western tip of the island. The Caronie Mountains are the dominant geographic feature, with peaks from 4,500 to 5,400 feet high, as well as massive Mount Etna itself, reaching 10,000 feet high and twenty miles in diameter.[2]

General Dwight D. Eisenhower commanded HUSKY, and the CCS appointed three British deputies to assist him. General Sir Harold R. L. G. Alexander served as deputy commander in chief and general in charge of the ground operations; Admiral Sir Andrew B. Cunningham commanded the naval forces; and Air Chief Marshal Sir Arthur Tedder served as air commander.

Two Allied armies were under Alexander: George S. Patton's Seventh Army and Bernard L. Montgomery's Eighth Army. The final plan called for both armies to land on Sicily's southeastern shore, and then proceed northward to seize Messina, thus cutting off the enemy escape route to the Italian mainland. While Montgomery (nicknamed Monty) was scheduled to land just south of Syracuse on both sides of the southeastern point of Sicily, Patton was to come ashore on seventy miles of beach along the Gulf of Gela.

In order to employ experienced combat units, Patton designated II Corps, still under Bradley, to spearhead the invasion, with the 1st Infantry Division again in the vanguard to seize Gela, and the veteran 3rd Division to attack simultaneously and capture the port and airfield at Licata. Other divisions, including the 45th Infantry Division, the 2d Armored Division, the 82nd Airborne Division, and a portion of the 9th Division, were also included in the force package. Elements of the 82nd Airborne were ordered to seize a vital hill mass that dominated a road intersection seven miles northeast of Gela.[3]

Patton's choice of the 1st Division was hardly surprising. Though he was personally infuriated with Terry Allen, whom he perceived was chiefly responsible for the lack of discipline in the division, he recognized that he needed him, "at least until the initial phase of the operation was consummated" because of the "critical nature" of HUSKY, the "conspicuous place" of the division in the invasion, and Allen's "experience as a combat leader."[4] As commanding general of the American contingent, Patton insisted that Allen's division be part of the troop list. "I want those sons of bitches! I won't go on without them," he declared on the eve of the invasion.[5]

D-Day for HUSKY was July 10, 1943, with the initial assault to be conducted by the airborne forces. At 0245 hours, the initial waves of the assault divisions came ashore. At Gela, General Allen employed a special task force of Rangers and combat engineers to delineate the four assault beaches. Thereafter, two regimental combat teams (RCTs)—the 26th, under Colonel John W. Bowen, and the 16th, under Colonel George A. Taylor—stormed the beaches.

Once ashore, Taylor's mission was to cut coastal Highway 115 and move along the road to Piano Lupo to join Colonel James Gavin's 505th Combat Team paratroopers before proceeding to Niscemi. In close proximity to the 1st Division's commanding general was Captain Joe Dawson, still serving as a liaison officer and a member of Allen's personal staff.

Writing on the eve of the invasion, Dawson described the complexity of amphibious operations and then voiced his personal fears that with each new battle, his chances "of going on to another were much less, as it took something out of you that could not be replaced." As LNO, Dawson assisted in coordinating the forward movement of the assaulting forces, as well as keeping Allen informed of the precise location of the attacking units.

It was a perilous mission fraught with personal danger as he landed behind the initial wave of the 16th Infantry. Though the 1st Division quickly established a beachhead against lighter than expected opposition, the enemy's Hermann Goering Parachute Panzer Division consolidated its forces on July 10 and launched a vicious counterattack that nearly drove the Americans back into the sea before it was thrown back by combined artillery and air and naval gunfire.[6]

Only after the beachhead was completely secure did Dawson pen a concise account of HUSKY's initial three days. Again, he prayed that the Almighty would give him courage to measure up to the task at hand.

Dawson to My Beloved Family

July 9, 1943
Off the Coast of Sicily

From the postmark, you will note that this is being written just before we step into the great unknown of D-Day and H-Hour. What it brings forth, I cannot hazard a good guess, but whatever happens, you can know that we shall do our best to live up to the heritage vested in us.

I must admit that the business of fighting is beginning to become a bit wearisome, now that we have been in actual combat for these many months and every one of us is beginning to feel the pangs of homesickness and a fervent desire to get back home. Nevertheless, the task before us is one that is truly awesome, and most anything can happen. That we will succeed is absolutely essential, and in this operation, it is do or die. We are prepared to do so.

There is little I can say here, for when this letter reaches you, the history will have already been written. Nevertheless, I pray that this letter will reach you and assure you that we are confident of success. Perhaps no military operation exists that is more strenuous than an amphibious operation, and to enumerate the multiplicity of detail that goes into such an endeavor would take endless reams of paper and would leave you more confused than before you started reading. Nevertheless, I have worked as hard as I ever worked in all my life in the preparation for this forthcoming event.

I feel that now that I have been through one already and am poised for a second one, that I am ready to let the other eight million soldiers we have come over for a whack at it. Not that my morale is low, for I know the deadly import of this war and the necessity for its end as soon as possible. It means, however, that every time I go into action, my chances of going on another are that much less for it takes something out of you that can never be replaced. Be that as it may, I am ready for it and I shall do my best. . . .

May you ever know that my heart is filled with unspeakable tenderness for you, and may you know that over here, as we approach the fateful hour . . . there will be many who will pay for freedom and the defense of all that we hold dear with their lives, we are trying to measure up. God grant that we may do our task.

Dawson to My Dear Brother

July 13, 1943
In Sicily

Our convoy moved along the shores of North Africa, and only the enemy and the rest of the world knew that we were on the high seas for with a force the magnitude of this one, it would have been impossible to hide it or make it inconspicuous. The enemy knew because of air reconnaissance, and also their submarines detected our presence. Fortunately, however, we had the good old U.S. Navy and the British Navy along with us, and they were able to keep the enemy from making any sort of attack while we were on the high seas.

All in all, it was a delightful cruise in the Mediterranean with only the grim knowledge of our mission to overshadow our thoughts and make the reality of the situation clear in our minds and hearts.

Throughout the last day, the wind blew with high intensity, and all of us felt the qualms of seasickness in addition to the realization that with the sea running as high as it was, that the chances of landing successfully . . . grew slimmer [by the hour]. But then the gods of fate stepped in, and by nine o'clock, the sea grew calmer and the winds abated in their velocity. The wind had been blowing from the northwest, and as we approached the island from the lee side under the shadows of the mountains that extend throughout the center of the island, finally ending in the great Mt. Etna, we found the necessary buffer to lay the sea enough to launch the small craft.

As we moved slowly toward shore, busying ourselves in preparations for debarking, we heard the drone of planes overhead, and soon the might of our air force became apparent as it struck the airdromes that nestle on the southern plains of the island. The whole sky was alight with the flames of the fires that were started by the incendiary bombs, and the intense flak of red and green tracers created the illusion of a gigantic skyrocket bursting in the sky. I can assure you that it was an unforgettable sight for it offered a prelude to that which was to come in a very short time, and we who have been through this before knew the implications to be gained from this spectacle. We knew that history was being written with a pen dipped in blood, and our destiny rested in the lap of God.

I landed just behind the assault waves and amid a hail of machine-gun fire and artillery shells. Three times, I ordered the coxswain to beach us, and twice we approached, only to be driven back to sea by the heavy fire. On the third time, however, we managed to get in without getting hit and quickly made our way up the dunes, seeking the security of the shallow indentations of the sand to protect us from the bursting shells.

It is a ticklish moment in one's life and can be likened to stepping into the Great Unknown, and only fate decides the issue for you, for the enemy was now fully alert, and the air was filled with flying steel. You don't have much time to think about anything except how and where to find some protection. At night this is always true because it is the Unseen that makes it so difficult to combat.

Fortunately, however, I survived without losing any of my men. I spent the next few hours accomplishing my mission, and by daylight, the first phase of the operation had been successfully completed. My lieutenant and myself were able to bag ten prisoners who were Italians that practically threw themselves at us in their haste to give up. And we also got four Germans who had sought to escape from the beach by way of truck, but it had bogged down in the sand, and seeing their hopeless position, did the only logical thing left for them to do.

All day long, we pressed the attack, meeting resistance all along the way, but not too heavy. I spent the morning dodging artillery fire, and after about two hours, I decided to wait for things to clear up a bit before I continued my running around the countryside. Unfortunately, I got caught in a counter-battery duel, and taking advantage of a foxhole, I caught about an hour's sleep while the shells landed around me. I was so tired, it really didn't make any difference at all.

Aside from this, the events of the rest of the day were not too exciting for the enemy air force did not make itself known until late that afternoon, and by then, I had a nice deep hole dug and could relax with impunity.

The past two days have been thrilling ones and also ones that have been unforgettable. I have seen more dangerous living in the past forty-eight hours than any other like period in my whole life. I have seen the *Luftwaffe* at its height, and believe me when I say it, those boys are rugged soldiers and absolutely fearless. Bombs have fallen constantly, and when they aren't bombing, they are strafing and only the charm I carry has pulled me out of some awfully tight spots. Would that I could relate in detail some of these experiences.

Then on top of that, they have been sending their tanks, assault guns and artillery against us, so that I can honestly say that their repertoire has been played all around me, without fear of contradiction. So it goes. I pray that everything will work out for the best and that soon this mess will end. We are doing our best and maybe someday, we will get a little relief from it all.

Well, brother, this is all for now. You can know that all is well with me as of this date, and though I am a bit battered and worn, I am still punching as best I can. Let me hear from you soon.

94

With the beachhead secure, Allen's Big Red One attacked north to seize Ponte Olivo and Niscemi, objectives that, according to the Seventh Army's plan, should have been taken no later than D + 1, the day after D-Day. According to an operational report prepared by Allen, General Patton was "wrought up" because the 1st Division had not yet taken Ponte Olivo airfield.[7]

Nor was the Seventh Army's commander pleased that the 1st Division had attacked without sufficient antitank and artillery support. Becoming increasingly dissatisfied with the 1st Division's senior leadership, he spoke to Allen and Roosevelt on July 11 and spurred them into action.

This was not the first time Patton expressed discontent with Allen and Roosevelt, both of whom he considered undisciplined. Early in the African campaign, Patton had humiliated Allen by urinating into his slit trench to demonstrate his contempt for the man's passive defense. Later, he chastised Allen for his slowness in the attack. A week prior to the invasion of Sicily, Patton reminded Allen "that the 1st Division is [not] the only unit in the show." On July 1, Patton's diary carried the entry that "Teddy [Roosevelt] . . . is a problem . . . as he is weak on discipline."

To II Corps commander Omar Bradley, Allen was not only poorly disciplined but also disobedient. On May 6, in the approach to Bizerte as the North African offensive wound to a successful conclusion, Allen ordered an attack across the Tine River against Bradley's expressed orders to hold in place.[8] Even Ike had counseled Patton on the poor discipline of the 1st Division.[9] Unbeknownst to the officers in the Big Red One, Allen's and Roosevelt's tenure of command was rapidly coming to an end.

Relationships among senior commanders of the American high command were far above the pay grade of Captain Joe Dawson. Within a week of the initial landings, Dawson requested and was granted relief from his duties on 1st Divisional staff and was reassigned to the 16th RCT as assistant regimental operations officer. This was the second time he had served on regimental staff.

Having turned down a chance to command a rifle company at the end of the Tunisian campaign, Dawson now recognized that duty with the regiment was the quickest path to company-level command. Still, his return was not without some misgivings. Reminiscing about the camaraderie that had once bonded the initial contingent of officers in the regiment prior to its deployment overseas in August 1942, he noted that the war had claimed so many of the officers who previously comprised this glorious regiment.

Over the course of several weeks of fighting, Dawson himself experienced a number of close calls. His duties at regimental level were far more dangerous than those associated with 1st Division staff. A review of the S-1 (adjutant) records for the 16th Infantry Regiment reveals that Dawson was frequently in the thick of the action. On July 10, he personally captured twenty enemy prisoners and escorted their commanding officer to division headquarters. Moving inland, he then coordinated air strikes on an enemy tank platoon. Accompanying the lead attack elements, Dawson informed the 16th Regiment of the precise locations of the forward rifle companies.

At Niscemi, he personally directed tanks forward to support the line units engaged with the enemy. Additional duties encompassed liaison with combat commands on the regiment's left and right boundaries and reporting strength levels to the regimental commander. By his own admission, he remained in personal jeopardy throughout the Sicilian campaign.

The fighting in Sicily was also changing Dawson in a number of ways. Having witnessed the intense fighting at Niscemi, where his close friend Ed Wozenski reconfirmed his reputation as one of the Big Red One's finest company commanders, Dawson now dehumanized the enemy as "sores that fester and erupt to create terrible consequences."

He was particularly disgusted that the enemy had used a ruse in which they displayed a white flag to lull a reconnaissance party he was accompanying into a false sense of security. Once the enemy was in range, they dropped the flag and poured a withering fire into the ranks of the Americans, killing nineteen of Dawson's men. Counterfeit capitulation, noted historian Gerald Linderman, threatened battlefield equilibrium, and Dawson's response was typical of most American GIs. His immediate assumption was German treachery; his immediate reaction was anger; and his immediate inclination was retaliation.[10]

As casualties mounted, Dawson's war had become a moral crusade in which the final outcome must be a world based on common understanding, lest the future lead to another blood bath that would make the current conflagration seem mild.

Additional changes to Dawson's psyche continued as the campaign mounted in intensity. Not yet thirty years old, he confessed he was nearing "old age," as fatigue that sapped "the old zip that was once his possession" was constantly present. Again, such reactions were typical of veterans who, within the span of several months in combat, claimed that they aged decades.

Still, this was hardly time to lose hope, and Dawson's letters reflected his desire to persevere. On more than one occasion, the young Texan yearned for the opportunity to do his part. As the 1st Division struggled up the center of Sicily, Dawson took renewed hope in ultimate victory by the news that Patton had taken Palermo and that Mussolini had abdicated. He expressed his hopes and fears in a series of letters that he wrote during the final week in July, as the soldiers of the 1st Division trekked across the mountainous terrain of central Sicily and approached Troina near the northern coast.

Dawson to My Dearest Family

July 23, 1943
Sicily

As this battle has been continuous and without surcease, I have had no opportunity to gather my wits together and put them on paper. But today, we are resting for the first time in two weeks, and I'm taking this chance to let you know that I am well though a bit tired.

As we push ever onward, I find that I need these moments of respite in order to rehabilitate both nerves and spirit. The ever presence of death and horror brings about a callousness to human suffering, for one becomes so wrapped up in self-preservation that it is impossible to sustain moral fortitude when one's own life is so constantly exposed.

Nevertheless, one experiences compassion even though the times are difficult to allow one to feel anything but cold hatred towards those who deny peace and human freedom, especially when it becomes intimate to one's own self and to those whom association through perilous times have brought into close friendship. It is exemplified by the growing feeling of urgency to get this dirty job over as quickly as possible before one loses the delicate balance that makes the difference between civilization and barbarism.

Here in Sicily, one sees the marks of war painted and etched in the faces of everyone. War has brought unspeakable suffering to these deluded and misguided people, and now that it is further enhanced by the power of our instruments of destruction, it makes their plight doubly terrible. Malnutrition painted luridly on the emaciated faces and bodies of countless little children afford pathos so striking that one must turn his head to maintain the courage necessary to face the task at hand.

'Tis a tragedy that only the swift termination of this war will alleviate the misery that dominates this side of the world. War brings disillusionment quickly when it actually comes to the homeland, and here, it tortures the imagination to assuage the past with the unutterable suffering that now exists. Perhaps it is well that we are faced with the startling picture for it brings forth the strengthening of purpose that assures our nation that such a visitation of horror must never reach our beloved land. Yes, it's an experience that will ever affect my life no matter what the future may bring forth. And though I cannot foresee the events to come, I can assure you that when the end comes, I shall pray constantly that I shall not be so deluded by this that my sanity of thought will be affected. God grant it.

I am now once more in the 16th Infantry [Regiment], having asked to be relieved from duty at Division. My duties and position at present are assistant S-3 of the regiment, and only time will tell what my ultimate job will be. There is only a small group of us left that once formed the officer personnel of this glorious regiment. War has taken a deep cut into this brave group of men, and the world can know that no unit has matched this one, and the history of this regiment will ever stand as a monument to the land of our nativity for bravery, courage and sacrifice. Those are empty words when one measures them in terms of the lives that have been given, but may all who make up our nation come to realize that the supreme sacrifice is a token that cannot be matched by anything else. Let us hope that these [men] have not died in vain.

There are countless stories of matchless heroism that I could recount, but one finds little solace or comfort when viewed in terms of life, but we preserve our hope and faith and courage by putting ourselves in the hands of God and trust Him to carry us through. One's religion in such places as this is basic and fundamental, and all cults and faiths are molded and melted into a common understanding. The differences and articles that segregate the various denominations appear inconsequential and selfish when compared to the tremendous need for unity.

I cannot keep abreast of world events when I am so completely concerned with this local scene of action, but the sooner we realize that the world must come to a common footing, the more quickly we will eliminate the sores that fester and erupt to create the terrible consequences that now embody our world. The crusade must begin now, and though one finds it a sort of idealistic premise when shells burst around you, bombs wipe out your friends, and misery and suffering dominate your life, yes it is difficult but more and more apparent to one and all.

The visions of the future must be based on the precepts of common understanding, but the world will see a blood bath that will make this war now existent seem puny in contrast. Only God can bring about a pause. It is my fervent prayer that sanity will rise with His help to prevent such a dreadful chaos.

Dear ones, this letter may have a solemn portent, but realize that I am seeing life in a measure far greater than one can envision from a distance. Know that it is you who must take up the torch when this phase ends. We who are fighting and dying on the battlefields must have the assurance that our nation will rise to the task of affecting peace.

Know that my tenderest thoughts belong to you and that through you is courage gained and maintained. God bless you one and all.

Dawson to My Dearest Ones

July 25, 1943

With another day in this island just ended, and the night is comparatively quiet, I will avail myself of the chance to write once more. Only the boom of the artillery breaks the stillness of the night with an occasional incoming shell to make us realize that all is not too peaceful on the other mountain. . . . One finds surcease only when night falls and the cooling breezes soothe one into a sleep of utter forgetfulness when the opportunity presents itself.

One adapts himself to these wartime necessities and instinctively seeks out odd moments here and there for a cat nap. Seldom does one get more than five or six hours sleep a day, so you see how one cultivates the *odd* moments. Only when I have been under extremely trying conditions or heavy artillery fire for long periods do I find a touch of insomnia. And this rapidly dissipates after a mental pep talk to myself. But with it all, I seem to be able to keep going without difficulty, though I find a fatigue constantly present and never the old zip that once was my possession. But then I am nearing old age anyhow, so that is to be expected.

We press on each day and have continued to make progress. Yesterday, our forces took Palermo, which clears the western portion of the island of all resistance and turns the battle zone to Mt. Etna and the Messina area. It is only the task of routing them out confronting us to end the struggle. . . .

Soon a year will have passed since I left America, and indeed as I pause to reflect all that has transpired, I begin to realize that life is truly short. It is difficult to think that I've been away so long, for in viewing time, one invariably asks the date from someone else, for the days melt into a oneness that erases the calendar completely, leaving only a span to reckon with, in terms of measure of deeds.

Never in all my years have my thoughts been so completely of you all. Perhaps this can be attributed to many things, but I prefer to think of it as being only the paramount one, namely my debt of gratitude for the privilege of being your son and brother. I fall so short of measuring up to you all that were it not from my knowing that I must, perhaps the story would be different. May you ever know that and be assured that I am striving and someday hope to fulfill the heritage vested within me. If God so wills, I know that I shall do so in part. . . .

Dawson to Dearest Sis et al

July 26, 1943

Today is rather significant insofar as the future is concerned because with Mussolini abdicating, I think the end is beginning to definitely assume clarity. Nevertheless, we still fight, and yesterday, the action was truly very stiff.

As we slowly move forward toward Messina, we meet growing resistance as the Germans and Fascists continue to attempt to delay our advance. However, I feel that events are shaping up, which tends to indicate that the pressure we exert is beginning to be felt and soon we should see the marks of real victory.

Sicily is really a tough battleground as the terrain is perhaps as rugged as I have ever seen. Having traversed nearly all the central and western portion of the island, I feel sure that I would not pick this as my residence if I had my choice. It's not anything to write home about, and as this is not a Cooks' Tour, I don't have the spirit to delve into the cultural or historical phases, but instead see stark realism and the horrors of the present, which do not make for an appreciation of the place. I hope it will end soon though.

Dawson to Dear Matt

July 30, 1943

Space only allows for a brief note to say I am still going strong, but now that I've been over the water a year, I am beginning to feel like a seasoned veteran. The other day, I had a narrow escape, and the event has only intensified my hatred for these people whom we are fighting.

I went forward with one of our reconnaissance parties to try and establish contact with the enemy. It was down a narrow winding road through a deep cut in the mountains, and as we moved toward the end of the cut where the terrain seemed to open up a bit, we ran into the Jerries. They displayed the white flag, and as our forward scout cars moved to them, they opened fire with an anti-tank gun and machine-guns, killing nineteen of my men, and only two of our jeeps escaped.

Fortunately, I was in the rear about 75 yards from the leading vehicle, so I managed to get out, though my driver was hit in the shoulder and the jeep was hit in several places. I can assure you that they will pay dearly for this dastardly trick. This is not the first time they have done this to us, but it's the first actual experience I have had. We will finish this job as soon as we can.

Dawson to Dearest Family

July 30, 1943

Now that I have been abroad one year, I find that Sicily is where I am now situated and still in a bitter battle. So far, we've pushed and pushed, and the truth of the matter is that we have been on the offensive continuously since November. It's grueling work, and I need not elaborate on the stark and sordid drama that is being unfolded in this forbidding country. The hills rise here, and as usual, we force our way ever upward. Someday, I hope we shall be able to fight downhill for a change.

I wrote Matt of an incident that occurred to me the other day so won't repeat. However, I am still going strong and though we are all getting a bit weary, we are hopeful that the end will not be too far away. With Sicily practically in our hands, and Italy tottering, the Axis is slowly being disintegrated, though there are many more bitter struggles ahead. Keep the home fires burning, and I'll be looking for the day when I can come home.

By the end of July, Montgomery's slow progress toward Messina necessitated a change in HUSKY's ground campaign. As Troy Middleton's 45th Division utilized the northern coastal Highway 113 from Palermo to Messina, Bradley pivoted II Corps 90 degrees to the right and directed Allen to spearhead the Seventh Army's drive to Messina along a parallel road (Highway 120). Soon, both the 45th and 1st Divisions encountered stiff opposition—the 45th at Santo Stefano and the 1st at Troina—approximately fifteen miles south of Middleton's advance. Though Manton Eddy's 9th Division landed at Palermo and was moving forward to relieve the Big Red One, Allen wanted to capture Troina before pulling the 1st Division out of the line.[11] The result was extremely bloody, as Troina rapidly emerged as the toughest fight in the entire Sicilian campaign.

On August 1, the 1st Division's G-3 (operations officer), Colonel Frederick W. Gibb, notified the 16th Regiment to prepare for offensive operations in the direction of Troina. The attack was expected to meet serious opposition because the city's defenders had already hurled back an attack by the 39th Infantry Regiment.

On August 3, the regiment was committed to action. Unfortunately, the attack went awry, with the 16th suffering heavy casualties. By 1410 hours, the situation was still unclear, as can be seen in the regimental report: "Colonel Matthews (2nd Battalion) is worried about E and F. E has two platoons missing. F had only one and a half platoons fighting strength. One squad of L went out, and we have no word of the squad. No word of Lieutenant Montague or Lieutenant Harris. Lieutenant Griffith was wounded and sent back. K lost men. I lost men. . . ."[12]

By 1635, the remnants of the 2nd Battalion streamed back; the companies were at less than 50 percent strong. That is the way it was at Troina—attack, counterattack, attack. It took the 1st Division until August 6 to clear the town. In his official report, Allen noted that the capture of Troina was finally accomplished after six days of heavy fighting, including five coordinated division attacks. The enemy fought desperately to hold Troina and launched twenty-four jarring counterattacks against the 1st Division's units. But the "continuing-day-and-night pressure, combined with the sharp maneuvering of the 1st Division units, finally broke the backbone of the stubborn enemy resistance."[13]

The battle at Troina ended the fighting for both the 16th RCT and the 1st Division in Sicily. The next day, elements of the 45th Division passed through the Big Red One's lines and continued the drive toward Cesaro and, eventually, Messina. After a month of constant combat, it was time for the 1st Division to rest and refit.

Although the 16th Regiment had performed valiantly in Omar Bradley's eyes, Allen had "flubbed badly." He had initially miscalculated the enemy's strength and was thrown back with heavy losses. Throughout the seven days of heavy fighting that ensued, Allen attempted to operate much as he had in the past, as an undisciplined, independent army, unresponsive to the corps commander's directives.[14] Such truculent behavior was anathema to Bradley's order and discipline. Not surprisingly, Allen's days in the division were clearly numbered.

Following the fall of Troina, Bradley immediately relieved Terry Allen as commanding general of the 1st Infantry Division and replaced him with Major General Clarence Huebner. Bradley also relieved Roosevelt, thus ending the Terry-Teddy era of the 1st Division.[15]

Prior to this change of command, Generals Allen and Huebner personally visited together all of the major subordinate commands of the 1st Division. The relief came as a bitter blow to Allen, who had emerged as one of the premier combat commanders of the war. He certainly had every reason to be proud of his command in the Sicilian campaign. During the first three days of the campaign, the Fighting First had effected a difficult landing, had repelled a vicious enemy counterattack, had "buttoned-up" the beachhead at Gela, had captured Niscemi and the enemy airport at Ponte Olivo, and had started its advance to the north.

During the succeeding twenty-four days, the 1st Division, by hard fights, fatiguing marches, and rapid maneuvers, slugged its way against determined German opposition through central Sicily. Its seizure of Troina capped a record of unsurpassed gallantry and conspicuous service. Allen attributed much of the unit's success, both in North Africa and in Sicily, to its skillful use of audacious night attacks. In summing up this particular form of infantry combat, Allen likened night operations to "the forward pass of the infantry units." Properly used, night combat could gain yardage at minimum cost. Improperly used, the commanding general noted that the assault units would "get a bloody nose," with nothing to show for it.[16]

If the 1st Division was so successful, why then was Allen relieved? Bradley explained it thus: Under its charismatic, hard-drinking commander, the Big Red One had become increasingly temperamental, disdainful of both regulations and senior commands. It thought itself exempt from the need for discipline because of its months on the line.

And it believed itself to be the only division carrying its fair share of the war.[17]

Though British General Harold Alexander found Allen "the finest division commander he had encountered in the war," Bradley found him "the most difficult man with whom I have ever had to work," a maverick, "fiercely antagonistic to any echelon above that of division."[18]

The II Corps commander then glossed over the real reason he fired Roosevelt too. In an attempt to justify relieving the son of an American president who was well liked by the army chief of staff, Bradley stated that there had emerged an unintentional rivalry between Allen and Roosevelt. Consequently, he had to relieve both men lest Allen's relief be perceived as a way to elevate Roosevelt at the expense of his former commander.

Beneath the verbiage lay the real cause of Allen's and Roosevelt's relief: modern warfare required teamwork, and in Bradley's mind, Terry Allen was not a team player. Allen was simply too full of himself and refused to acknowledge that the Big Red One was not the only true fighting division in the U.S. Army.

Nor was he Bradley's type of commander. Like Patton, Terry Allen was a swashbuckler whose fondness for fighting and profanity alienated the more taciturn Bradley. In his postwar memoirs, Bradley expressed misgivings about Allen's leadership style prior to the invasion. Though Patton overruled him on keeping Allen in command until "the initial phase of the operation was consummated," Bradley was instrumental in having Patton tone down his commendation for Allen's service in Tunisia by adding, "He's a very poor disciplinarian."[19]

Lack of discipline in a frontline division was abhorrent to Bradley and he held Allen responsible. Roosevelt too was a maverick who refused to play the game. Both perceived themselves above the playing field. Bradley desired team players in his command, and Allen and Roosevelt were not team players in the mind of the II Corps commander. In short, Bradley felt that both commanders had sinned by loving their division too much.

Seventh Army commander Patton apparently agreed, for he too previously had several run-ins with Allen and Roosevelt in North Africa. In March during the advance toward Tunis, Patton repeatedly pressured Allen to move harder and faster than Allen thought was prudent. Allen's chief of staff remembered that Patton would arrive daily in the early hours of the morning to Allen's tactical command post for a situation report.

On one occasion, Patton initiated his conversation with Allen by stating that the 1st Division was "doing a poor job, lacked courage, was poorly led." When Allen bristled and countered Patton's tirade, Patton shouted him down. Allen then got his Irish-Spanish anger aroused, turned on his heel, and simply walked away from the II Corps commander.[20]

It was an incident that reflected poorly on both commanders and one which both regretted. Still, the entire affair did not bode well for Allen's future as a commander in Patton's army. Not surprisingly, Patton remained intent on relieving Allen at some opportune date, but not before HUSKY was assured success. Because of his former association with Allen and Roosevelt, he requested the relief of the 1st Division's two senior officers, but "without prejudice on the ground that their experience will be of great value at home and that they are now battle weary."[21]

Allen's and Roosevelt's relief also deeply affected the officers who had served with them since the deployment of the division overseas. The combat veterans of Tunisia and Sicily—and Dawson certainly fell into this category—felt the loss keenly, as many had served with Allen and Roosevelt since the days at Camp Blanding.

Having served closely with them throughout North Africa, Dawson was perceived as one of the general's "fair-haired boys." As aide-de-camp, even on a temporary basis, Dawson developed a growing admiration for the independent-minded commanding general. He was not alone in his opinion that Terry Allen was about the most admired senior officer in the Mediterranean Theater. News correspondent Quentin Reynolds wrote, "Never in my life have I seen a man so worshipped as Terry was and is not only by his men in the First, but by every war correspondent who has ever come in contact with him."[22]

In later years, Dawson characterized Allen as "a wonderful leader whose absolute capacity to inspire *esprit de corps* was unmatched by any man whom he had ever known. Allen was loved by everybody in the 1st Division because he was a soldier's soldier." The vast majority of junior officers revered both Allen and Roosevelt and thought Bradley's action was completely unwarranted. At the same time, they understood that such events clearly fell under the umbrella of the "fortunes of war." While most officers kept their opinions to themselves, Dawson reflected on his own combat experience and unburdened himself of his frustrations in two letters to his family.

Dawson to My Dearest Ones

August 6, 1943
A little Sicilian town

It is almost midnight and the end of an epochal day, one that marks another milestone toward the end of this war and the defeat of those who have sought to create a living hell on this earth. With it has come the feeling that another corner has been turned and ere long, the traveling should be down the straight road, for today ends a battle that has been the bitterest we have ever fought. The concept of its impact cannot be measured in words of description for it has been too terrible, too exhausting and costly.

Tonight, one feels that a pall of death surrounds us and literally penetrates the marrow of the bones. The rubble of shattered homes, buildings and creations of many who long since have passed on, and the little mounds hastily placed over those who fell, dotting the steep slopes of these forbidding peaks, bespeak the destruction wreaked on life and the things wrought by man. The swollen, misshapen bits of human flesh yet unburied, lying amid the stones and weeds that cover the barren hillsides, are mute testimonials to the appalling tragedy of this vicious and horrible holocaust.

The pockmarks of the shells that mar the face of this terrestrial surface, as if some scourge had left its ravages imprinted indelibly on all who have lived and seen it, causes the bravest of us to utter a silent prayer to Him for seeing us through. At long last, the night comes and with it, a haunting stillness pervades this valley of death, and I find it difficult to calm my nerves that have been stretched to the breaking point by the strain of the eon of time that bespeaks this past week. I find my voice uttering nonsensical and empty thoughts in a subconscious effort to assuage the torment of physical and mental exhaustion. So I seek solace in writing these words to you and unburden the tight skein of jumbled feelings that enmesh my being.

Be patient and know that in living hand in hand with death, the human mind and body undergo a test beyond the realm of understanding, and the aftermath of the task accomplished brings forth a letdown unlike any other in the scale of human emotions. There is a marriage of those who remain, and the souls of those who have fallen and now lie sleeping on this bloodstained soil, and the faces of these comrades dwell intimately on the screen of your minds and remind you forcibly of the brevity of this human existence.

We hear the lilt of their voices and their laughter. Yes, dear ones, life becomes mere nothingness, and the stark drama that now unfolds gives pause to those of us who seek to carry on. We will walk softly in their memory. But I cannot help but reflect tonight on the events of the past twelve months and the toll that has been taken on those of us who left America and all that we hold dear, in order to give our all for its protection from that which we now are grimly forcing into ignominy and utter defeat. Some here, some there, Oran, Ousseltia, Kasserine, Medgez, El Bab, Gafsa, El Guettar, Bijo, Tunis, and these terrible mountains of Sicily, where every mile has been a struggle, bitter and costly. I now begin to realize the great demands that are exacted from those who do the actual fighting, and the price is high.

Yesterday, I was under a terrific artillery bombardment that lasted over two hours without a let-up, and from past experience, I can only say that there are few things that are more nerve wracking than an artillery shelling. The whine and swish of the big shells as they whiz through the air, and the flying steel that fills the atmosphere, where the shell lands nearby cause a sense of futility to exist because there is absolutely nothing one can do about it except hope that one doesn't land directly on you.

The best thing to do under such conditions is to try and get a little sleep, for in this way, the nervous tension is allayed somewhat, and one relaxes a bit. Men who have not learned this little trick often become so unnerved that a breakdown of control over their feelings is their unfortunate lot. You learn these little things the hard way!

Terry left tonight, and with him went a record unequaled by any general officer in the divisions of the U.S. Army. We've been through a lot and we all feel keenly sad about his going, though it is to a higher post of duty. I should like to be with him.

Our new C.O. is a grand soldier of the old school from all accounts, but I'll reserve judgment 'til I see him in action.[23] Terry leaves with the end of this bitter battle today, and I somehow feel that this one was the toughest we have yet had. It is a mark of great credit to him that we have always delivered in the pinches and have lived up to our creed, "No mission too difficult; no sacrifice too great." We've many more battles ahead and campaigns to fight before the end, but those of us who make up this branch of our army will keep going somehow 'til the job is done.

Each of you will aid the cause immeasurably if a few moments are devoted to this business of writing. Though you perhaps find that you are pretty busy each day, I must remind you that with all the infernal machines of death ravaging the environs wherein I work and fight, I still manage a line or two to someone of you. So do drop a line more often. One letter is all I have received during the past thirty-six days. That is not very good!

Dawson to My Dearest Ones

August 8, 1943

Just a brief respite from the battle to catch our breaths after the past month of constant fighting. I only wish time, space and censors would allow full explanations of the battles we've fought over here. They have been arduous and difficult on all, but we've done the job. We landed at a little village called Gela and since then, it's been uphill all the way.

I'm well and in fairly good spirits, though Terry left yesterday after we had won a great battle for him.[24] We all hate to see him go! I'm still here in the Regiment, and what the future holds, *je ne sais pas*, but whatever it is, I'll be pitching as best I can.

For Dawson, early August also brought a more important change of venue. At long last he was assigned command of a frontline rifle company. Casualties had greatly reduced the number of available captains in the regiment to a precious few, and this time, Dawson readily accepted command. With an additional month of combat under his belt and with Allen no longer on the scene, he felt less inhibited about any perception that he had been the commanding general's and the regimental commander's "favorite son."

If he thought he would be welcomed with open arms, however, Dawson was sadly mistaken. Upon arriving at the company, he received about as cordial a welcome as that given to Huebner when he replaced the popular Allen. Huebner later observed of the men of the 1st Division, "They respected me; they loved General Allen."[25]

That assessment pretty well summed up Dawson's situation when he assumed command of his unit. In command of G Company, 2nd Battalion, 16th Infantry Regiment, prior to Joe Dawson's arrival had been Captain Edward Wozenski, who had earned the Distinguished

Service Cross during the fighting around Niscemi. Wozenski had not only achieved the respect and admiration of the troops, but their affection as well.

In the eyes of G Company, Wozenski was the calmest officer under fire in the entire 16th Infantry, and that spirit of trust and confidence permeated the ranks. None was happy that Wozenski left G Company to assume command of another company in the same battalion to make way for a staff officer untested in combat. Now, in came Dawson, a staff officer who had never commanded a combat unit, including a rifle platoon, where successful leadership was deemed the prerequisite for promotion to the grade of captain and assignment to the most critical organization in the U.S. Army for ground combat.

Dawson was hardly the only officer who experienced apprehension on assuming command of a battle-hardened infantry company. In many ways, he was indicative of officers who arrived in Europe after the invasion of France the subsequent June. Charles MacDonald, a captain just twenty-two years old, arrived in I Company, 23rd Regiment, after the unit had stormed ashore in Normandy on D + 1. The company then fought ferociously at St. Lo and stormed a string of pillboxes at Brest. By the time that campaign was over, merely fifty soldiers survived from the initial contingent that deployed to the Continent a month earlier.

And the army, in its infinite wisdom, then assigned a "shavetail" lieutenant to command this company of veterans. Several months later, MacDonald received command of a second rifle company whose former commander, like Wozenski, was a devil-may-care leader who had previously received the Distinguished Service Cross for heroism in combat.[26] MacDonald, like Dawson, had to demonstrate to his men that he was "worthy" to lead them into combat.

With respect to organization, G Company was similar to all rifle companies in the U.S. Army. According to the new Army Ground Forces tables of March 1, 1943, the smallest infantry unit, the rifle squad, remained a team of twelve men, armed with ten M1 (Garand) rifles, one automatic rifle, and one M1903 (Springfield) rifle.

Three such squads formed a rifle platoon. Three rifle platoons were then grouped with a weapons platoon to form a rifle company. The weapons platoon had two .30-caliber light machine guns and three 60-mm mortars as its primary weapons. In addition, the platoon had three antitank rocker launchers, more commonly known as bazookas, and one .50-caliber machine gun, the latter for antiaircraft defense.

Personnel in a rifle company totaled 192, though senior headquarters frequently attached additional personnel depending on the type of operation. In the 1st Infantry Division, there were twenty-seven rifle companies, consisting of 5,184 men, around whom the rest of the Big Red One was built.[27] When Dawson took command of G Company, the unit's strength was nearly 60 percent of its authorized total.

With cessation of hostilities, Dawson acknowledged that his greatest challenge was to keep the troops occupied. He realized all too well that an idle soldier was more prone to grumble and complain than an active GI, so he initiated a strenuous training program in the hopes of imprinting his own personality on the company. Not surprisingly, he achieved mixed results.

Soldiers who had just completed a rigorous campaign in difficult terrain were not happy to take orders from a "staff puke" whom they felt was placing far too much emphasis on bathing, cleaning uniforms, getting haircuts, and general experience. By the third week of August, however, the new commander noted that the company was beginning to perk up and adjust to the new chain of command.

Dawson's efforts to obtain fresh vegetables and fruit to augment the daily diet did wonders to improve troop morale. As with Napoleon's *Grande Armee*, G Company's morale was "focused on their stomachs." Dawson also successfully lobbied for the delivery of delinquent mail, including his own, which he noted had "been scarce as hen's teeth" since the onset of the campaign.

Dawson to Dearest Family

August 13, 1943

Just a note to say I'm still gazing at Mt. Etna and soon I pray that we will have this island. I am now commanding "G" Company, having assumed this new job several days ago. . . . Drama and pathos reign supreme over here, and one is forced to avert the things that are not absolutely necessary for the task at hand.

Dawson to My Dear Family

August 15, 1943
Sicily

I am sitting under a shelter half suspended by German field telephone wire and glancing every now and then at the crown of

Mt. Etna, watching the gray clouds form as the heat emits from the cone and condenses the moisture in the air above. The mountain itself is most dominating and completely encompasses the entire countryside. It is a very symmetrical shape, with its eastern and western slopes almost vertical, while its northern and southern slopes seem to stretch great distances at an angle of 45 degrees, creating an imaginative prehistoric creature sprawled beneath a brilliant sun with a tiny fire exuding from the apex of its hunched backbone . . . though history shows that this has been a battleground many times in the past, there has been indelibly etched on the face of this island the ravages of warfare undreamed of in days gone by.

Everything is in shambles, fields barren from scorching fires, homes, churches, buildings of every description, nothing but rubble—and the ever-present odor of death. What a merciless demon is modern war. The measure of it is reflected in the entire landscape and burned into the mind of each of us for *we know* how diabolical and heinous it can be. Men are as putty in such a holocaust and only the years to come will offer the hope that from this carnal debauchery, something good will be born.

The roads and trails are lined with crosses of friend and foe alike, [and] act as silent reminders to we who still remain that something must be settled once and for all, so another war cannot ever ravage this earth. *We think a lot of things over here!*

I was most interested in the column in the Dallas news concerning . . . the expressions made by the Dallas pastor. . . . Religion on the battlefield is so basic and elementary that all facets of denominationalism [sic] and creedism [sic] seem false and superfluous. You merely pray to God that you can have the strength to carry on and place your being in His Hands for He alone decides our destiny.

How else could a man say a prayer in one breath and the next moment damn an enemy by words and deeds, killing without remorse or thought? Only [through] the stern acceptance of a righteousness unto death itself can I preserve my moral conscience. Though you probably will never understand, you must know that though my outward expression of religion is not very satisfactory, my inner feelings are *well grounded* and on a *firm conviction.*

So end[ed] the Battle of Sicily, and once again, we have succeeded. The cost has been high, but I trust well worth the sacrifice.

What the future holds will be seen in the weeks to come, but you can rest assured, I'll be in there somewhere.

I have urgently requested several items in letters past, but have not received any of them. So if you have not acted before, *please* send me without delay: 1. *letters*, 2. *film*, 3. *candy*, 4. *fountain pen*. There should be plenty of money in the bank for such simple things, so please send them to me. Also, if you will, send me the Sunday paper so that I can keep up with local activities.

Letters are still scarce as hen's teeth. Know my heart is tenderly occupied with you *all*.

Dawson to My Dearest Family

August 21, 1943

The company is beginning to perk up as a result of the cessation of hostilities, so my trouble really starts now, for it means keeping all the men in line and also trying to find suitable means of relaxation. That is a real problem because after living a carnal life on the battlefield, subordinates' moral ethics (if any) [deteriorate] so the iron hand must be used occasionally.

Dawson to Dearest Family

August 22, 1943

Sunday and a brief interlude that affords a time for pause in the week and things personal can thus be attended. We are now in the throes of trying to *impress* the men to start shaving and get their hair cut and clothes cleaned, as well as their bodies. Also the shaking down of the men newly joined. My worries are now purely personal as these 200-odd souls are my sole responsibility, so I'm kept busy. . . . One thing I'm doing is *stressing good food,* and my patrols range countless miles in an effort to supplement the normal issue with fresh vegetables, meats, etc. So far we are doing all right!

Dawson to Dearest Ones

August 22, 1943

Deep in the heart of the regiment, I am lost as to the "big" picture as my time is well occupied with details on the functioning of this company of mine. We are just now beginning to relax from the nerve strain of battle and the result is I must have plenty for my men to do in order to prevent unrestrained "relaxing." We are now in the throes of bathing, delousing, and clothes washing and house keeping, but the men are doing swell.

Tonight, Bob Hope is entertaining the entire division, but I am holding down the fort and straightening out some accumulated items. Terry got the DSM for his doings (& ours) in Tunisia and Oran. Guess they'll give him the Congressional Medal [of Honor] for Sicily.[28]

My new men range from an Ottawa Indian to an Italian who became a citizen in 1935. Others include boys from Michigan, Pennsylvania, Alabama, New York, New Mexico, and Massachusetts. Such is the cross section. Will be in there fighting though. When the time comes, *write!*

Dawson to Matt & P.L.[29]

August 23, 1943

Next to me, you two are about the world's worst correspondents due to the fact that you dip the gifted pen about once every blue moon. But I'll forgive you because Mother sends me the latest photos and general news. . . .

Sicily continues to be my habitat, and having covered practically every inch of it, I am about ready to seek other scenes and terrain. I feel sure Uncle Sam will give me the chance soon enough! But I'm enjoying myself for the first time in months, and have had a great time reorganizing my outfit and getting it back in shape. What with those killed, wounded and missing, I've had to start pretty much at scratch. But the nucleus is here, and the will is imbedded in everyone, and with a lot of hard work, we'll round into shape—or else!

Dawson to Dearest Family

August 24, 1943

Having a bath today for the third consecutive day makes me feel quite renovated, and with other things, life in Sicily becomes more endurable. Perhaps the days to come will bring forth some form of recreation, but meantime, I'm engrossed in teaching men to shoot straight and take care of themselves.

Still, the world rocks over here with the din of warfare. I go to sleep each night with the hollow staccato sound of a night flying *Messerschmidt* that seems to have taken a fancy to us with an occasional bouquet of bombs to remind us that he is still mad at us. However, now after so darn many of these, I merely grunt and roll over to a more comfortable position in my sleeping bag.

Sure miss Terry these days. Really, times have changed since his departure. Well, we keep plugging along. Get in the habit of writing for a change!

Dawson to Dearest Family

August 25, 1943

Today is much like a Sunday morning there in Texas. The warm sun beams down from a cloudless blue sky, and the sound of Protestant hymns merge with the incantations of the Catholic Mass. Though this is a rough and rugged group of fighting men, the attendance is truly outstanding. Perhaps you can understand how we come to depend on spiritual help, and though religion is not worn on the sleeves of the men, their hearts and souls are filled with a consciousness of God. It's a simple faith, but an enduring one.

The week past has enabled us all to relax and rest. The men are all beginning to show visible signs of perking up a bit, and I've been scouring the countryside for grapes, cantaloupes, honeydew melons, watermelons, peaches, eggplants, onions, green peppers, fresh eggs, beef and Italian spaghetti. In truth, the men are eating as well as anyone in the U.S. Army. Like Napoleon, I feel that morale is focused in the stomach. . . .

Operation HUSKY officially ended on August 17, 1943, with the Allied capture of Messina. In the final analysis, the U.S. Army had come of age during the campaign in Sicily. With respect to the strategic picture, the campaign demonstrated to the British that the Americans could execute a highly successful campaign against veteran German divisions and emerge victorious.

Patton's dash to Palermo and then to Messina, though derided in the British press, convinced many senior Allied officers that the American army would no longer be content to play second fiddle to the British. The balance within the Atlantic Alliance was beginning to shift in favor of the Americans. The campaign, however, had not been without cost. In accomplishing the objectives laid down by the CCS at

Casablanca, the Allied forces inflicted casualties that included 12,000 German dead and captured and 147,000 Italian dead, wounded, and captured. The cost to the invading forces was slightly less than 20,000 men: 7,402 in the Seventh Army, 11,843 in the British Eighth Army. Total 1st Infantry Division casualties totaled 267 killed in action or died of wounds, 1,184 wounded, and 337 missing.[30]

On a personal level, Dawson had also come of age. Combat had toughened him. He noted that he had not seen anything of value in Sicily that was worth the trouble to send home, but he acknowledged that he had found "a lot of hard earned experience" during the campaign. The combat itself "had been grueling. We marched and fought clear across the island in practically nothing flat."

As for the GI, he "doesn't think in terms of grand tactics. All he's thinking about is that next little hill." Troina had been the worst battle he had experienced since El Guettar, though Niscemi had also been a bloodbath. In short, this firsthand experience prepared Dawson to command a rifle company. He was also fortunate to assume command of an experienced outfit, one whose record was known throughout the Big Red One.

The relatively long period of inactivity between the end of the campaign and the debarkation of the 16th Regiment for England in November presented Dawson with the opportunity to familiarize himself with the strengths and weaknesses of G Company before he led them into combat. The respite also gave him a chance to collect his wits and view some of the countryside before tackling the next operation.

A visit to the western extremity of Sicily in late September gave him particular joy, even while he lamented the loss of so many close friends who had perished in the preceding campaign. His letters home during this period were devoted almost exclusively to family affairs, with only occasional references to the fighting occurring on the Italian mainland. The fact that the 1st Division was not committed to the Italian peninsula in the early autumn hinted that Eisenhower had something more important in store for the Big Red One.

Dawson to My Beloved Family

September 4, 1943

With the toe of Italy receiving the brunt of the onslaught, we on the island sense the news with firm belief that the climax in the Mediterranean is coming soon. It will be difficult to say when the final capitulation will be, but I am confident that it is not too distant.

These days are glorious in the comparative manner in which we occupy ourselves. Though the elements of war surround us, the booming of the guns does not shatter our peace of mind. With autumn coming, I feel sure that we shall see the turn of the tide, but I cannot hide the fact that it will be a blood bath that has no parallel.

Little in the way of outstanding news for the days passes with no cause for events of great importance. I am well and am busy. The temper, however, needs firing once more, so I feel the natural letdown. Be that as it may, it's good to be alive and filled with the knowledge that I've got a most wonderful family.

Dawson to My Dear Family

September 27, 1943
Sicily

The weekend provided a slight diversion from the routine of camp. Feeling the need to get away from everything and everyone, I fed my jeep an extra portion of oats and struck out for Propani, Morsala [sic] and points west. As my habitat has been largely concerned with eastern and central Sicily, I was all the more anxious to go west, for I have had hopes that somewhere on this island, there would be a spot that would be pleasing to the eye and also restful. . . . Of late, the constant and ever-present timetable of duty has wrought a strain on this heretofore free and independent soul. As a consequence, I struck out with no other purpose in mind than to get off by myself.

Now some people say Sicily is beautiful and picturesque. As a general statement, I feel that the person asserting this apparently comes from an awful neighborhood and has never enjoyed the really interesting and pleasant spots on this earth. And by slight digression, I must confess that it has proved to be the most disappointing country I have yet visited since I left America.

It is true that the little donkey carts, brightly painted, and the horses and mules and donkeys that pull them bedecked in tassels and colorful ribbons and the clap, clap, punctuated by the jingling bells, all add up to a degree of the unusual. Then no matter where the shore may be, the Mediterranean provides an unforgettable sight with its symphony of color.

But the impact of war is omnipresent throughout the whole terrain and the never-to-be-forgotten days of fighting over the

rugged, bitter and forbidding mountains, overshadows one's aesthetic senses and denies one the same feeling as that shared by a
tourist. The towns, nestling on the sides of the rocky crags, prove
interesting only at a distance for upon close examination, the vicious scene of indescribable filth and the gaunt, emaciated faces
of the inhabitants removes all vestige of beauty by the starkness
of reality.

Then those towns through which the path of war passed are
not fit to be called habitations. The crumbling rubble that once
was homes to countless numbers of men, women, and children
now encase their rotting flesh, from which exudes the stench of
death, so horrible and real to those of us who have lived with it
saturating our olfactory senses for these many months. The few
who are alive are nothing more than ghosts that stare through
eyes dulled to the breaking point by the tragedy that has enmeshed
their earthly existence.

To some who may view this awful sight with compassion, I
feel sure their hearts would bleed at such a terrible scene, but
always my thoughts burned with the memories of Bill Cole, Will
Janney, Jack Krumn, Phil Martin and the countless other friends
of mine who met their death from some of the many terrible weapons that are our constant source of misery.

'Twas this land and that of our foes that spawned these people,
and they alone decided our fate, as well as theirs. So to me, who
faces them across the field of battle, I see a decided partiality to
my own comrades, as well as having the ever-present knowledge
that my own life is always in danger. . . .

Sunday morning, I journeyed on to my ultimate destination—
a tiny little village perched high on the crest of a mountain that
rises sheer from the waters of the sea. From this grand height
(3,000 feet), the eye views Palermo in the distance, Marsala,
Trapani and all the western half of the island. Unsullied by the
ravages of war, it retains all of its prewar loveliness. Surrounded
by a lovely forest of towering spruce and firs, it provided a real
spot for peace and quiet.

I remained all afternoon, gazing into the distance and erasing
from my mind the horrible and carnal scenes that have predomi-
nated. A lovely open-air restaurant afforded a delicious dinner
that made a perfect climax for such a wonderful day. I returned
home refreshed and more at peace than I've been in months. . . .

Dawson to Dearest Family

October 12, 1943

The campaign in Italy is progressing OK and as yet, I have not had to do any work over there. However, I have been keenly interested in its outcome and have followed it closely. From all accounts, the going is pretty stiff and doubtless will be an all-out slugfest when the battle for Rome takes place. These lowdown creatures are still about as tough as I care to take on, and they still have plenty of fight in them. The trouble seems to be that the world is suffering from the delusion that they are already beaten, but from my own personal observations, they are not finished 'til the final shot is fired.

The day following Dawson's final letter from Sicily, the 16th Regiment conducted a shakedown inspection that presaged that the unit was preparing for another deployment. Two days later, G Company packed and crated its equipment, a sure sign that Dawson's command was not destined for combat on the Italian mainland.

Rumors about their ultimate destination permeated the ranks. As Ernie Pyle remarked prior to his own return to the United States, the number one rumor in every outfit was that ships already were waiting to take the troops back to the good 'ole USA. Other rumors had the 1st Division remaining in Sicily as occupation troops, going to England, going to China, and—ugly thought—going right on as the spearhead of the next invasion.[31] Unbeknownst to the GIs of the Big Red One, General Bradley once again had selected the combat-hardened 1st Infantry Division for the biggest show of the war.

5
Preparation for D-Day

There will doubtless be many who will suffer death as a result of the next big conflict, but the final achievement will indeed be worth the price.

With the fighting in Sicily over, planning turned toward the invasion of the European continent. Because of the Big Red One's battlefield experience, American planners under Omar Bradley's personal direction selected it as one of the divisions to spearhead the invasion.

Bradley, newly designated commander of American ground forces for OVERLORD, stated:

> Much as I disliked subjecting the 1st Division to still another landing, I felt that as a commander I had no other choice. . . . I felt compelled to employ the best troops I had, to minimize the risks and hoist the odds in our favor in any way that I could. As a result, the division that deserved compassion as a reward for its previous ordeals now became the inevitable choice for our most difficult job. Whatever the injustice, it is better that war heaps its burdens unfairly than that victory be jeopardized in an effort to equalize the ordeal.[1]

General Dwight Eisenhower concurred wholeheartedly with Bradley's selection of the Big Red One and soon cabled General George Marshall, saying that in both the line of communications and in the combat troops, "I would feel happier if a wider combat experience could be represented."[2] The Supreme Commander was less convinced about the potential of General Clarence Huebner, who had not led them in combat, but he deferred to Bradley, in whom he had the greatest confidence.

Deployment to England began in the autumn, with the 16th Regiment sailing on October 23. The voyage took the regiment from Sicily to Algiers, then along the North African coast, where they passed through the Straits of Gibraltar. For Dawson, these were familiar waters that conjured up both a time and a place when life had been more carefree.

Images of parties at General Terry Allen's headquarters and front-line inspections with Teddy Roosevelt Jr. seemed ages past. Now in command of a rifle company, Captain Joe Dawson had far different responsibilities from the previous year when he served at headquarters. No longer was he going to war as an individual; he was now personally responsible for the care and welfare of roughly 150 American fighting men.

On the eve of the invasion he wrote that few positions in the army provided greater joy and sorrow than command of frontline soldiers. Though he had witnessed the joy of their success and the heartbreaking sorrow when "the gods of war snuffed out the life of American soldiers," things were different now. G Company belonged to him, not Ed Wozenski, and upon Dawson's shoulders rested their entire future.

After nearly two weeks at sea, England appeared on the horizon, and the reaction among the GIs was one of jubilation. On November 5, the oceanic journey ended at Liverpool, where the 16th Regiment received a raucous welcome from the local inhabitants. There was no time to dally, however, and the regiment immediately entrained for Dorchester, some three hundred miles from the port.

Just as soon as he established G Company's bivouac area at Walditch in Dorset, Dawson wrote a letter that he hoped would reach his family by Christmas. He described the voyage, as well as his growing friendship with Captain Ed Wozenski. He had known Wozenski since his own arrival in the 1st Division and had respected him as one of the premier company commanders in the 16th Regiment. Now they shared the same campsite, which delighted both commanders immeasurably.

Dawson to My Beloved Family

November 28, 1943
A Christmas Letter 1943
Somewhere in England

Receipt of this letter will probably be very near Christmas Day, and I do hope that it will provide you with a little understanding of what has transpired since my last letter and also a bit of tender love from many miles away.

The tale in all its detail will eventually be given when I return home and recount all those things that are prohibited at this time, but from the pertinent extracts of this letter, you will be able to arrive at some idea of my doings of late.[3] The above [address] will indicate somewhat the great contrast that has taken place in environment in the past two months. Then get your map and examine the distance between the two points and the fact that the war has altered the airline route a great deal. . . .

I'll start this little narrative from the time I last wrote regularly. The olives were turning ripe and the almond season had passed some weeks before, as well as the melons and grapes. Early morning had a noticeable tang and sharpness that bespoke the snow and ice that had begun to make itself felt on our men in the Italian Apennines. October was nearing end, and the sunny hills of Sicily were turning brown as fall approached. Our trip to the port was a sharp reminder that the days of warm sunshine were about ended for us, and I could not help but feel a bit disconsolate at the thought of winter and its suffering that swiftly was descending.

Arriving at the port, I could not help but feel a sense of awe come over me as I remembered in ages past the glorious city that once dominated this portion of the world and how modern war had wreaked such destruction on the priceless relics of this long past civilization.[4] But amid the wreckage-strewn harbor and beneath the barrage balloons lay the great ships that were to take us on our voyage to the next phase of destiny. How good it felt when I boarded her and bid farewell to the land that holds too many memories to ever make it appeal to me in the years to come. The story is written in all our hearts and perhaps will never be fully disclosed.

Then the loveliest of all voyages began. Sailing along past the *djebels* of Tunisia and all the memories they awakened was indeed a tribute to our concept of life, for they spoke a solemn eulogy to those who rest there beneath them. Yes, you sort of felt that "something" had been accomplished, as it was from this point that the tide of victory began to flow.

A brief stop at Algiers, nestled in all her majestic loveliness in a crescent of azure blue was another reminder of days that will ever live in my memories. Then as we passed the coast beside Oran, I felt a faint note of nostalgia for here was the only place that held for me any happy moments since my departure from home. The interlude will always be remembered though never will it be renewed.

Then on past Gibraltar, and my only sorrow as I passed this famous landmark was the fact that the Prudential Insurance Company still has its sign dimmed out—owing to blackout, wartime regulations, etc. Someday, I hope to again pass this portal and see such a monument of American self-expression adorning this spot.

Just a word about the ship and some experiences thereon: It was a real beauty, and I enjoyed a marvelous stateroom with private bath and a real bed with clean white sheets! A doctor, a Catholic chaplain and another company commander were my fellow roommates. All of us have been together in the regiment since Camp Blanding, so we have much in common. . . .

The thought of once more seeing England made us all so happy that no one suffered any ill effects during the voyage. However, I must add that we did not encounter a single day of rough water and even the *Queen Mary* would not have been any more enjoyable. And when at long last we arrived at this beloved spot, I can assure you that I did just as all the men did, raise a shout that could be heard almost to Berlin. A lump rose in my throat and a tear or two joined in with the ever-present English "mist" as I saw the docks slowly come nearer. Only when I get to see the old lady in New York harbor will I feel so much a spirit of homecoming. And when the band struck up the tune of "Dixie," then "Sidewalks of New York," you can imagine the crescendo that crushed the ears of all within miles. Yes, war has its compensations.

The train journey was long, and yet how wonderful it was to see the loveliness of this, my "adopted" home. All it lacked to be perfect was a realization that the destination was not Texas! But this is second best, though Doc still argues that Italy is the garden spot of the world.[5] My idea, however, is based on not only the physical beauty of the landscape, but those who live and create here as well. For me, the Italians will never be anything in my category of peoples, whereas I believe my love for the British is practically a reincarnation of my long dead ancestors. They are real!

Now a word of what has occurred since my arrival. To say that I have been busy is a mere word usage that could not adequately express the true picture. Honestly, aside from censorship restrictions, I have not had a moment to call my own, nevertheless, it's been great sport, and I've been enjoying myself to the limit.

Ed Wozenski and I have our men together in a camp, which is all our own, so we have sought to make it as we wish to make our own homes. We are proud of it, and I must say, it is the very best camp anywhere around. If you look up some of the issues of *Time* magazine and read the story of the Battle of Niscemi, you will read of [Wozenski's] exploits.[6]

At that time, he commanded my company, but I took it over at Troina, and he was shifted to E Company. We are great friends and have our quarters together. Then we have a mess that is the finest in the army. The food is an epicure's dream, and I can vouch for it being good because it is a banquet every meal— breakfast, lunch and dinner. At least we are being fed as never in history. . . .

So this brings me down to now. The mail has descended in a glorious deluge, and all of two months accumulation is providing me with great joy. . . . Above all, though, are the dear letters from all that bring me closer to you one and all. How tenderly do I love you, and as this Christmas should provide hope for peace as no other ever before, may you know that I am grateful beyond all words to my Heavenly Father for the privilege of being your representative in the fight for those things that form our foundation of life on this earth.

God bless you Mother, Dad, Alice, Leighton, Donna Booch, Matthew and all the other members of my beloved family.[7] Know that God is watching over all of us and someday soon we shall be together.

Although the 1st Infantry Division did not officially join Bradley's First U.S. Army until February 2, a First Army training directive that emphasized perfection of maneuver exercises and special direction toward the conduct of amphibious operations governed training in England. The First Army also ordered instruction in the detection of enemy mines and booby traps, and in the neutralization of mine fields, requiring that at least ten mine detector operators be trained in each infantry unit.

In addition, the training program prescribed that all company-grade officers of infantry and engineers be given instruction in the technique of adjusting artillery fire using forward observation methods. Firing-range facilities were limited compared to the large size of the force to be trained for the upcoming invasion. Sufficient large training areas to hold exercises on a regimental or divisional scale were not available, though the acquisition of Slapton Sands in southern England compensated for the limited facilities of the Assault Training Center at Ilfracombe on the northwest coast of Devonshire. In the months preceding the invasion, all units conducted large-scale amphibious exercises at Slapton Sands; the commands designated for the initial assault waves utilized the facilities several times.[8]

As the training intensified, Dawson's company was reinforced with a number of replacements. He had arrived in England with 125 GIs, but 1st Division policy added an additional 15 percent of the authorized strength in anticipation of casualties. The integration of the replacements was relatively smooth as the veterans from Sicily provided a cadre, or nucleus, among whom to incorporate the recent arrivals.

On a personal level, Dawson had to win the respect of his veterans, many of whom still regarded him as an interloper from regimental headquarters. In the months ahead, he experienced some difficulty in overcoming the fact that he had been a staff officer, not a combat officer. Realizing that the only way he could achieve success as a commander was to earn the respect of his men, he set about establishing a rigorous training program.

From the company's arrival in England until it embarked on the ship that would take it across the English Channel, Dawson welded his team into a cohesive fighting force, physically and mentally. "I didn't spare the horses," he later recalled. "I tried to instill in them an understanding and awareness of the gravity of the situation and the necessity for total teamwork, for each of them had to rely on the other in order to achieve whatever success or whether they would survive." He reminded them, "This will be a battle of survival."

The long days and nights of training did not endear Dawson to his men, but there was no alternative to preparedness for combat. He later recalled, "I could not do anything about that except to covenant with God and my own self that I was going to be the one who would lead them when the time came."[9]

Dawson to My Dear Family

January 6, 1944

Today came V-mail dated December 24 saying all is well . . . also I am happy to know that mail has finally arrived to allay your fears concerning yours truly. I shall try and keep you informed as best I can of my whereabouts.

Now that Christmas and New Year's have come and gone, we are spending our time most intensively for the future events that will forth come. You can only know that it will be a terrific battle before the final victory. . . .

Last night I journeyed to see "This Is the Army" and enjoyed it immensely. Irving Berlin was in it, as you know, and his music is still grand. I missed it while I was in London and was glad I finally saw it. I will review in detail the highlights of the past few weeks this weekend when I hope to find time to catch up on my letters. Am well and in good spirits.

Dawson to Dearest Family

January 13, 1944
London

News is beginning to come along quite well now, and I have received letters as late as December 29th, so I now am well aware that the holidays produced most enjoyable hours for all. . . . Over here in England, there seems to be ample evidence of the fruits of war, though from all outward signs, the men-folk are all away to the battlefronts. In fact, I seldom see any girl that is not married— all the rest are serving in the forces.

It's really amazing. It has really been a treat to be here again and my time occupied to the fullest, which perhaps explains my writing not being as prolific as before. In fact, I have been terribly busy working, and what time off I have had, I've spent being with friends or taking trips. I spent five heavenly days in London that really compensated in a large degree for the months I spent in a fox hole and eating Spam. I stayed at this fine hotel and enjoyed every second of my leave. . . .

I reached London late on a Saturday night and at a station I was not familiar with. I tried to locate a taxi, but none was available, so I struck out walking in the blackout, lugging my suitcase that seemed to weigh a ton. At the stroke of midnight, I finally staggered into this hotel where I astonished the clerk by asking him for my room reservation. He demurred by saying that he had expected me several hours earlier, but as I had not arrived, he had to give my room to someone else. I raised the roof then and demanded the manager. He soothed my feelings by immediately bringing forth a key that gave me a spot that was an answer to my fondest wishes. Only a person who has lived in the open for months could enjoy this luxury as I did, for the bed was so soft I really felt as though I was immersed in a billowy cloud.

I braved the cold rain and fog Sunday morning by venturing to St. Paul's [Cathedral] for the service there and found it quite interesting, as well as inspiring. You would have been amazed at the number of American officers and men who comprised the audience—in fact they seemed to be in the majority. Then [we enjoyed] a wonderful dinner in the grillroom, then back up to my little nest for a nap.

Well, I started calling on the phone all my friends of the year before, and to my keen disappointment, couldn't locate a single one! Old man gloom began to descend, so I decided to go out for a walk and chase away the blues. Down in the lobby, I ran into Drew Middleton, whom I hadn't seen since Sicily. . . . You can know that our conversation was a most interesting one and filled with reminiscences of the events that were so entwined in our personal lives. . . .

Visits from senior commanders have always been morale boosters for fighting men, and in mid-January, the 1st Division hosted General Sir Bernard Montgomery, soon-to-be-designated commander of the land forces for the impending invasion. Monty left London on a five-day tour of Bradley's First U.S. Army on January 14. He visited both the 29th Division and the 1st Division, the two assault divisions destined to land side by side on Omaha Beach.

As was his custom, Monty arranged to address the men in large groups of three- to four-thousand strong, roughly brigade strength. He traveled from command to command, speaking from the hood of a jeep by means of a loudspeaker. His intent was to talk to the GIs, let them see him; in this way, he hoped that he might establish mutual confidence.

His message was simple: "Now get gathered round here fellows—this is how we're going to knock the Germans all to hell."[10] Monty made a particularly favorable impression on the 1st Division GIs since he said that of all the American divisions he had seen, he would rather serve with the Big Red One. Such talks were huge successes and did much to eradicate the national barriers that existed between the two principal partners in the Atlantic alliance.

Nor was Monty the only senior commander to inspect the American troop commands. From February 1 to June 1, Eisenhower visited twenty-six divisions, twenty-four airfields, five ships of war, and numerous depots, shops, hospitals, and other important installations. The Big Red One's turn occurred on April 2, when the Supreme Commander, accompanied by General Huebner and assistant division commander Brigadier General Wyman, came to inspect, present awards, and deliver a speech to the division at the Cricket Field in Bridport.

Any illusions of returning to the States were dispelled when Ike said, "The First Division will be one of the last to go home. If nothing else, I'll just keep you around for good luck."[11] Bradley followed shortly thereafter on the 11th and lectured all of the officers of the 16th Regiment on the importance of the upcoming invasion. Such visits, sandwiched between a seemingly endless series of conferences and staff meetings, were necessary and highly valuable in conveying to the troops the commanders' concern for their health and welfare.[12]

For Joe Dawson, the order of the day focused training on basic soldier skills as well as small-unit combat drills. It was tough, grueling work, noted the regimental history, but the task ahead was the greatest and the most ambitious of the war. Commanders placed renewed emphasis on marksmanship and physical conditioning. With the large number of replacements on hand, quick reaction drills monopolized squad and platoon activities as small-unit leaders wove their respective units into cohesive fighting forces.

Dawson attempted to convey some of the blistering pace in correspondence, in which he stated he was "gittin" ready. Another time, he stressed that "things are moving along these days, and we're working pretty hard." Consequently, his family should not expect many letters. What letters he did write discussed the inclement weather and his personal concerns that the nation was not as supportive as it ought to be of the impending crusade to rid the world of Nazi tyranny.

Seldom did he mention the intricacies of his unenviable task of preparing soldiers for combat. Rather, he chastised his mother for asking too many questions concerning his whereabouts, and chided himself for his own carelessness at revealing intelligence that might prove beneficial to the enemy if the Germans penetrated the veil of secrecy surrounding the Allied troop concentrations.

Dawson to My Dearest Family

February 17, 1944

With the duties here on the warfront steadily increasing and the foreknowledge that we will engage the enemy this year, there is little time for sentiment or nostalgia to play on one's emotions. Nevertheless, I am often brought back to reality just by reading a letter from one of you. The physical, of course, is impossible, but the mental contact afforded by these letters is always the highlight of the day for all of us. . . .

Of course, weather provides a topic of conversation all over this world, and perhaps that is because it affects every single one of us. I have been able to withstand the cold with a great deal more comfort this winter than any of the past three. I attribute this to the fact that I have some very dear loved ones, who have wisely and thoughtfully provided me with substantial contributions toward a winter wardrobe. Also the army has begun to get conscious of the need for heavy clothing, and I'm fixed with field, as well as dress wear.

I also practically bought an entire new uniform upon my return here and though most items were purchased through the army with the cost at a level as low as possible, the prices still made one wonder just what a dollar is worth. Items that formerly were $25 are now $65 and $75. . . . Dear, old Leighton, with his marvelous sense of reality, sent me my prize possession—a pair of fleece-lined gauntlets that have been worth their weight in gold. I am the envy of the regiment and I would not part with them for love or money.

Your analysis, Mother, concerning my station here was interesting, and my only comment is you read my letters carefully and then you won't have to spend so much time trying to dope it all out. Also, remember that in war, the enemy relies on sympathetic and non-military minded individuals to gain vital information. Though there is a tendency for more news to leak out from the topside, it is necessary for all of us to exercise security constantly.

Frankly, I'm amazed at myself for the slip-up. Though you cannot realize security of military information 'til you become an integral part of the army, you can take the posters you see displayed to heart and know that they are true. The enemy learns vital information when he can find out such seemingly harmless things as the fact that my unit is now in England. From our past performances, he can draw sharp conclusions that mean a lot to him as he prepares for the big day. So I urge you to refrain from over-enthusiasm concerning my whereabouts and keep such knowledge to yourself. . . .

I wish I had time to develop a number of thoughts that are present in my mind right now, but limitations of time necessitate my ending this little letter. Will try to find time again soon. Meantime, remember your own thoughts directed this direction afford me a far deeper blessing than you could ever know.

Complaining has always been the prerogative of the American citizen-soldier, and Dawson enthusiastically joined the crescendo emanating from soldiers with too much time on their hands. As with the majority of soldiers who fought in World War II, the later stages of the conflict led to a lengthy indictment of the home front.[13] Civilians seemed to view military life and the sacrifices endured by the GIs as inconsequential compared to the ordered life of the domestic front. Moreover, the inequity of sacrifice startled the GIs, who kept tabs on events in America via *The Stars and Stripes* and letters from home.

In Dawson's case, he was particularly appalled at the dissension, personal selfishness, and the seeming indifference of the American public to the needs of the war. The reports of power strikes, transportation upheavals in the railroad and airline industries, automotive strikes, making a fast buck, stories about "petulant womanhood" that failed to flock to the ranks of the newly organized women service organizations, the list continued ad infinitum.

Such half-hearted participation undercut the war effort and seriously affected troop morale. Dawson echoed popular sentiment among the soldiers that the emphasis on material wealth had to end immediately, lest the country find itself torn asunder by "cold and merciless civil strife." It was now time for the civilian populace to get on board.

Nor did "slackers" and "gold-brickers" escape Dawson's scrutiny. Service on a court-martial has always been one of the more unpleasant duties that most commanders experience during their military careers. Courts-martial spanned a myriad of crimes, but two of the most heinous to combat officers were desertion and cowardice under fire.[14]

While in England awaiting the onset of the invasion of the Continent, the army sought to clear the docket from past offenses dating back to the Mediterranean campaigns. One such crime involved a young GI who had gone AWOL on the eve of the invasion of Sicily. The presiding officers reckoned that the soldier simply failed to do his duty and deliberately jeopardized his comrades by his absence at a critical juncture of the impending battle. The board of officers sentenced the GI to death, but all such sentences had to be personally approved by General Eisenhower. In this case, the sentence was commuted to forty years of hard labor and forfeiture of rights and citizenship.

Having witnessed death so frequently in North Africa and Sicily, Dawson regretted the commutation of the court's verdict, but took some satisfaction that the offender had to pay a heavy price. In his mind, forty years seemed insignificant when weighed against the soldiers who paid the ultimate price in battle.

Spring 1944 also marked Dawson's thirtieth birthday, prompting him to reflect on the preceding year's events, as well as to contemplate the upcoming invasion. The year 1943 had been "fraught with danger and trial," but he had survived the ordeal and emerged stronger because of it. Having seen the horrors of war close up, he clearly understood that operations in Tunisia and Sicily would pale in comparison to the hellish combat he envisioned on the continent of Europe.

Most importantly, the months preceding the impending invasion gave Dawson a break from the tensions of frontline combat and time to recoup his spirits. Not surprisingly, his letters reflected his growing apprehension of what it would take to win the war and totally eradicate the Nazi menace from the face of the earth. The correspondence also revealed his immense pride as a combat infantryman and in the GIs with whom he had served in North Africa and Sicily.

Dawson to My Dearest Family

February 27, 1944

Another eventful and busy week has passed, and with it have been days cold and miserable and filled by tasks that bespeak the ordeals of combat. . . . The war is becoming more and more devastating, and when the final phase does take place, it will bring about even greater chaos. I shudder to think of it, for my knowledge of both the composite as well as the limited outlook is quite detailed, and I'm frank to confess that it is a dreary picture.

One's conception of the forces at work both on the individual and on the nations themselves is much clearer over here than back at home, and the agony of readjustment will equal, if not surpass, the tragedies now being enacted. One sees it in the news accounts, as well as through personal contact with peoples of the various nations of Europe.

Morality oftentimes suffers a terrific setback in times like these, and this exemplifies itself most pointedly by the reports that reach us from America. Even now, while the figures of wartime tragedy mount with unbelievable rapidity, we who fight on the battlefront are amazed to find dissension, personal selfishness and seeming indifference to the needs of war exemplifying our nation's thought. The people of America will someday find themselves in a state of cold and merciless civil strife should such attitudes continue to dominate our domestic life.

The men who shoulder the burdens over here and in the South Pacific have come to know the meaning of life to a degree unparalleled in American history. Indeed, it angers and hurts them most deeply to see the material side of life still dominating the National thought while they are facing a hell indescribable. The day of half-hearted participation is long past, and the sooner labor and capital realize this, the easier it will be for all concerned in the days to come.

Recently, I was a member of a general court-martial that sat and rendered justice to men of the army guilty of certain war crimes. On one man, we imposed the sentence of death because he went absent from his organization three days prior to our embarking for Sicily. By his act of desertion, we on the court felt that he did not feel his duty or obligation worthy of the sacrifice that one has to make when he faces the enemy face to face. Although the case was remitted to forty years at hard labor and forfeiture of all rights and citizenship, I feel that justice in a small degree was granted.

One lives a lifetime in a matter of seconds on the battlefront, and many are those who have paid with their lives in order to protect the precepts of life for which we fight. Is it then fair to them to let one enjoy these blessings that shirks his responsibility and duty when others have paid so dearly? My only regret is that our judgment was not upheld.

The same attitude is felt toward those so-called Americans back home who pervert these ideals that are being bought daily in blood. The all-mighty dollar sign continues to predicate our every action—witness the power strike in Los Angeles, the railroad strikes, the plane and automobile strikes, the tremendous profits of the vast industrial combines, the petulant womanhood of America as they answer the call for the auxiliary armed forces— Wacs, Waves, Spars, the bureaucracy of Washington, and finally the countless thousands of able-bodied men of America who place their evaluation of life solely upon their own personal ambitions and desires. War to them is still something for someone else to bear the hard way.

God knows I entered this thing realistically and with my eyes open, and though I've been fortunate in that the bullet with my name on it has yet to strike, I've been through a hell that has burned away the falsities of life that veiled my outlook as a youth. I have had fear clutch at my vitals 'til I felt my inner soul almost strangled, yet throughout it all, a calmness of conscience kept me at my post and pulled me through.

But I have also seen cowardice displayed that hurt my heart more deeply than a knife stab, for it demonstrated the weakness that is the gravest of all mankind. Seeing it expressed in men of America cuts at one's very life. Such is true of so many who fill our ranks with the attitude, "Service to country—but please, Mr. President, make it a safe place." Yes, that, too, crops up on all sides. It's because mothers, fathers, sisters and wives and children are all too precious to part with, even though their very lives are in the balance scales of destiny. Such lack of moral stamina is of course attributed to the fact that war still remains a nebulous unreality to the people of America because they haven't suffered the true vicissitudes of the horrible, dirty, bloody, nasty holocaust. It's still a bad dream for someone else to confront.

Such emotional outbursts must be controlled, I realize, and seldom do I indulge in these expressions. But today, as I stand on the threshold of 1944 and look into the future, I see the horrors to come and I only pray to God that my feelings toward these seeming expressions of Americanism are false, and the things that I sublimate are the true essence of America and truly worthy of the sacrifice that will be made.

Dawson to My Dear Ones

March 1, 1944
England

For the past two weeks, the bitter wind and sleet has kept me seeking the stove constantly, and I hope it was the swan song of winter and warmer weather soon to be here. Indeed, it has been a very rough winter everywhere, and I am grateful that I've been so fortunate in being out of combat the past bitter months. I truly sympathize with the men in Italy and know they have had a rough go of it. Indeed it has been a very quiet stay here in England and only an occasional returning bomber that has had a few holes put into it recalls the nearness of "Jerry."

Also, a one-night stand in London recently was like the eventful night of June 3, 1943, when I was in Algiers and the biggest AA barrage in history was fired.[15] London can really put on a show that even dwarfs that one in Algiers. It sorta [sic] made me feel pretty good, though, to hear some honest to goodness shooting for a change. I was beginning to get senile and self-complacent. As usual, I didn't get hit or even a close one, so it was all very good to watch. The poor devils that got it, though, perhaps felt a bit different. . . .

I note that Dick Wood has been in Alaska. Is he a lieutenant commander or just what? Of course, we in the ground (infantry) forces get promoted when the next higher rank gets killed or wounded, so sometimes promotions are a bit fast or slow, depending on where we are and what we're doing. However, I'd not swap a Captain's bars in the Infantry for a silver leaf in the Air Corps or any other branch, so don't look for anything on that score from me.

Dawson to My Dear Family

March 19, 1944
England

Once more, I am reminded that a year has passed into Eternity and another milestone has been met in earthly existence. Perhaps no year of all the thirty [years] I have lived has been so fraught with danger and trial, yet I find myself still possessed with a body that is whole, although scarred a bit by the tests it has met.[16]

Vividly, I recall the year ago today when I was sitting, huddled in a slit trench at El Guettar, listening to the symphony of war playing the prelude to the great battle that began on that day. Also, I remember midst it all, how I had thrust into my hands some letters from each of you that bespoke your tender thoughts to me. Indeed, it was a most timely inspiration and they served me well during those terrible days.

Now, with the comparative peace of the past five months to restore my courage and renew my determination to fulfill my mission, I am aware that the year has matured my thoughts as well as my physical being much more than any other year of my life. The task ahead has sobered my outlook considerably, and all the past trials have assumed slight insignificance in comparison. But that is true of all life I guess, and I am grateful that I was fortunate to come through this far and still be able to continue the fight. It has meant many hours of fear and anguish on my part, but I've always been able to hold on to my belief that it is worthwhile.

During these long, cold, English winter nights, there have been many occasions when a group of us would foregather in our little clubroom around the fire and discuss topics concerning our lives and our outlook on the general scheme of things. Indeed, it has been most startling how Ed Wozenski and I share the same attitudes, and we have amazed each other by expressing orally the same identical thoughts that may be running through the other's mind at the very moment. It is a priceless gift that we treasure deeply, for in the days to come as we fight alongside each other; this mutual confidence will be of inestimable value. How seldom is this the case! Even on maneuvers this past month, we have seen it work to a degree most satisfying to all concerned.

One thing above all that has created this feeling between us has been an agreement of our minds on the necessity of making this the final and last war that will encompass our nation and the world. One thought has dominated our thoughts and actions throughout the past few years, and indeed it has proven a point to both of us that destruction of the enemy in his entirety is necessary before final and lasting peace can be affected.

It is ever a source of wonderment to me how the average American can complacently compromise his morals by simply working up a physical dislike for the enemy merely because the enemy has forced him into uncomfortable surroundings. Personally, I would never be able to take human life if I merely shot in self-defense at some German who happened to be shooting at me. If America could ever learn to hate commensurate with the demands made on one's moral nature then I feel sure the war would quickly end.

One has to feel completely a sense of righteousness in order to take human life because it threatens some things that are higher than mere individuals. The average American is sore at Germany because she threatens his economic and social security and is content to wage war against them only so long as she maintains such a position. Were Germany to sue for peace tomorrow, I am afraid that there would be all too few who would care to continue the struggle until the end, when it would be impossible for Germany to ever wreak the destruction and devastation upon the world in the years to come.

I, myself, am of the feeling that this must end all wars, and this can only be done by total and complete disintegration of the German Nation. She has disrupted the peace and sanity of the world ever since time began, therefore, she cannot be trusted ever again. What does it profit if one has a cancer and has only a portion of it removed while the core remains intact to continue its devastating growth? Again, what does it profit the world to see hosts of its youth and lifeblood destroyed and then a score of years later, see the terrible scene reenacted? As I have said many times before, there is no place for sentimentality in war for it is too brutal, horrible and tragic for human weaknesses to dominate thought or action. 'Tis far better to end the thing once and for all, rather than leave the seeds of hate to flower again. And such will be the case if we don't finish the task now. . . .

I am, perhaps, a bit garbled in my expression because whenever I seek to utter these thoughts, I am consumed by the subject in an intensity of feeling that is difficult to express. Nevertheless, you may gather from this that there are certain forces at work within me that certainly are different from the same person I was five years ago. What destiny may decree for me in the days to come I feel that I have gained a strength of purpose if nothing else, from this war and my only hope is that it will bear fruit for the betterment of all.

Twenty months ago, I left America, and indeed as the months pile up, I often wonder how I will fit into the family circle if I return. To be sure, no family has stood by one with greater loyalty, and I am ever aware of my shortcomings and weaknesses as compared with each of you. Yours has been a life dedicated to the betterment of life through the highest medium, whereas I have sought the same goal only through a harsh, bitter and loathsome manner. Nevertheless, may we each pray that our efforts will achieve the same end and from our lives will spring a better existence for those who follow after us?

Surely with all that has come to pass in the years gone by, there is some unfulfilled destiny awaiting me that will prove my worth, and I only hope I shall be able to accomplish it before the inevitable end that claims us all. Be aware of this hope and realize that my obligation to you is recognized and someday will be reflected in actuality. . . .

The arrival of spring also heralded what Dawson hoped would be an improvement in the dismal weather that had characterized the unit's stay in England. "Beautiful springtime here and how lovely is the countryside. Such greenery and flowers make war seem a great distance away sometimes," he ruefully commented, "but war never is completely lost from sight."

Easter arrived and passed quietly "with lovely music," though he could not help but feel a bit nostalgic in recalling the events of the preceding year and the terrible bitterness of Tunisia. Still, he remained thankful for the respite from combat during the past six months, but saw the necessity of gearing himself up for the final showdown with the forces of the Third Reich. Ever present was his concern that he would measure up to the standards both his family and he had set for himself.

Dawson to My Dearest Ones

April 23, 1944
England

Another eventful week has passed into the realm of recorded history, and with it, has brought a growing pressure on all of us who actively participate in the manual of arms. The many duties comprising army life are most heavy when a period of preparation occupies the main center of our stage life. How demanding upon our nerves cannot easily be explained, but I assure you it is about the most difficult task we have.

To those who possess imagination, it is doubly hard because one envisions the worst, and as a consequence, the moments of self-analysis are oft-times filled with presentments of the future based on the most terrible moments of the past. However, it will be essential that the final showdown come soon and the end be accomplished as quickly as possible. . . .

General Bradley paid us a visit recently and honored me with a review of my men executing some simulated battle exercises. The last time I had seen him was when we shared a foxhole during an air attack at Gela. Now that he's got a promotion, I hope he won't outstrip me too far, as I seem to be temporarily stymied in the rank of captain!

As always, amphibious training provided the focal point for the assault divisions' training schedules. In some cases, selected officers and men attended the British Battle School at Woolacombe, England, to refine techniques of fire support and coordination of operations from ship to shore. As for Dawson's 16th Regiment, the unit spent two weeks in early February at Devon conducting amphibious rehearsals under simulated combat conditions. March found elements from the 1st Division at Slapton Sands on the coast of Devon, southwest of Dartmouth, for additional training.

These exercises culminated in two dress rehearsals for the invasion force: Exercise TIGER, conducted at the end of April for VII Corps units scheduled to land at Utah Beach; and Exercise FABIUS I, conducted the first week in May for V Corps units scheduled to land at Omaha Beach.[17] During these exercises, minor technicalities were overcome and revisions were made to enhance the success of the landings; however, the basic organization and the techniques as evolved in the Assault Training Center remained unchanged.[18]

According to one battalion commander, the rehearsals proceeded smoothly with one exception. The naval control officers and boat crews who participated in the exercises were not the same ones who would land the 16th Infantry on Omaha Beach. Many of the actual participants in D-Day arrived in England too late to take part in the rehearsals. Still, the rehearsals did answer one question that small-unit commanders had been debating for weeks: "When can the boatloads of troops be reorganized into regular infantry units?"

Because of the capacity of the assault craft, company commanders had to improvise special organizations in order to get troops from the ship to the shore. This unique organization was of limited utility once the unit landed, and had to be discarded as soon as possible. Upon completion of FABIUS I, however, planners determined that the organization of boatloads would continue until the assault regiment had been passed through by subsequent units. While such a decision would materially reduce the effectiveness of the assault units once ashore, it would be impossible to reorganize any size unit in the face of the enemy defenses anticipated on Omaha Beach.[19]

In spite of the intensified training, there still remained ample time for rest and relaxation before the troops would be sealed in their marshaling areas, pending Ike's decision to launch the invasion. Regimental commander Colonel George Taylor ensured that the troops were afforded ample opportunities for movies, tours, and dances. Commanders also needed recreation, and Dawson took several days' leave to visit London and the surrounding countryside.

He was excited by "certain people who had crossed his path of life" over the course of the preceding weeks. In April, he was the guest at a little party hosted by the residents of a small village. One particular family lived in Singapore until the very end, and succeeded in leaving only a short time before the Japanese entered the city in

December 1941. Their opinion of the Japanese was akin to that of the average American, Dawson noted, though he himself did not share the same feeling toward them as he did toward the Germans. To the commanding officer of one of the assault companies, the Germans remained "Public Enemy No. 1."

All in all, these cultural exchanges fascinated him, and as a small-town boy from Waco, he enjoyed the banter with members of the upper crust of British society. "What arguments we do have!" he stated in a brief note to his family. "These arguments are the outgrowth of their natural resentment toward Americans, whom they fear are assuming the dominating role in this world, and as they represent the upper British caste, they are reluctant to see themselves take second place." Still, such diversions were pleasant distractions from military life and the all-consuming responsibilities of command.

But social gatherings and excursions to the countryside were just that—pleasant distractions that provided temporary relief from Dawson's primary mission. More and more, his attention centered on G Company as it entered the final month of preparatory drills. He was pleased at the company's progress, having directly supervised virtually every aspect of training. The men, as well as their still-unproved commander, were ready to take the fight to the Germans.

Dawson's subsequent letters reflected his pride in the company's battle worthiness. The correspondence also reflected his assessment of his own potential to command soldiers in combat.

Dawson to Dearest Family

Sunday, May 1, 1944

Today is a really an outstanding one from the natural beauty standpoint, and I'm very leisurely occupying myself in luxuriant relaxation and rest. Under stately elm and oak trees that have been here many years, I am quite at peace with the world in general, though the roar of planes overhead as they wing eastward toward the Continent upsets reveries a bit and makes me realize the portent of the future. However, I am singularly optimistic about the whole thing and I know that it will be a great show because I've got a group of men that are as good as they come in anybody's army.

Yes, I'm sorta [sic] proud of them and if I likened them to a football team, I would say they are a coach's dream! We're ready this time, so I can assure you success! When the whistle blows

138

for the kickoff, you can know that I'll be in the big middle of the scrimmage and not cooling my heels back in some supply depot far removed from the playing field.

And though, dear ones, there are many who have had greater glory in this war than I have, none have had any more front-line action than I have, and I'm glad I've had this privilege. When it's all over, there won't be any regrets nor will there be cause for any criticism for the part we Dawsons have played in this war.

All I ask is that when the big show starts, you not worry about me because I am convinced that regardless of the outcome, it will all work out for the best. There will doubtless be many who will suffer death as a result of the next big conflict, but the final achievement will indeed be worth the price. Just know that and pray for its speedy fruition. . . .

This is all for now, but know I'll try and keep you posted as time passes.

Dawson to My Dear Family

May 11, 1944

Well, the month of May moves along, and even now, my bones are still chilled by the wintry winds that seem to persist spasmodically. First, there's a swell spring day, then a dreary, cold, wet one, so I still wear my "long handles." But with it all, I am in excellent health and physically and mentally prepared for the future.

My problems, of course, are my men, and they are constantly occupying themselves in diligently pursuing their duties both from a military and social standpoint. Unfortunately, several of them persist in being as strenuous in their social life as they are in their military, so I am kept busy twenty-four hours a day. But I am becoming both realistic as well as philosophical about the whole thing, and hope that their energy and colossal physical powers will be on the same level when the shells start playing tit-tat-too amongst us. . . .

Ran into an awfully nice fellow from Corpus the other day who is a bombardier in a B-26. He hopes to locate Roy for me. We spent a couple of days together, and he and I enjoyed our mutual interest in Corpus. Guess Roy will be over soon, and if so, I hope we can see each other. Would indeed be swell if we could see the show from the air and ground both. In that way, you would be able to get a pretty complete picture of it all. Then when Brothers

Matt and L. B. report from the Navy, I guess everything will be covered, except the Marines, who are nothing more than 2nd class infantrymen anyhow!

Dawson to My Dearest Ones

May 16, 1944

Life continues full and most absorbing. Letters indeed are gratefully received, and I trust you are receiving mine . . . the war is such a minute-to-minute proposition that the thought and action of the whole world changes with each new social or military incident. Strange, indeed, how unstable the convictions of life remain, even at this stage of the war.

Odd that I no longer feel so intense a desire to save the world from its downfall, but more am I becoming deadly realistic concerning life and what constitutes my idea of freedom. Well, events to come will doubtless bring about an understanding of just what I mean.

Trust all is well with each of you, and now that Matt has joined the Navy, I presume you will be occupied with many interesting things pertaining to him. But don't forget "GI Joe."

With the invasion less than three weeks away, G Company and the rest of the assaulting force made final preparations. General Huebner addressed his troops on May 19, and a week later, all leaders were briefed on the specifics of the operation. It was now problematic concerning just when the actual invasion would occur.

Although the coastal area had been closed to visitors since April, now the concentration areas themselves were isolated from contact with the surrounding countryside. At Eisenhower's request, the British government halted all traffic between the southern part of England and the remainder of the United Kingdom, and then took the unprecedented step of arbitrarily stopping all diplomatic communiqués from the United Kingdom to foreign countries.

Additionally, a host of two thousand Counter Intelligence Corps men guarded the marshaling camps closely lest enemy agents decipher any pertinent intelligence concerning the invasion. Local officers enforced strict camouflage discipline to avoid detection of the troop concentrations.[20]

For the small-unit leaders and the average GI, the actual date of OVERLORD was insignificant. All of them knew from the very time they had arrived in Liverpool on their return to England that they were preparing for the cross-channel attack.

It was not a mission for which the individual rifleman would have volunteered. The majority of soldiers in the combat units would have wholeheartedly concurred with Dawson on the eve of the invasion of Sicily when he stated that the 1st Division had been through two amphibious invasions already, and now it was time for "the other 8,000,000 soldiers to come over and have a whack at it." Still, the GIs of Tunisia and Sicily recognized that they were a special organization with the most combat experience of any division in the U.S. Army.

Most, including Dawson, wrote final letters to loved ones in the event they would not return. A more personal letter to his beloved mother followed one sent to his family as a whole. In both letters, he reiterated his devotion to his family and asked each to say a prayer for his officers and men that they might measure up to "the great task confronting the forces of life they represent."

Dawson to My Beloved Family

May 29, 1944

Two wonderful, warm, sunshiny days, the nicest I've experienced since leaving North Africa and Sicily, have just been completed. Indeed, you can understand how that would be an item worthy of several lines!

But that isn't what I intended to mention in this little letter. It's just a way of opening that leads me to assure you that my heart is filled with unmeasured warmth and tenderness for each of you and especially Dad and Mother. Even a calloused old soldier finds a spark of human tenderness when it comes to his loved ones, and as I am fast maturing into that category, I just thought I better reassure you of this.

Now that the tempo of war beats faster and faster, and soon the crescendo will climax this holocaust with an impact that will leave us all breathless, I want to reiterate my devotion to you, who mean more to me than anything else in the world. The life we've led together has been blessed with a happiness and joy that has been a privilege that few families ever can possibly match. I so feel that I have been the one who has had a measure more than all the rest of you, for never has one family been so loving, kind, considerate and understanding to one as you have to me. May God bless you one and all and ever keep you in His care.

Dawson to My Precious Mother

May 30, 1944
England

Your dear letter of the 21st came today and gave me a joy of heart that is truly hard to describe. Few people in this world have the ability to write as you do, and none provides the inspirational pleasure that yours does. Always know that I have a niche in my heart for you that will ever be the most precious treasure I possess.

Through the years, the warmth and tenderness of your devotion to me has been the abiding source of comfort that has helped me meet the tests, and I have found unspeakable strength came from your character and personality. I shall never be able to measure up to you and Dad, but in my humble prayer, I hope that God will somehow find my destiny a reflection of credit to you both.

Living as I do in a day of horror and travesty on the finer precepts of life, one cannot reveal in action all that is found within the heart and soul. However, I hope that someday I shall be able to return to normal and somehow make my personality felt in a manner that will do honor to those who have been my greatest partisans.

The destiny of life is an elusive thing that is never shaped until the moments have passed and formed the shape of events that create our lives on this earth. So it is never measured 'til all the facets are patterned and thus analyzed in detail. So it is with the approach of awesome events that will shape the course of all our lives in the years to come. One cannot dwell too much in the past and recall too much of the sordid details that comprised the moments of the past two years. Fate has served me well, and indeed, I've been fortunate to have lived with death so closely and yet carried on without serious physical hurt. And now that again the demands of war are upon me, I only pray that I shall be privileged to live 'til my destiny is achieved.

I am truly conscious of the responsibility that rests upon all my men and me. In your prayers and communions with God, I beg of you to remember each of my men and officers to Him that they may have His living care and protection. There will be many who will join Him for there has never been a greater task confronting the forces of life that we represent than the one that lies before us. But I am comforted that each has a deep and sincere appreciation for the job ahead, and I know that they will do the task and well!

There are few positions in the army that provide greater joy and sorrow than a command of front line troops. I say joy and sorrow because it is a privilege to be with them in success and a heartbreaking sorrow when the gods of war snuff them away from this life. I've seen this often in the past, but never before were they my own men. Now, I am their leader, and upon my shoulders rest their entire future. I tell you this for it will give you in part the responsibility that is mine. So now as never before I ask that you remember me to God's care and pray that I shall have the strength to do the job.

The warm sunshine sifting through the lovely beech and elm trees of this beautiful English countryside is indeed a pleasure to me, and my heart is infinitely tender as I recall spring at home and all the wonderful memories of the Texas abloom in June. But I do not let myself go too far from the realities of the task ahead, for it will mean a softening to the sterner necessities that now occupy my life. However, I only wish to say that America is indeed a wonderful land, and one worth every sacrifice necessary to keep her free and safe from the forces against whom we are pitted.

When the big day comes, you will undoubtedly be wondering about me, and where I am, and how I fit into the show of shows. All I can say, dearest ones, is that I shall be giving everything within my power, and the enemy will know that there is one outfit led by a long, lanky Texan who means business. Later, as time unfolds, all the story will be revealed to you, so keep your curiosity down and your spirits high, 'cause you know that I shall let you have the details just as soon as I possibly can.

There's really little more I can say, dearest Mother, at this time, except that you are ever dearer to me with each passing second. Know this always, and I'll be thinking and loving you as only a devoted soul could worship the most wonderful mother in all this world.

Having made peace with his Creator and with his family, Dawson and G Company moved to the final embarkation site at Weymouth Harbor. Once on board the ship, he went around to all his men and spoke to them individually, telling them that he wished them all the best and that he expected the best from each of them.

Was the pep talk effective? He wasn't sure, noting, "I had a mixed reaction from them. I think I still was an outlander and, frankly, to be perfectly honest, I didn't know when I landed whether I was going to get shot from the back or the front." In any event, there was no time to contemplate his personal fate. The Allied Expeditionary Force was about to embark on what the Supreme Commander termed "a great crusade."

"The eyes of the world are upon you," read Ike's order of the day to the troops. And the eyes of G Company rested entirely on Captain Joseph Turner Dawson, an officer who had never exercised command in war. How would he react under fire? Would he measure up to the challenge? The answer to those questions rested on a four-mile stretch of sand in the Calvados region of Normandy known as Omaha Beach.

Captain Joe Dawson upon his return from the fighting on
Dawson's Ridge.
Joe Dawson private collection

Lieutenant General George S. Patton Jr. (left) and Brigadier General
Theodore Roosevelt Jr., assistant commanding general, 1st Infantry
Division, conduct an impromptu field conference at a street corner
in Gela, Sicily, during the island's invasion in July 1943.
*U.S. Army Signal Corps photo, courtesy of the U.S. Army Military History Institute,
Carlisle Barracks, Pennsylvania*

After six days of fighting, advance elements of the 16th Infantry Regiment enter the town of Troina, Sicily, to clear it of snipers.
U.S. Army Signal Corps photo, courtesy of the U.S. Army Military History Institute, Carlisle Barracks, Pennsylvania

Dawson surveys a Mark IV tank near Troina, Sicily, after the
fighting ceased.
Joe Dawson private collection

Dawson conducts marksmanship training after
assuming command of G Company, 2nd Battalion,
16th Infantry Regiment, in August 1943.
Joe Dawson private collection

Captain Joe Dawson in England on the eve of the invasion of Europe. His letters reflect a constant concern whether he will measure up to the crucible of combat.
Joe Dawson private collection

Lieutenant General Omar N. Bradley inspects Dawson's company in the spring of 1944. Bradley visited every company in his command prior to the commencement of Operation OVERLORD.
Joe Dawson private collection

Sixteenth Infantry Regiment conducts preinvasion amphibious training at Slapton Sands. Dawson's company participated in two 1st Infantry Division exercises there prior to D-Day.

U.S. Army Signal Corps photo, courtesy of the U.S. Army Military History Institute, Carlisle Barracks, Pennsylvania

Army troops aboard an LCT prior to the D-Day invasion, June 6, 1944.
U.S. Army Signal Corps photo, courtesy of the U.S. Army Military History Institute, Carlisle Barracks, Pennsylvania

Major General Clarence Huebner, commanding general,
1st Infantry Division, at the time of the invasion of Europe.
U.S. Army Signal Corps photo, courtesy of the U.S. Military Academy,
West Point, New York

American assault troops in a landing craft huddle behind the protective front of the craft as it nears Omaha Beach. Smoke in the background is from naval gunfire support of the D-Day landings.
U.S. Army Signal Corps photo, courtesy of the U.S. Army Military History Institute, Carlisle Barracks, Pennsylvania

Army troops land on Omaha Beach during the initial landings, June 6, 1944. The ridge, which Dawson's company climbed under fire, is in the background.
U.S. Army Signal Corps photo, courtesy of the U.S. Army Military History Institute, Carlisle Barracks, Pennsylvania

An American medic bandages the hand of a GI who was injured while
trying to land on Omaha Beach.
*U.S. Army Signal Corps photo, courtesy of the U.S. Army Military History Institute,
Carlisle Barracks, Pennsylvania*

Six days after the initial landings at Omaha Beach, American combat engineers construct a roadway as the Allies rush reinforcements to aid the units on the front line. By D-Day + 6, Dawson's company remained under fire from snipers as it recuperated from the fighting on June 6.
U.S. Army Signal Corps photo, courtesy of the U.S. Army Military History Institute, Carlisle Barracks, Pennsylvania

On July 2, 1944, General Dwight D. Eisenhower, Supreme
Commander, Allied Expeditionary Force, pins the Distinguished
Service Cross on Captain Joe Dawson for heroism under fire
at Omaha Beach.
U.S. Army Signal Corps photo, Joe Dawson private collection

German civilians flee Aachen in October 1944. Aachen was the first great city in Germany captured by the Allies. While the fighting raged within the city, Dawson and his men held the Verlautenheide Ridge outside Eilendorf. For its staunch defense of "Dawson's Ridge," G Company, 2nd Battalion, received the Presidential Unit Citation.

U.S. Army Signal Corps photo, courtesy of the U.S. Military Academy,
West Point, New York

On the fiftieth anniversary of D-Day, Joe Dawson shows President Bill Clinton the route along which he led G Company up the bluffs overlooking Omaha Beach. Later, Dawson introduced the president at ceremonies commemorating the veterans who landed on D-Day. With Dawson and the president are D-Day veterans Walt Ehlers and Bob Slaughter.
Official White House photo, courtesy of Joe Dawson private collection

6
Normandy

God is my witness that the men of my company lived, fought and died in true glory.

For the Big Red One, movement to the marshaling areas in the vicinity of Long Bredy, Dorset, began on May 7 and was completed four days later. Once in the encampments, the troops were "sealed" in their camps, pending deployment to the points of embarkation. On June 1, embarkation began at Weymouth Harbor, and by the third, all of the assault troops had boarded their craft.

The 16th Regiment's 1st Battalion climbed aboard the USS *Samuel Chase*; the 2nd Battalion, containing Dawson's company, went aboard the USS *Henrico*; and the 3rd Battalion sailed on the HMS *Empire Anvil*. The next days brought nervous anticipation, awaiting the decision of the supreme commander to launch the invasion of France. In the opening hours of June 5, General Dwight Eisenhower confirmed that D-Day would be Tuesday, June 6. By that time, the largest armada in history was already at sea.

The general plan of the First Division called for attacking with two reinforced RCTs abreast—the Big Red One's organic 16th Infantry Regiment on the left, and the attached 116th Infantry Regiment from the 29th Infantry Division on the right. Dawson's 16th RCT was to land on Omaha Beach in areas designated as Fox Green and Easy Red at H-Hour, with the 2nd and 3rd Battalions abreast. The 1st Battalion was in reserve.

The objective of Dawson's 2nd Battalion was to reduce the beach defenses in its zone, capture Colleville-sur-Mer, seize and hold assigned objectives, dig in and establish defensive positions to repel anticipated enemy counterattacks, and cover the landing of the remainder of the 1st Division. Providing naval gun support to the Big Red One were the battleships *Arkansas*, *Texas*, and *Nevada*, plus three cruisers, the *Bellona*, *Black Prince*, and *Glasgow*. In addition, there were ten destroyers and a large number of smaller vessels, including nine rocket-launching craft. The 9th U.S. Air Force provided tactical air support.[1]

As the vast armada moved toward the Normandy coast, news correspondent Ernie Pyle took copious notes for a column that he was preparing to write as soon as he went ashore. Pyle noted that those aboard the ships had secretly dreaded the voyage, for they expected attacks from U-boats, E-boats, and—at nighttime—from aircraft. But nothing happened because minesweepers had swept wide channels between England and France.

Escorting the fleet was the largest contingent of ships than "any human had ever seen before at one glance." There were "battleships and all other kinds of warships clear down to patrol boats. There were great fleets of Liberty ships. There were fleets of luxury liners turned into troop transports, and fleets of big landing craft and tank carriers and tankers. And in and out through it all were nondescript ships—converted yachts, riverboats, tugs, and barges."

The best way Pyle could describe the vast armada and the frantic urgency of the traffic was to suggest, "You visualize New York Harbor on its busiest day of the year and then just enlarge that scene until it takes in all the ocean the human eye can reach, clear around the horizon. And over the horizon there are dozens of times that many."[2]

For those soldiers, sailors, and airmen who experienced D-Day, it was a moment like no other in history. H-Hour in the 16th Infantry Regiment's zone of Omaha Beach was 0645 hours, with G Company scheduled to land in the second wave at approximately 0700. At 0115 hours, the company was alerted and began preparations for disembarking into their assault craft. Breakfast, consisting of bologna and luncheon meat sandwiches and coffee, was given to all personnel.

After they secured their equipment, Dawson called the six boat teams to their respective debarkation stations and began loading the landing craft, vehicle and personnel (LCVP).[3] In light of the lessons learned at Slapton Sands, the standard organization for all assault companies called for the unit to be organized into six assault sections with approximately thirty-seven men in each craft. This unique organization for OVERLORD was never replicated for any subsequent operation, although minor equipment differences existed throughout the assaulting divisions.

Dawson personally commanded G Company's headquarters section. Lieutenants John D. Burbridge, Eugene A. Day, James A. Krucas, Marvin M. Stine, and Kenneth "Den" Bleau commanded sections one through five, respectively. An over-strength platoon remained under command of a Lieutenant Lange, who was later dismissed from service.[4]

On June 6, the Channel was extremely choppy, which created considerable delay in loading the personnel into the assault craft. Loading was finally accomplished by placing all heavy equipment and ten men into each assault craft before lowering the boats. The remainder of the boat team then climbed over the side of the *Henrico* by scramble nets.

By 0415, all assault teams were loaded, and the boat wave began forming approximately five hundred yards off the starboard bow of the *Henrico*. Thirty minutes later, all boats met in this position and proceeded toward the distant shore. One commander remembered, "There was the usual racing around for well over one hour, during which every man was completely soaked, and many, sickened."

On schedule, the assault wave reached the line of departure two thousand yards from the beach at 0635 hours and deployed with all boats abreast. As the boats moved closer to shore, the men passed a few men tossing about in the water in life belts and small rubber rafts, and then more and more. At first, the assault wave thought these men were downed airmen, but they soon realized they were crews from tanks that had floundered in the heavy surf.

Observers noted the intense enemy fire falling on the beach, and as G Company came within a thousand yards of Omaha, they came under small arms fire that intensified as they moved closer. The second section's boat then hit a sandbar seven hundred yards out, but the coxswain told the men to stand steady, and he bumped his way through. The rough seas and withering enemy fire caused the coxswains of the landing craft great difficulty in maintaining the boats' formation, but the company reached the water's edge relatively intact.[5]

The story of Bloody Omaha has been told a thousand times. Nothing in the First Division's history or Dawson's experience could have prepared the men for what they encountered on that beach. The 2nd Battalion landing plan called for E and F Companies to land abreast, with G Company in reserve and H Company in support. Because of the tidal drift, few units landed on the desired beach. E and F Companies drifted from position and landed to the east, on Fox Green. Only one platoon, commanded by Lieutenant John Spaulding, landed where it was supposed to, on Easy Red. There, accompanied by two boat sections from the 29th Division that landed far out of sector and five DD tanks from Company B, 741st Tank Battalion and eight standard tanks from Company A, 741st Tank Battalion, began firing on enemy positions.

As the first wave of the 2nd Battalion Landing Team struck Fox Green, however, intense enemy fire virtually decimated the two lead companies. Both assault companies sustained nearly 50 percent casualties in the initial minutes of the assault. The men were subjected to machine-gun and antitank fire as they waded toward shore. One LCVP received a direct hit from an antitank gun, burst into flames, and exploded.

On Fox Green itself, beach obstacles were plentiful, consisting of hedgehogs, tetrahedrons, log ramps, curved rails, and stakes. In the actual battalion zone, there were no DD tanks to cover the advance of the assault companies, nor were there any bomb craters on the beach in which the men could take cover from enemy fire.

Captain Ed Wozenski, who commanded E Company, remembered, "Men were falling on all sides, and the water was reddened with their blood. The survivors still moved forward and eventually worked up to a pile of shale at the high water mark. Unfortunately, most of our guns were jammed with sand, but every arm was brought to bear on the enemy. Men armed with pistols alone were firing back at machine-guns in an effort to cover the company's men still struggling ashore."

Other men, displaying the best in courage and devotion to duty, stripped and cleaned their weapons while under heavy fire. Enemy snipers mercilessly mowed down anyone attempting to return to the water and drag their wounded comrades to the base of the shale. By the time Wozenski's men reached the summit later in the morning, a rough check revealed that well over one hundred men out of the 183 who landed were killed, wounded, or missing.[6]

Utter chaos reigned, Dawson recalled, "because the Germans controlled the field of fire completely, and the first wave was totally disorganized by their tremendous number of casualties."[7] Most of the first wave lay dead or dying, the equipment and the wreckage of battle clogging the shoreline. The initial wave had become pinned down, "mentally if not physically," Dawson remembered, as "there was no coordinated fire from the Americans ashore. They were bunched shoulder to shoulder and were huddling on patches of ground, which gave them partial cover from the enemy's fire."[8]

These were the remnants from Wozenski's company, together with soldiers from the 116th RCT, who had landed on the wrong beach and had become demoralized in part by that error. The inferno of Omaha consumed everyone and everything that touched its shore.

Landing under extremely heavy fire in his designated zone on Easy Red, Dawson was first off his LCVP, followed by his communications sergeant and his company clerk. As he jumped, he later recalled that an artillery shell struck the boat, wiping out the remaining thirty-three members of his headquarters platoon, including the naval officer who was the fire control officer assigned to coordinate the fire from ships offshore.

Within seconds, soldiers from the company's five remaining assault crafts landed. The boats were hurriedly emptied, the men jumping into water shoulder deep while under intense machine-gun and antitank fire. Fortunately, the division's initial assault wave had reduced a number of the beach defenses in G Company's zone, but enemy fire remained heavy. Remarkably, most of Dawson's company, consisting of 219 officers and men, survived the initial landing intact, but German small-arms fire quickly reduced that number.[9]

G Company suffered most of its casualties—63 in total—in getting from the waterline to a small shingled mound about ten feet high that enabled the company to secure a slight amount of defilade from fire raking the beach from the flanks and immediate front. Dawson's casualties fell mainly from mortar and bullet fire, the artillery having been shifted to succeeding assault waves.

Overwhelmed by the sheer horror of the spectacle, Dawson seized the initiative and took command of the survivors, who by now huddled under the protection of the sandbar that marked the high water mark of the beach and provided the only cover available from direct fire. He realized, "There was nothing I could do on the beach except die. I knew no one else was going to do it. Some things one does automatically, some by circumstance, but I knew it had to be done. There is no other way to say it."[10]

Unless Dawson could galvanize his men, G Company would meet the same fate as its sister companies. Fifty years after the war, Dawson reflected on D-Day, stating that leading his men off Omaha Beach was the toughest decision he ever made as a company commander. "I was fortunate enough to realize that there wasn't any point in me standing there and, frankly, I felt the only way I could move was forward, and to go up and see if I could get off the beach," he recalled.

At one point, Dawson found a sergeant and two soldiers who seemingly refused to advance. He exhorted them strongly to follow him and then he moved on. Looking over his shoulder, he saw the trio still huddled behind one of the beach obstacles. Returning to the men, he again shouted to them to come along when, suddenly, he realized that all three were dead. The encounter only stiffened his resolve to get off the beach.

The distance from the sandbar or shingle to the crest of the bluff was approximately 750 yards to G Company's front. At the shingle, Dawson met Lieutenant Colonel Herbert Hicks, his battalion commander, who immediately ordered him to advance and seize the high ground to the immediate front. Once atop the bluff, Hicks directed him to deploy the company from the right to clear the crest. Hicks merely confirmed Dawson's own intentions. Collecting his men at the base of the shingle, Dawson moved rapidly forward.

Beyond the shingle was wire—two double aprons and concertina, about ten feet high. Positioning his machine guns on top of the shingle and the company mortars at its base, he prepared to advance. Suddenly, he saw a path, blocked with obstacles and obviously mined, leading toward the crest that dominated the beach. The veterans from North Africa and Sicily knew exactly what to do. With Dawson were Sergeant Ed Tatara and PFC Henry Peszek, who quickly fastened two bangalore torpedoes together, shoved them under the strands of concertina, and blew a gap through which Dawson and a small contingent of men passed.[11]

Beyond the wire lay the minefield. Two dead GIs littered the mined area. The men of G Company raced through the field over their fallen comrades, figuring that this was the safest route. Having survived the dangerous stretch from water's edge to the foot of the bluffs, Dawson now began the dangerous ascent. German bullets "sounded like a bunch of bees that seemed to swarm everywhere," he later recalled.

Midway up the slope, Dawson and PFC Frank Baldridge found themselves caught between the fire of their own men and that of an enemy machine-gun nest at the head of the draw. Both men flopped next to a fallen log for cover, and then Dawson instructed Baldridge to "leave your equipment here and go back and get the rest of the company." Simultaneously, Dawson met Lieutenant John Spaulding with the remnants of his platoon from E Company. Spaulding, one of the first junior officers to make it across the seawall, had traversed the swamp and beach flat and had ascended the bluff.[12]

Directing Spaulding to cover his advance, Dawson proceeded up the draw toward the summit. As he neared the crest, the terrain became almost vertical for about ten feet. The change in topography provided complete concealment from observation by the entrenched enemy on the summit. On the crest, a machine gun was busily firing at the beach, and Dawson could hear rifle and mortar fire coming from the bluff.

"There was a machine gun about thirty feet to the east of where I thought we would be able to get through," he remembered. "I knew he had to be taken out if we were going to reach our objective. I was able to get within a few feet, below him where he couldn't see me."

Gathering a few men, he caught his breath, tossed two grenades, and silenced the enemy crew that was creating such havoc on the beach below. Without waiting for reinforcements, Dawson and his men pressed on until they eliminated the remaining German positions. To his knowledge, no one had penetrated the enemy defenses until this moment. It was approximately nine o'clock in the morning.[13]

Finally, Dawson's small group halted and waited at the brow of the ridge for the company to come up. As the platoons reached him, he rapidly deployed them on line and moved in the direction of Colleville. By now, enemy fire had temporarily slackened, so G Company moved more quickly. As soon as his remaining men were assembled, Dawson debouched from that point, firing on the retreating enemy and moving toward a gate in the right corner of an open field.

A dirt roadway led from the field directly to Dawson's front through a heavily wooded area. Entering the wooded area, G Company immediately encountered German small-arms fire. It was nearly noon before they reached the outskirts of Colleville. En route to the town, Staff Sergeant Joseph Barr sneaked along a hedgerow and captured eight prisoners, routing them from a dugout. They were Germans and Poles.

As with most Norman villages, the dominant building was a church, with its steeple serving as an observation post. Collecting a sergeant and a private, Dawson and his men entered the church and killed the three German defenders, as well as the forward observer in the tower.

When he emerged from the church, Dawson sustained his first wound when an enemy sniper fired from across the wall. The bullet went through his carbine, shattering the weapon's stock and sending its fragments through his kneecap and the fleshy portion of his right leg. Pausing only enough time to bandage the wound, he then led his company through yet another "very severe fire fight" on the outskirts of the village. By now, it was approximately mid-afternoon.

Shortly thereafter, G Company suffered seven casualties as a result of friendly fire. U.S. Navy ships lying off the Norman coast suddenly "bloodied us from one end of the town to the other." Dawson was angered beyond all measure because he thought it was totally disgraceful that his own navy would be so careless to fire without confirmation that the Germans still held Colleville. Having lost his naval fire coordinator in the initial assault, he was unable to send the coordinates of his forward elements as expeditiously as he would have liked, and it took more than an hour for battalion headquarters to reach the offshore batteries.[14] By that time, the 16th Regiment had suffered sixty-four casualties. With the exception of the men who died on Dawson's landing craft, this was the worst tragedy that befell G Company on D-Day.

By nightfall on June 6, the Americans had landed 35,000 men on Omaha, "but it took 250 to open the way," Dawson recalled at the end of the most important day in his life. He took justifiable pride in what G Company had accomplished, yet he still trembled with emotion whenever he thought how bravely they had accomplished their job when other companies were seemingly overwhelmed by the awesome and grim enemy defense. Company casualties on June 6 alone numbered 14 killed, 32 wounded, and 3 missing in action.[15] Casualties, including attachments, numbered 60 killed and wounded. Not once had his men faltered under his personal leadership.

Other commands had performed equally well, but G Company had been one of the first to penetrate the enemy defenses. In retrospect, Dawson attributed his success to poor German marksmanship and his own ability to control his command, both in landing together and maneuvering up the bluff as a fighting unit. Only on the beach for ten minutes, he took advantage of the opportunity when subsequent boat waves attracted the enemy fire, and for the first time, his men could see the enemy clearly.

Other factors beyond Dawson's control certainly contributed to his success. German defenses were more dispersed along Dawson's front than on other sectors of Omaha, and divisional engineers had cleared some of the obstacles to his front. G Company also profited from the small defile directly in the path, and this feature facilitated Dawson in initiating the advance inland. Once his men reached the summit, they engaged the enemy with direct fire, which forced the Germans to cease the concentrated rifle, machine-gun, and mortar fire with which they were sweeping the eastern part of Easy Red and a portion of Fox Green.

What Rommel termed "the longest day" also changed Joe Dawson. Aboard the *Henrico*, he wondered if he would survive the next day's battle, whether he would be shot from the front or the back. He had now proven himself in combat as a frontline commander, and G Company took special pride in his leadership by example. As he gathered his survivors around him in the church courtyard in Colleville, he noticed that an eerie calm had descended upon his men.

As he moved from one man to the next, Dawson became aware of a difference among them, a change that he might not have noticed had he not known them so intimately. The majority of the company had taken part in its first action. They had killed during those hours and observed violent death for the first time.

Marine veteran Phil Caputo expressed similar sentiments a generation later, after his troops had seen the cruelty combat aroused in men participating in their initial combat. Before D-Day, G Company fit both definitions of the word infantry, which means either a "body of soldiers equipped for service on foot" or "infants, boys, youths collectively." The difference now was that the second definition could no longer be applied to the GIs in Dawson's command. Having received that primary sacrament of war, baptism of fire, their boyhoods were behind them.[16] As with Caputo's marines, Dawson's soldiers were no longer boys, but men, men who had killed and been killed.

"I think a mutual respect began to develop," Dawson recalled, "and it was almost incredible. I felt it in every one of my men. We had casualties. We had lost men there on the beach. We had two or three [casualties] suffered in this battle." More importantly, a bond emerged between the commander and the soldiers entrusted to his care. A subtle change had occurred in the minds of the men, particularly the veterans of the Mediterranean.

Virtually unnoticed, D-Day witnessed the quiet transition from Wozenski's company to Dawson's. The company of veterans had discovered what they had in their youthful, inexperienced CO.[17] Their leader had proved his mettle in combat. Moreover, he had seized a fleeting opportunity and led them from the beach. Of all the companies that had landed in the first two waves, G Company suffered the fewest casualties in proportion to what they had accomplished. In the words of General Omar Bradley and by the deeds of Captain Joe Dawson, every doughboy in G Company now served in a company of heroes.

Dawson had paid a personal toll in his company's success. By midday, June 6, his knee had swollen to twice its regular size, and the medics felt he would have a better chance of survival if he were treated in a hospital rather than in the field. Evacuated on D + 1, he was transferred to a hospital in England. X-rays revealed that Dawson had suffered a superficial wound, and he immediately declared himself fit to return to duty. A doctor determined otherwise, and after a surgical staff removed the fragments, the physician placed Dawson on several days' bed rest. Dawson would have none of it; the very next day, he obtained a pass to go to town and promptly caught a train to Bournemouth, where he pleaded with U.S. Navy personnel to take him across the English Channel to Omaha Beach. "I thought I belonged with my company," he later insisted.[18] Meanwhile, the hospital sent out a frantic call for its missing patient.

Dawson's immense pride in his company was reflected in his initial letters after returning to his men following his short respite in England.

Dawson to Dearest Sis

June 12, 1944

Just a line to say I'm OK and have managed to get along this far. The news has covered the situation pretty well, though words can never describe the hell that was created on the beach that I stormed. God was with me, and I survived to get the job done, but it was terrible.

Am returning to the front after having a little medical attention to a couple of items that I received D-Day.[19] Am fit as a fiddle, and I'll be paying my respects to Jerry again soon.[20]

Well, darling, just keep your fingers crossed, and know that everything goes well over here. We're on the final road now, and it shouldn't be too long before we manage to finish the job.

Dawson to Dearest Ones

June 12, 1944

Well, the big show is now on, and as I had a front line ticket, I can only say that the papers have made no understatement as to the fury or the bitterness of the struggle. I will try and find time to let you know more of the details later, but I wanted you to be assured that all is well and I am fit.

There never was nor there never will be a more wonderful group of men than those who make up my company. There were many that suffered from the initial ordeal, but those of us left were able to do the job assigned us, and we did ourselves proud. Somehow, I can only feel that the Lord was walking beside me and spared me, for which I am eternally grateful. Well, you are getting the news from the papers as to how we are progressing, so just feel that we are getting on with our job.

The same day Dawson wrote home, Ernie Pyle also sent the first of three columns from Normandy. Pyle had come ashore at Omaha Beach on D + 1, just after the fighting had moved inland. A two-year veteran of war, even Pyle was astonished at the chaos and debris that littered miles of shoreline. Spending three days with the troops,

154

he attempted to describe the horror of all that he had seen: "Submerged tanks and overturned boats and burned trucks and shell-shattered jeeps and sad little personal belongings were strewn all over these bitter sands. That plus the bodies of soldiers lying in rows covered with blankets, the toes of their shoes sticking up in a line as though on drill. And other bodies uncollected, still sprawling grotesquely in the sand or half hidden by the high grass beyond the beach."

It seemed to Pyle that it was a pure miracle that the GIs had taken the bluffs. For some of the American platoons it was easy, but in this special sector where Pyle found himself, "our troops faced such odds that our getting ashore was like my whipping Joe Louis down to a pulp."[21]

For the next several days, Pyle, as did Dawson, collected his thoughts and contemplated what General Dwight Eisenhower had called "a great crusade." The sheer spectacle of D-Day still dwarfed anything in Dawson's memory. As individual reinforcements filled G Company's ranks, he gave his personal account of the previous ten days and the specific role his men had played in the Allied success.

Dawson to My Dearest Family

June 16, 1944
An Apple Orchard, Normandy

You must forgive me for not writing a detailed letter to you before now because there were certain things that occurred to prevent me from gathering my thoughts together long enough to inscribe them. My slight incapacitation is now coming along nicely and offers no presentable difficulty, so I am once more with my men and my heart is happy. One never realized the utter loneliness of separation until he has had the privilege of living and being a part of the finest group of men on the face of the earth.

The platitudes of those who spend their lives recording the deeds of courageous men are in truth the expressions of the artisans of literary word-binding compared to those thoughts that can never be put into words by the men who see and live the intimate relationship of mutual sufferers in this greatest of ordeals.

What I'm trying to say is that justice can never be properly accorded to the magnificent fortitude and heroism of the fine American soldier and man. He is without peer, and these past few days have implanted in the hearts of all a realization of the true greatness of these men. I say this because I've had an honor never to be equaled in being a part of a group that will ever stand as a symbol of greatness to all who witnessed or know how they measured up to the supreme test without faltering or wavering. I cannot say more for my heart forbears it, but God is my Witness that the men of my company lived, fought and died in true glory.

The story of our coming to France has been told a thousand times over by all the newsmen of the world, and tales of individual heroism are recorded for all to read and become inspired. But none surpassed, either in deed or action, "my" men. I shall not be able to give in detail all that did transpire, but with restrained license of censorship you can judge for yourselves just how we met and overcame our enemies.

Tarawa and all the other terrible beachheads of this war have nothing on the murderous hell that descended upon us as we touched the shores of France. All the many weapons of war seemed to be concentrated on that naked, exposed bit of sand, and the miracle of it all was the fact that I still cannot tell just how I crossed it or how my men managed—but we did! Though many fell as we moved through this storm of steel, they didn't falter an instant, but came on without stopping.

My company pressed on, however, and only pausing a few seconds to get their breath, stormed the heights commanding the beach, and with this successful assault, we were able to secure the beach for the other units to come ashore. Throughout that day and night and the next day, we were constantly busy, and at times, were engaged literally eye-to-eye with the Jerries. All I can say is we were able to stand on our own and hold our ground against his constant attacks.

I took a short leave to get a piece of adhesive tape for my knees, and the darned medics kept me on a Cook's tour for about five days before I was able to elude them and return home.[22] Now, after three days with the constant shelling and firing all along here, I am once more restored to a good, nervous state. Nothing is more nerve-wracking than being attended by a bunch of solicitous nurses and doctors, though, seriously, they are the unsung heroes of this war, and their marvelous work of caring for the wounded and suffering is something without parallel. They were simply magnificent.[23]

All of which brings me down to the present, and here, amid the apple trees of this bit of France, with the symphony of war encompassing me, I have found peace of heart and soul never before attained in all my life. For here, I am with the bravest, finest, grandest bunch of men that God ever breathed life into. Before it's all over, you will know that this is true and that this company is my life.

God bless you one and all.

For the remainder of June, patrolling dominated the activities of Dawson and the 1st Division. The situation of the 16th RCT eased somewhat when other elements of the Big Red One passed through the regiment to continue the main attack. As the division moved inland, they encountered the Norman *bocage*, the fabled hedgerows that stymied the American advance. The hedgerow country of Normandy became a killing field that consumed thousands of American lives and hardened the American soldier.

Dawson remembered that before D-Day, the "boys were still fighting a civilized war. It took the drive, drive, drive of the Normandy hedgerows, where they saw their buddies shot down in a sickeningly constant stream of losses, to educate them to war." Ernie Pyle concurred, telling his readers: "This hedge-to-hedge stuff is a type of warfare we've never run into before, and I've seen more dead Germans than ever in my life. Americans too, but not nearly so many as the Germans. One day, I'll think I'm getting hardened to dead people, dead young people in vast numbers, and then next day, I'll realize I'm not and never could be."[24] Warfare had taken on another, more brutal dimension. Dawson remembered, "By the time we broke out of St. Lo, the boys knew what to do with Germans. Now they are cold, businessmen."

Why had the First Army not developed an offensive doctrine for offensive action in the hedgerows? The answer lay at both the operational and the tactical levels of war. Operation OVERLORD was the most complex operation ever undertaken by the U.S. Army. OVERLORD included not only the amphibious assault against a hostile shore, but also the buildup of a lodgment area as a prelude for subsequent operations. The amphibious assault was correctly deemed the most dangerous, and army planners applied a disproportionate share of their efforts to the problem of establishing the beachhead, and too little to what lay inland.

It was not that they were unaware of the existence of hedgerows. For the previous four years, British agents and the French Resistance had provided literally thousands of photographs of virtually every square mile of the Norman countryside. Still, planners did little to address the necessity of combined arms operations, particularly infantry-tank operations.

The reason was different in the frontline companies. Whereas the First Army after-action report noted that infantry-artillery doctrine had been firmly established in North Africa and Sicily, the infantry-tank team required more attention in the training period than had been provided. Far too many infantry commanders possessed insufficient knowledge of the proper employment of tanks as an infantry support weapon in restricted terrain, and insufficient opportunity to familiarize themselves and work in conjunction with separate tank battalions.

The most effective method of attack proved to be in the combined coordination of infantry, artillery, and tanks, with many of the tanks equipped with dozer blades or large steel teeth in front to punch holes through the hedgerows. The tanks then laid down a base of fire as the infantry advanced. In smaller units, a satisfactory solution of the problem of liaison between tanks and infantry was found to be in the company commander's assignment of one infantry squad to work with a tank platoon at all times.[25]

Other obstacles besides hedgerows confronted soldiers in the rifle companies. German sniper activity also increased significantly, even in the rear areas where the 16th RCT remained in temporary reserve. Omaha Beach itself was not declared secure until June 9, when the 3rd Battalion, 23rd Infantry Regiment, killed the remaining snipers. No area seemed safe from the sniper threat. Before any unit bivouacked for the night, patrols had to eliminate the snipers, who seemed to hide in every building, every hedgerow.

As one officer noted, "individual soldiers have become sniper-wise before, but now we're sniper-conscious as whole units."[26] Constant patrolling was the answer to the sniper problem. The night of June 22–23 was fairly typical. In a report to division headquarters, the regimental intelligence officer reported: sixty patrols—POWs taken—no casualties—no additional information.[27]

The lull in activity also gave frontline commanders time to reflect and prepare for the upcoming offensive, designed to break what was rapidly emerging as a bloody stalemate. For Joe Dawson, it was time to bring his family up to speed on activities on the front, as well as to reflect on his own chances of surviving the ordeal.

Dawson to My Dear Family

June 21, 1944
A Beech Grove in Normandy

Having just finished a breakfast of dried eggs and cold mush, my stomach is partially appeased, and I'm relatively free of one of the four horsemen at the moment—hunger. Then, too, the atmosphere is very heavy this morning, with visibility almost zero, and the whole world seems to be dripping with the heavy fog that is peculiar to this country. However, the compensation of it all is the relative quiet pervading the battlefront. The big guns are quiet, and the silence is all the more sharpened by the absence of the drone of aircraft overhead. Only a staccato tattoo of machine gun fire in the distance recalls the imminent presence of the Hun.

So there's really nothing to do at the moment, so here I am wrapped in a blanket deep in my foxhole with a sputtering candle to afford just enough light to see to the inscribing of this piece of paper. I'm in the mood for a little dissertation anyhow, as I failed to awaken all night long, so I am fresh and strengthened by the first night's sleep in several days. All night long, the guns pounded with shells falling all around, but oddly enough, that is when I can relax best, so I slept like a babe. Only once did I awaken, and that was when a shell burst nearby and rudely spattered dirt all over me and into my mouth, but this inconvenience merely caused me to seek a more comfortable adjustment of the bones.

It all boils down to the fact that after two years of dodging shot and shell, I've become fairly steady in the face of all this discomfort, so my pains are more physical than mental. Were I to resort to analysis of several dominant thoughts concerning war, I would be a bit upset by the turn of events, but after all said and done, there is compensation in the satisfaction of knowing one's capabilities can meet the tests and do the required tasks.

The whole tenor of this invasion is sparked by an enthusiastic propaganda of a religious crusade designed to save the world from the Infidel. Now to be frank, I must confess that the abiding strength that impels me through this mess is based on my own belief in the rightness of it all, and the necessity to protect certain freedoms that are inherent in my Christian life.

Yet, the taint of political and social corruption that constantly manifests itself through the medium of self-expression on the part of many of the so-called leaders of our times gives one a tinge of doubt as to the truth of the crusade idea. . . . Thank God that Ernie Pyle exists to write the true picture of this glamorous life we lead, and perhaps let some few realize that the doughboy suffers no illusions of romance when it comes to this business of war.[28]

I must be getting soft, though, because last night I spent in wondrous slumber, and dreamed the whole night through. Countless faces passed through my mental screen, and scenes of lovely homes and happy people awoke in me a deep sense of desire to someday find myself in such surroundings. How wonderful it would be to recapture the loveliness of life once more, where friends and loved ones make life decent and happy. I have had a life abundant, it is true, and how often I have thanked Him for the countless blessings of life that have been mine. Yet with it all has been a well of loneliness and unrest that has thwarted my true destiny of life to a degree that has caused me great wonderment and questioning as to just what course life will bring to me. . . .

No letter is complete without mentioning one's physical condition, so I will report that all is well with me. I limp a bit from the old knee, but only when the shells are not falling—when they begin to whine close by, I hop around like a West Texas jackrabbit with a hound at his tail! This damp weather seems to make me a bit stiff in the joint, but that's understandable, and forty years from now, I'll never know the difference.

There is one thing that makes me quite happy and proud and that is the fact that the regiment is to be given a Presidential Citation for the D-Day job. That will help a lot of the men to know that there is real pride and esteem held for it and them by the people who know what this outfit has done.

Well, I must close for now, but with the reminder that my heart is filled with unutterable tenderness for you all, my beloved family.

Dawson to My Dearest Family

June 25, 1944

On this beautiful Sunday afternoon, I'm peacefully ensconced beneath an ivy-covered hedgerow that affords defilade from the artillery that drops in every so often and reminds me that there's a war going on. The azure blue sky filled with warm sunlight is truly the answer to my express desires. How nice it has been to bask in real warm sunshine for a change. The contrast of sound is indeed strange, also, because one minute, the air is filled with the blast or crash of an incoming shell or outgoing one. Then silence, and in the distance, the soft mellow tones of the church bells sounding vespers creates the wide separation of conflicting emotions of war.

A wonderful night's sleep last night has restored my nerve and strengthened me immeasurably. Believe me, it's nothing so satisfying as well-earned sleep. The amazing feature of it all was when I awoke this morning, my executive officer informed me that we had the heaviest shelling yet experienced in the past week! Oh well, after two years of this, I'm becoming somewhat used to all this. . . . I'm fit as a fiddle and the old leg is really about well.

Dawson to My Beloved Family

June 26, 1944
Cold & Wet, Normandy

Perhaps your state of anxiety was allayed somewhat by the news account disclosing my participation thus far in this campaign. . . . The [newspaper] account was fairly accurate, though I still feel a bit jealous of the fact that it was my company that succeeded in fighting through the beach and emerging victorious. I still tremble with emotion whenever I think of how bravely and nobly they did their job when others were seemingly overwhelmed by the awesome and grim defense the enemy had. Not once did my men falter, so it was that we achieved where others failed. Our price was great, but the Lord certainly was hand-in-hand with good old "G" Co., and we turned defeat into victory.

Now today, I've spent in mere routine dreariness that marks so many days of warfare. It is cold and raining and most uncomfortable with the shelling of the "heinies" adding torment to discomfort. But there's nothing to do but huddle a bit closer in the ground and believe me my hole is plenty deep! I somehow get a little comfort, however, and if the wet, damp, cold would lift, I'm sure my leg would lose its stiffness. It's coming along fine, and I feel sure that in a few more days, everything will be tip-top shape. . . .

Well, everything moves along, and Cherbourg is about ready to fall.[29] There's been a heap of things going on over here, so don't be disillusioned by the fact that the reports may indicate "all quiet on the Western Front." Right now, there's enough noise around me to require cotton in my ears all the time, just from the guns firing.

Dawson to My Dearest Family

June 30, 1944
Normandy

Well, I have become a bit calloused by the innumerable spectacles of war that have etched themselves upon my memory, so tonight I cannot elaborate too fully on the goings on at this moment. However, the papers will doubtless emphasize and glamorize in the full account. Reading various accounts in *Time* and *Newsweek*, it appears that the coverage is a bit better edited than it was in North Africa and Sicily, and less adulteration of fact. In real fairness, the essence of every one of these stories is basically true and vital to those who experienced them, hence, one temporizes his reactions to the slight inaccuracies that may crop up. The essence is there, and the undeniable hell attendant to each of them makes the whole picture stand out in everyone's mind.

Now, here I am ensconced in a hedgerow with a self-propelled 88 playing tit-tat-too rather near, while in the distance the air is filled with planes as they make a bomb run—flak smoke like ink spots on the blue canopy of the sky—a flash of flame then searing, smoking, fragments from a riddled plane plummeting downward in its final dive—the dull, resounding crump of the bombs as they effect their destruction, a high throated whine of a diving Spitfire spraying machine gunfire below—a jarring crash of a heavy artillery barrage going out overhead—then deathly silence. In the distance, the panther-like coughing of a machine gun merges in with the rat-tat of answering rifles. All this, the symphony of war beneath the apple trees where oddly oblivious to it all lies yours truly, penning this little note.

My spirits have been none too high these past several days, and my thoughts have constantly intruded into my inner recesses causing at times wonderment. To see strong, brave men meet death and hurt with a smile that is placed there only because they have lived in the sustaining confidence of their convictions is indeed the benediction upon this complete travesty against human decency. But recalling to mind the futility of it all, and the business and depravity created through this medium makes one stop at times and wonder. For those who have shouldered these tasks of human destruction these past two years, there are many times one feels the importunity of it all. It somehow makes you a bit bitter at some of the falsities of life that are bared by the stark realism of days of combat.

Disillusionment is the most disheartening of all the reactions one assumes. The erasure from the soul of all manifestations of idealistic emotions somehow brings the galling bitterness into sharp, caustic doses of life-killing poison and causes one's remnants of sanity that remain to question the terrible price this requires. To me, I've somehow felt that there must be a justification for my efforts and deeds, and I've been facing each bitter day on the belief that from this will emerge a cleaner, better, more decent life for those whom I most deeply cherish. This has withstood all the trials and tribulations that have befallen me and enabled me to continue as best I could. One cannot help but reflect at the barbaric animalism that closes the mind to the cruel task of taking human life. Yet, without a deep sense of duty to everything that means a thing to me in this life, I know that I would never be able to go on.

The reason why I've felt so keenly a moral letdown these last few days is because I've seen those who have stood alongside me throughout these bitter months abroad, fighting and giving everything within their scope of life toward the task at hand, become embittered and cruelly disillusioned by the frailties of our social and moral structure. To them and to myself, this war has been unbelievably real and personal. What little satisfaction gained from it has been the belief that it all was worthwhile, and that this was shared by all our loved ones and those who represent our nation in society and government alike. . . .

Yet when you see the ranks thin each day that passes, and yet another comes to take their place, the limitations of life come into sharp relief, and you wonder if it would be right to seek a lesser task and personally enjoy some of the life that remains. No one is indispensable in this world, and how expendable we infantrymen are really is reflected by the ever-growing list of comrades who have fallen. The ties that bound us inseparably throughout these past two years are rapidly dissolving through the never-to-be-satisfied appetite of the war gods.

How totally impersonal life has become in all its social phases, for no longer does the familiar, friendly hello of all my intimate friends help to bolster my courage and steadfastness. They are gone, and a feeling of aloneness oft times of late has threatened to engulf me. Yes, even with a million men surrounding me, there come these dreadful times, and they tear at my heart and soul, bringing into sharp focus the moments past that have been so devoid of the sustaining strength of comradeship. That of course is merely a self-commiseration that brings in sharp clarity the whole vacuum of my earthly existence because of my base self-ishness. But as in *The Tale of Two Cities*, [sic] my life so parallels the character who said, "It's not what I am, but what I might have been"—that is my tragedy, and that is why I am alone so much in my own heart.

All life has seemed to stand in bold relief these past three and a half weeks as never before. The fact that through it all, I've somehow felt a little vindication for my being on this earth has sustained me and brought a feeling that come what may, I've been able to do a little toward attaining my destiny in life. The men who through the dull, monotony of the winter months of arduous training now see clearly why some things were done and because of this, they are still alive. Many paid their lives these weeks here, but there still remains some because of their willingness to bear the burdens together. The reward has been in their looks of con-fidence in me—that has paid me the highest tribute life has ever given me. That is what will keep me going in the days to come, because I'm closing my heart and should to all others.

With this strengthening, I shall withstand the tests to come. God grant that I shall measure up. In your prayers to Him, that must be your request. Though honors can never pay for their glo-rious sacrifice and service, I pray that they will be rewarded with the most precious of all things—life once more at home!

Forgive me, dear ones, but with this little outburst, I have some-how been able to release in part the stress that builds up occa-sionally.

As June faded into distant memory, July brought news of a major attack to break out of the hedgerow country. The first order of busi-ness, however, was to recognize the heroism of the soldiers—Dawson among them—who had performed so valiantly in the invasion of Europe. On July 2, General Eisenhower, accompanied by Lieutenant General Bradley, V Corps commander Major General Leonard T. Gerow, and 1st Division commanding general Major General Clarence Huebner, presented twenty-two 1st Division soldiers with Distinguished Service Crosses for heroism under fire. Two other soldiers received the Legion of Merit.[30] Dawson took immense pride that his battalion commander and regimental commander were among the recipients.

Dawson's own citation read:

Captain Joseph T. Dawson, 0452348, 16th Infantry, United States Army. For extraordinary heroism in action against the enemy of 6 June 1944 near Colleville-sur-Mer, France. Captain Dawson, in the initial landing on the coast of France, disembarked under a hail of enemy machine gun and rifle fire, and with utmost calmness, proceeded to organize a large group of men who were floundering near their bullet-riddled craft and led them ashore. However, upon reaching the beach, he found that his company was pinned down by direct fire from three enemy machine guns, which were placed in an enemy strongpoint in a cliff immediately beyond the heavily mined sands. With absolute disregard for his own personal safety, Captain Dawson moved from his position of cover on to the mine field, deliberately drawing the fire of the enemy machine guns in order that his men might be free to move. This heroic diversion succeeded, and his combat group crossed the beach to move into the assault on the enemy strongpoint. During this action, Captain Dawson was wounded in the leg. In a superb display of courage in the face of heavy enemy fire, Captain Dawson, although wounded, led a successful attack into the enemy stronghold. The gallantry and outstanding leadership of Captain Dawson reflect great credit upon himself and were in keeping with the highest traditions of the Armed Forces of the United States.[31]

In addition to bestowing individual awards, Ike recommended the 16th Regiment for a Distinguished Unit Citation for its achievement on D-Day. The citation noted that the 16th Regiment, under the most adverse conditions, assaulted the coast of France against "a long-prepared, determined and powerfully-emplaced enemy. After suffering a third of the assault strength as casualties, the officers and men gathered the remnants of their units and slowly began to develop from a confused, hurt mass into a cohesive, determined fighting force."

Throughout D-Day, innumerable acts of gallantry were performed in the face of the superior enemy fire. Referring to what G Company had accomplished, the citation stated that "a breach was blown in the wire, and the Regiment advanced . . . and with grim determination, suffering terrible casualties, the Regiment forced its way forward in a frontal assault . . . and engaged the enemy, and, in a magnificent display of courage and will to win, destroyed them. The breach opened by the 16th Infantry Regiment was the main personnel exit for the V Corps for forty-eight hours."[32]

Once on the bluffs, the 16th drove back a fanatically resisting enemy and repulsed five separate counterattacks by numerically superior forces until the 1st Division and V Corps beachhead was secured. Individually and collectively, the members of the regiment "turned threatened catastrophe into a glorious victory for the American army."

As one of the company commanders who had first breached the enemy defenses, Dawson beamed with pride as the supreme commander then gathered the award recipients around him.

> Men . . . I'm not going to make a speech, but this simple little ceremony gives me opportunity to come over here and through you, say thanks. You are one of the finest regiments in our army. I know your record from the day you landed in North Africa and through Sicily. I am beginning to think that the First Division is a sort of Praetorian Guard which goes along with me and gives me luck.[33] Although many of you wanted to go home, I demanded when I came here that you should also be here for this tough job. You have proved that you have what it takes to finish the job. If you will do me a favor when you go back, you will spread the word through the Regiment that I am terrifically proud and grateful to them. To all you fellows: Good luck, keep on top, and so long.[34]

Returning to G Company following the ceremony, Dawson wrote several letters to reassure his family that all was well and to say once again how proud he was of his company of GIs.

Dawson to My Dearest Ones

July 3, 1944

Yesterday, I had a rather enjoyable time visiting with all the old friends at Division Headquarters. It is a bit different from the time I served there, and the old familiar Teddy and Terry no longer shed their warm personalities around or make one completely at ease as they so ably could. However, the other friends are there and the present high command has been quite interested in this fine company and is most generous in their interest in me. But the close friendships and attachments made through North Africa and Sicily are the ones that somehow drove me back to the fold, and it does one good to hear them solicitously inquire about my welfare. . . .

All my officers are now back with me after being in the hospital for a few weeks. Thank God they were not seriously hit and are back in good shape. Their strength has proved the salvation of so many of my men, and it's really swell to have them back home. Strange it is how these men have gone through all the campaigns and been hit several times yet never too seriously to warrant a return home to America—just arms shattered, etc., yet some people go after seeing two days in the South Pacific! The highest command over here remarked that the 1st Division was the "Praetorian Guard," but believe me, the faces have certainly passed through these ranks in great numbers since leaving New York a decade or so ago . . . [35]

There is really nothing to write about today, but thought you might like a little idle chatter. Had a good meal of beef today, thanks to an artillery shell carving it into steaks for us, and naturally, we couldn't afford to let it spoil or go unheeded. This bit of change of menu was most welcome, as the field diet is pretty harmless, as you have probably noted from other letters. . . .

Dawson to My Dearest Family

July 5, 1944
Normandy

Well, "old folks Joe" is now back on his two legs with everything in top shape. The knee is healed, and aside from the early morning cramps and stiffness caused by months in the field, this old bag of bones still is in better shape than most of the so-called "body beautifuls." The old ticker never misses a beat for you, and consequently, I have no troubles. The news is constantly becoming more favorable, and I don't believe the war will continue more than another decade anyhow!

Last night, we celebrated the Fourth of July with a little show of fireworks, and today, everything is extremely quiet. Only in the distance can you hear an occasional volley of artillery, but here, all is quiet (at the moment)!

Dawson to Dearest Grandfather

July 5, 1944
France

Here in France, we are sitting around beneath the apple trees and occasionally moving the enemy out from the next hedgerow, thus taking a bit of ground each day. This is slower than we experienced in North Africa and Sicily, but still, the guns have their bite and sting here as well.

We are now in command of Cherbourg, and I am sure that this will bring great events in the future. Our men are never so deeply desirous of finishing this job, and I have every belief that the end is not too far distant. . . .

Dawson to My Dearest Ones

July 9, 1944
In the woods, Normandy

I find that a few hours of sleep often works wonders, and today, I feel like a new man because of a few hours of uninterrupted rest. I was so tired that I finally dropped off into a state of coma. . . . shortly after my writing yesterday, things began to happen around here, and as a consequence, I was rather busy 'til the wee hours this morning. Today being sort of a cloudy overcast period again means little activity except for artillery and mortars with only an occasional rattle from a machine gun.

I was amused at a visitor just now who "braved" the dangers of coming up here to see me from the Ordnance [Corps]. He was so nervous he found it impossible to even hold a cup of coffee and discuss the subject that he came to find out about! Oh well! I get scared, too, but it sometimes makes one wonder if this constant exposure is worthwhile when such examples as this come before your sights.

A poor bedraggled cow was last seen disintegrating into nice loin steaks as a result of a mortar round falling out to the front. Naturally, I feel a bit better now that I know the delicious results of this fortune of war. Thank the Lord that Spam has no longer become my prime hate in life. Seems the army has reduced the amount.

While Dawson never complained in combat, his letters frequently reflected his consternation with army bureaucracy and its failure to

168

support the frontline GI. Complaining about chow has always been the prerogative of any soldier, and officers were hardly the exception. Disgusted with the constant supply of canned beef, the American infantryman relished the opportunity to take advantage of Norman beef, which was plentiful in the countryside. Thus, stray cattle were not killed solely by artillery or mortar shells; many a rifle round found its mark whenever a unit tired of the usual diet.

Other traditional complaints included lack of mail, poor weather, and boredom. As did many of his soldiers, Dawson repeatedly chastised his family for not writing more. The lack of mail, coupled with the daily loss of life, eroded his morale to the point that he wondered if he could go on. Dawson was clearly breaking under the strain of combat. How much longer he could endure remained a constant concern. After a month of intense combat, he was slipping into emotional and physical exhaustion. Not surprisingly, he sought other outlets to relieve his frustrations.

For the commanding officer of G Company, that meant a return to the scene of his company's D-Day heroics and a visit to division headquarters, where his diminishing circle of close friends from North Africa were still on staff. Both visits proved to be sobering experiences, yet he found temporary relief in the pride he held in his beloved G Company. How any of his men had survived the battle was beyond his comprehension.

It was also beyond the comprehension of James Jones, the American novelist who later worked as a screenwriter on Darryl F. Zanuck's epic film "The Longest Day." Jones had occasion to tramp all over the D-Day beaches "until I got to know them very well. . . . [At] Omaha, I climbed up and sat a while on the edge of the bluff, and looked down into the cup-shaped area with the sea at its back." As Jones visualized D-Day, he pictured himself near the machine-gun nest that Dawson destroyed in his ascent to the crest of the bluffs.

Jones described the scene thus:

It was easy to see what a murderous, converging fire could be brought to bear on the beaches from the curving bluff. Especially to an old infantryman. And it was easy to half-close your eyes and imagine what it must have been like. The terror and total confusion, men screaming or sinking silently under the water, tanks sinking as their crews drowned inside, landing craft going up as a direct hit took them, or grating ashore to discharge their live cargo into the already scrambled mess,

officers trying to get their men together, medics trying to find
shelter for the wounded. . . . I sat there until my friends began
to yell at me from down below, and I fervently thanked God or
Whomever that I had not been there.

Omaha Beach, he concluded, had been "a bloodbath" of mon-
strous proportions.[36]

Jones's lucid prose captured Dawson's sentiments perfectly.

Dawson to My Dear Family

July 19, 1944
Normandy

After several days, I again take a little time to review a few thoughts
to you. With the constant strain upon one, there are times when
one's mind goes rather blank, and a tendency for self-
commiseration takes place. To be sure, I find this quite natural,
and only the few thin threads remaining to my sanity prevent a
complete breakdown both mentally and spiritually. This cannot
be fully appreciated by anyone outside the sphere of military cold-
ness and brutality. Such are essential characteristics to wage successful warfare, but at times, the impact becomes so strong that
you pause and wrack your feeble brain for a satisfactory answer.

Can it be that there is actually a limit to one's physical and
mental capacity? Now, after so long a time at this task, I'm beginning to weary, oh so much, and the utter futility gives rise to innumerable speculations as to why one must go on. Of course, I shall
never give up nor will I despair for the future, but I find that life
assumes a complexity that leaves one's soul stripped and shorn
of all the higher ideals and reduces the entire outlook on life to a
baseness common only to the animalistic urge for existence!

The whole span of life that is concentrated into the short
space of time when the fate of one's life hangs in a delicate
balance is an experience that removes all vestige of glory from
war and reflects its cruel, heartless agony. The loneliness is therefore heightened, and one wonders if the price is aware to those
that will profit from the sacrifices. Disillusionment comes when
this question dominates the pattern of one's inner thoughts, only
comforted by the fact that [in] those who share with me these
responsibilities I find the needed strength to carry on, but I pray
the end will come soon.

Well, so much for the deeper thoughts. Had a nice v-mail a few days ago, which was most gratifying. [The writer] commented on the fact that I had received a D.S.C., and that you had been notified to that effect. It was given to me by General Eisenhower and General Bradley on the 2nd of July, being a result of D-Day. Frankly, there have been many times in North Africa and Sicily where I probably deserved such a thing as a pat on the back, but this was a real surprise to me because I can see little that I did to be so rewarded. I just happened to do a job, and my men followed me, and that's what I get paid to do every day. My only regret is that all who went through that indescribable hell could not receive adequate reward. The London *Daily Mail* must have confused me with Superman from their write-up, which was sent to me by friends in England. . . .

Yesterday, I took a little trip to the rear—my first since my return from the hospital. With my executive officer, Lieutenant [Stanley] Karas, we revisited the scene of our landing and walked over the ground over which we fought.[37] Indeed, my heart stood still as I placed myself in the enemy positions. How I came across that beach will ever remain the unshaken realism that God alone so willed it.

From a purely abstract point of view and as a military problem, I would say that such a place could not be successfully taken by assault troops. It was just too perfect a defensive position, so don't ask me how it was done because that will ever remain an unsolved riddle. That chapter is now long closed anyway, and since then, we've struggled on, but far less spectacularly. But it has taken its toll and will continue to do so till final victory. We continue to exact from the enemy a terrific price, but even so, he in turn inflicts damage and death to us as well. Perhaps the forces will finally become so strong that he will crack.

Incidentally, keep your eye peeled for some stories and pictures about three of my men. 2nd Lieutenant Bleau, Sergeant Baldridge and Sergeant Sternik were all interviewed recently by the press, radio and films, and should show up in some of these channels. They were an index on what makes this outfit great, and I'm happy that they were able to have this recognition. I put Bleau in for the D.S.C. and the other two for Silver Stars, so that will be nice for them.[38] In case you run across anything on them, please send me the dope so that I can give it to them. . . .

Must close now, but with a pointed reminder that letters still cannot be received unless written.

Dawson to Dearest Family

July 20, 1944

Took a wonderful trip yesterday throughout the entire beachhead, and took stock of all that has taken place since our arrival in France. Naturally, the devastation caused by total war can never be fully envisioned unless one actually sees it in all its terrible waste, but you can be assured that every inch of the way has felt the terrific impact of modern weapons. Though the Germans labored themselves and countless thousands of conscripted slaves for four long years to erect the most strongly fortified positions in the world, they have been overcome by much "blood," much "sweat," and many bitter "tears."

The thing that also struck me and has ever been a bit of an enigma to me is the varied aspect of reception accorded one by the French. I cannot say what will be the case further inland, but I'm prone to feel that the bulk of those who remained in these coastal sectors were rather sympathetic to the Germans. That is purely a personal observation, but is based on several evidences that I know of.

Well, the war moves ever onward, and with it all, I find more and more occasion to reflect upon just what it all will accomplish in the end. It is far from over, and there will be many bitter months still lying ahead. These who have lived through such awful bitterness and who have been touched so deeply by it will find small compensation initially. Let's hope for the best though.

Dawson to My Dear Family

July 23, 1944
Wet Normandy

Much can be said pro and con concerning receipt of mail, but needless to say, it is vital to one's good spirits and essential for high morale. Things are black enough in the middle of the combat zone, but without mail from those who provide the incentive to carry out these deadly tasks, the old spirit quickly dissolves. Needless to say, this is a rather pointed reminder that there has been a great vacuum or void created these past several days due to this cause.

The weather has proven most disagreeable of late, and though at the moment, there is not actual rain falling, the skies are still overcast, and the air sorta [sic] oozes with damp humidity. A lull in the activity of war is offset by the fact that one is completely miserable due to the wet and cold, especially at night. Maybe this means little, though, in the grand strategy, but if it takes such things as this to make the necessary frame of mind to wage successful war, then I guess we're about ready to take Berlin. The only real gripe, though, is the fact that rheumatism has set in on my knee, and I got to do calisthenics every morning for about ten minutes before the joint will function. But that's a small item, and I guess I can't worry too much about that. . . .

There is much optimism reflected in the news of late, and naturally, it means much to us over here. With the impending civil war in Germany and Tojo's resignation, it might appear that the enemy is *beginning* to crack.[39] I underline the word, beginning, because there still remains the final *coup de gras* [sic] to be administered, and you can be assured that it will be most sanguinary.

Also, for your information, I shall doubtless continue in the middle of things 'til the final blow. Fate has decreed I remain in such a status, so am no longer wondering where I'm going, but how long I'll last on the way! I've used up all the luck of a dozen blokes, and the Lord and I just happen to be awfully good friends, else I would never have left Africa. Someday, when Jerome and little Joe are grown and past their twenties, I only hope and pray that the world will have been sufficiently bathed in blood this time to prevent their participation in such a mess. That's about the only consolation one gets nowadays, and perhaps someday, it will be realized by all.

Well, so much for today. Now I'm a bit busy so must end. Know my heart is filled with devotion for you all—even if you don't write!

The false optimism concerning the impending German collapse to which Dawson referred was also reflected in *The Stars and Stripes*. Issues throughout the summer of 1944 mentioned that the U.S. Army was set to open five centers for discharging GIs. In August, the paper stated that the army, anticipating an early end of hostilities with Germany, had begun oiling its demobilization machine. The army announced that officers and enlisted men had completed training to organize and operate "reception centers in reverse" throughout the country, where hundreds of thousands of discharged veterans would exchange olive drab uniforms for civilian tweeds.

Under the proposed War Department plan, demobilization would be on an individual basis rather than by units. Theater commanders would be informed of the details of a "point system," by which points would be awarded for each month of service, for each month overseas, for major combat engagements, for decorations, for being married, for each child or other dependent, and for age. Had the plan been put in effect immediately, Dawson would have been one of the first to go home since he was in the upper echelon in most categories. The War Department later expanded the number of reception centers to eighteen by early September.

Exiled political leaders also predicted the Nazi defeat. The Czech, Belgian, Greek, Norwegian, Dutch, and Yugoslavian governments were prepared to return home at a moment's notice. John Parris, a staff writer for United Press International, predicted that the Nazi regime would crumble within sixty days of the German defeat in Normandy.[40] Such optimism might have prevailed in the rear ranks, but the GIs in the forward battle area knew differently.

After two months of horrific bloodletting, however, the campaign in Normandy was rapidly drawing to a close. On July 24, the U.S. First Army under Bradley held an east-west line that ran from Caumont to St.-Lo to Lessay on the Channel. Beyond this line lay open fields and rolling hills, ideal for mobile warfare. If the Americans could pierce the German defenses, they would be out of the hedgerows that had hindered their advance throughout the summer. The Americans were now six weeks behind schedule.

To breach the German lines, Bradley developed Operation CO-BRA, a massive infantry and armor attack preceded by a tremendous aerial bombardment on a narrow front. After several delays caused by inclement weather, COBRA kicked off with a bang, but not before mishap. Instead of flying parallel to the American lines, the bombers flew perpendicular. Too many bombs fell short, resulting in 111 GIs killed and 490 wounded. Among the dead was General Lesley McNair, former chief of the Army Ground Forces, who was in Normandy to observe the attack.

Still, the effect on the Germans was devastating. With no reinforcements available, their lines began to crumble under the weight of the Allied onslaught. General "Lightning Joe" Collins, the VII Corps commander entrusted to achieve the breakthrough, committed his armor reserves on July 27, and the enemy defenses snapped. Here was the golden opportunity to deliver a fatal blow to the *Wehrmacht* on the western front.

The massive assault during the final week in July produced the effect Bradley had envisioned. Huebner's 1st Infantry Division moved by motorized column first to Tribehou, then to Marigny, west of St.-Lo. Dawson's battalion was again in reserve of the 16th Regiment, but by late in the evening on the twenty-seventh, it too was committed to action. Along with its sister companies, G Company met only scattered resistance. Traffic congestion, as much as enemy fire, impeded the American advance.

All indicators pointed to the complete disintegration of the German army in Normandy. Following another week of heavy fighting, Bradley activated the Third (US) Army under George Patton. By August 1, the COBRA breakthrough had evolved into a breakout, with the remnants of the German army fleeing to the east. Dawson took a moment to report the changing nature of warfare.

Dawson to My Dearest Ones

August 3, 1944

The juggernaut of war moves swiftly on to a climax, and each remaining terrible hour brings us closer to our final objective. With it also comes the bitter destruction of the enemy though the toll mounts for us as well. But here in France now is being enacted the same type of warfare that has characterized the Russian front for these many months. How it can best be described is not within my limited vocabulary for its vastness and power is unprecedented in the annals of America's military endeavors to date.

Here is the first time that we have been able to combine all our military resources into one cohesive striking force, and its impact is truly overwhelming. Like some tornado that tears a deep gash of devastation through the countryside, our columns have broken through his defense, and woe has befallen thousands who vainly sought to stem our advance. They lie by the wayside in untold numbers as evidence of the puny insignificance of the individual in this great struggle.

To each, it was quite personal and yet the grinding, smashing jaws of modern war reduces them quickly to dust. The only tragedy that appeals to those of us long encased in bitterness toward the enemy is when one of our beloved group is snapped into the other world by these who have brought such suffering to us all. Beloved homes, villages and great cities are nothing but shattered ruins, blackened and charred by fire and the instruments of war.

No matter how hardened one becomes through months and years of intimate combat with the enemy, these mute evidences to the terrible cost of war give pause to pray for an everlasting peace that will insure against any future repetition. And as we move on to the final battle, we do so, trusting that somehow the Lord will see fit to keep us. Each of my men has come to be such a part of me that it is difficult to forbear when death takes them. Yet they continue to fall and serve only to deepen our resolve to end this thing once and for all.

A few days ago, one of my officers fell, and somehow I just lost my self-control, for it epitomized all my men who have died so far. All night long I couldn't sleep for the awful hurt that gripped me. I prayed earnestly for God to somehow relieve me of the oppressive burden that sometimes weighs so very heavily. 'Tis indeed something that cannot be placed in words on a letter—this responsibility of men's lives, yet it becomes so personal and heartbreaking now, after so many months of this.

Throughout Tunisia and Sicily, I somehow managed without having these feelings, because then I was responsible only for myself and little can I feel should my turn come, but when so many entrusted to my care die or become hurt, it is then that life becomes bitter, beyond words. It somehow nurtures the suggestion within your heart to hope that others bear the cross that goes with each intimate clash because each time is etched in one's memory and heart by a fallen comrade.

Yes, dear Mother and Dad, the road to glory is a one-way road, each milestone a monument to the fallen.

Don't think me poetic or in any wise, seeking to glamorize war or my place in it, but how my heart is filled with loneliness these days. Believe me, I have come to appreciate the love and comradeship of a few who share like burdens, and when the final chapter is written, I only pray that men like Ed Wozenski and Stanley Karas will be able to enjoy the rest and peace that we all are so earnestly seeking.[41]

The alert sounds once more, and I'm on my way. May God bless you one and all.

By the end of August, the campaign in Normandy was over. The question confronting the senior commanders was whether they could concentrate their forces in sufficient numbers and end the war in 1944. For the GIs in the front lines, the question was simple: Would they survive? As commanding officer of a frontline rifle company, Dawson determined to do everything within his power to ensure that he brought his boys home safely. The road ahead proved bloody and long.

7
Breakout and Pursuit

I must temper my resolution to meet the final tests with a realiza-
tion that I'm growing awfully weary and must not falter.

ate summer 1944 proved to be heady days for the Allied Expeditionary Force. With the *Wehrmacht* in complete disarray following the Allied forces' wildly successful campaign in Normandy,
the Allied armies advanced rapidly across northern France and into
Belgium. Allied strategy as expressed in pre-D-Day planning looked
toward the ultimate objective of Berlin, but General Dwight Eisenhower
also wanted an economic objective, which, if reached, "would rapidly
starve Germany of the means to continue the war."

That objective was to capture the Ruhr industrial area, the loss of
which would deprive Germany of 65 percent of its production of crude
steel and 56 percent of its coal. In considering which axes of advance
were best, Supreme Headquarters (SHAEF) selected four routes: (1)
the plain of Flanders; (2) the Marbeuge-Liege-Aachen axis north of
the Ardennes; (3) the Ardennes; and (4) the Metz-Kaiserslautern gap.
After considerable discussion, SHAEF selected the second and fourth
options.[1] Newly assigned to Lightning Joe Collins's VII Corps, the 1st
Infantry Division and Dawson's company deployed along the
Marbeuge-Liege-Aachen axis in pursuit of retreating Germans.

Now refitted and reorganized, the 16th RCT conducted one of its
longest uninterrupted moves of the war, traveling to the neighborhood of Lardy, south of Paris—a distance of ninety-six miles. The Big
Red One then took up the chase the final week in August, and Dawson
reflected on the changing nature of warfare. He was ecstatic that the
Normandy hedgerows were far to his rear. Now was the opportunity
to restore mobility to the war.

So unbelievable and rapid was the Allied advance that at times, he
was frequently unsure of his exact location. Several letters were noted
simply, "somewhere in France." More significantly, he commented on
how few casualties G Company had suffered as they continued to pressure their German adversaries, who remained scattered and totally disorganized, seemingly incapable of establishing a coordinated defense.

Still, the G Company that left Normandy in mid-August was not the same outfit that had landed on Omaha Beach on D-Day. Casualties had thinned its ranks significantly since its arrival on the continent, and replacements had altered the group's composition. The company, like the 1st Division, reflected a truly national flavor—a far cry from the onset of the war, when the vast majority of the men were from the eastern United States. Over the course of the summer, Dawson's command suffered twenty-one dead, including one officer, and fifty-six wounded. Company morning reports listed three other GIs as missing in action, but presumed dead.

Experience had also altered the unit's perspective, but the nucleus of noncommissioned officers who had served in the Mediterranean Theater and in Normandy quickly brought the individual replacements up to speed. Fortunately for G Company, all of the officers, save one killed by friendly fire in midsummer, were still on hand. More important to the unit's combat effectiveness was the presence of a strong corps of noncommissioned officers who survived the initial carnage of D-Day.

Dawson to My Dear Family

August 11, 1944

Deep into France, we now are putting into practice the true application of mobile warfare. The elements involved are still the same as in other types, but things are much more fluid in action. Nevertheless, there are bitter clashes that are short and final. With it all comes the belief that the end is not too distant, and I only trust that it will be possible to see it through. . . .

Am sorry that things are so confused at present, but I'm rather busy these days, so don't be alarmed if I do not render a letter a day. Will do my best to keep you informed, but I am really having a hard time getting my own thoughts together. But if the pressure is on us, think what it is on the enemy.

Dawson to Dearest Family

August 26, 1944

The pace of this present campaign is about unbelievable to everyone, and I can only comment on the fact that I have not been idle! It's truly "somewhere in France" now, so just know that all is well, and as soon as all the Germans are run back into Germany, maybe the war will enable me to sit down and catch up on my correspondence.

The good letters from each of you give me much joy, and be assured that I will find Roy if it is humanly possible to get a few hours off from the actual task of fighting.[2] Naturally, I am still in the thick of things!

Haven't seen Paris yet, but will doubtless run in there some-day soon for a little respite from chasing the Hun all over Normandy.[3]

While the Big Red One bypassed the French capital, others, including Ernie Pyle, visited the City of Lights. Pyle described the liberation of Paris as "one of the great days of all time," and reckoned that he was part of a richly historic day. On entering the heart of the city, he witnessed "pandemonium of surely the greatest mass joy that has ever happened. The streets were lined as by the Fourth of July crowds at home, only this crowd was almost hysterical. The streets of Paris are very wide, and they were packed on each side. . . . Everybody was throwing flowers and even serpentine. As our jeep eased through the crowds, thousands of people crowded up, leaving only a narrow corridor, and frantic men, women and children grabbed us and kissed us and shook our hands and beat on our shoulders and slapped our backs and shouted their joy as we passed."

Fearing that he had not done justice to such an auspicious event, Pyle addressed the celebration again in his next column, remarking that on the day of liberation, "from 2 o'clock in the afternoon until darkness around 10, we few Americans in Paris on that first day were kissed and hauled and mauled by friendly mobs until we hardly knew where we were." America's favorite correspondent confessed that the reception had been so big, he "felt inadequate to touch it—I don't know where to start or what to say. The words you put down about it sound feeble to the point of asininity."

On the second day of liberation, a city-wide festival occurred to honor the Americans. You could tell, said Pyle, "that the women had prettied up especially. The old men had on their old medals, and the children were scrubbed and Sunday-dressed until they hurt, and then everybody came downtown . . . the pandemonium of a free and lovable Paris reigned again. It was wonderful to be there."[4]

As for Dawson's company, on they went, across the Seine and the battlefields of World War I, across the historic Marne, beyond Chateau-

Thierry, where the Americans had halted Ludendorff's spring offensive of 1918, beyond Soissons, a town steeped in 1st Division lore and where the 16th Regiment had fought bitterly in the last war. Nothing seemed to impede the Allied advance except an occasional sniper or small-unit engagement.

Forty miles a day seemed typical of the regiment's progress as the once proud *Wehrmacht* struggled to escape the ever-closing iron ring that strangled it. Dawson visited Paris immediately after its evacuation by the Germans, but the event left him rattled, and he promised to return to the City of Lights under more favorable circumstances.

On the twenty-eighth, elements of E and G Companies engaged the enemy at Aunet sur Marne in force and inflicted a crushing defeat on the Germans. That same day, a fleeing German column struck back and isolated one of his platoons, prompting Dawson to collect one platoon and two tanks and come to its rescue. He was delighted that friendly casualties were light, but lamented the loss of four men. The firefight also served as a bitter reminder that war remained a dangerous business.[5] As Dawson ruefully noted, "lifetimes were lived in such incidents as these." Approaching the Belgian border, he then established his command post in a chateau that had formerly housed a German headquarters, and Dawson reflected once again on the rapid pace of war and his fear of not measuring up to the high standards expected by his men.

Dawson to My Beloved Family

September 1, 1944
A Fortress in France

The swift movement of this modern war prevents one from collecting his thoughts long enough to even take adequate consideration of the tactical situation, much less inscribe a few lines homeward. Nevertheless, the Hun was thrown out of here by my men yesterday, so I find a brief respite this afternoon to allow a little time to pass on to you that all is well.

This juggernaut of power that now is in full swing will go down in the military annals of the ages, and the destruction it has wreaked upon the enemy truly defies adequate description. Yet with it all has come a firm conviction that ere too long, the final objective will be reached and peace will be assured. It cannot be overstated, however, that the demands upon physical and mental resources sometimes threaten the breaking point, but we try to be good soldiers and carry on. We're comforted by the knowledge that though it sometimes seems to be more than human resources can stand, still the enemy finds the forces of fate completely encompassing them, and there is an unrelenting attrition that bespeaks a quick total disintegration of their house of cards. The flame of righteousness continues to burn, though I cannot utter the relief that will come when it's all done. Like some gigantic pendulum that is motivated by the weight of gravity, we continue to swing ever onward.

Time forebears a detailed analysis of this past month, for each second is filled with a new situation—so fast has been the tempo of life. Each successive day has brought changes of scenery, changes of action—and changes of life. Sharp, bitter, terrible clashes with the fanatical diehards of the *Waffen SS* bring a mounting toll of our own men, but their losses are ghastly beyond reckoning. A fallen doughboy lies tattered and torn beside a charred and shattered gun, marking still another who has done his job and in the near distance, the burned and crumpled wreckage of a once terrifying and powerful Nazi tank, with its crew strewing the ground in disemboweled shreds are the reminders that he did not die in vain. And all along the road are these mute reminders that justice is now being inflicted in a measure that can only bring the cost so high that the enemy must cease his vicious efforts.

Yet on we go—on we go. How can I inscribe the heartbreak, agony or suffering that is written on all of us, yet how proud I am when I read in the souls of these who are doing their job, the grim resolve and undaunted purposefulness that *this will be the last time!*

A boy trudges down the hot, dusty road with fifty-five pounds of equipment on his thin shoulders; his feet are bleeding from the blisters that make each step a searing, soul-stabbing pain. The others exhort him to carry on. We say, "G Co. never drops out!" He bites his lips and tears of pain stream down his face as he says, "Captain, I'll be there even if I gotta crawl!" Dear God, how can one measure up to such as this?

The mission is to capture the small little village in the distance, high on the wooded hillside with only the beautiful spire of their beloved cathedral to guide us through the verdant hedgerows. Our artillery pounds the roads to prevent the enemy from withdrawing. We move cautiously, furtively glancing to right and left, forward and rear, to assure that no sniper will surprise us. Even with such efforts, a sudden burst from a rapid firing machine gun breaks the unearthly stillness—a cry as its bullets strike home—then we strike back, swiftly, powerfully, finally, thus another nest is wiped out completely and forever.

We go on inexorably and as we reach the little town, the fleeing remnants of the garrison shower us with a last parting volley. We order our tanks forward, and soon, the spires of smoke billow skyward, marking the spot where destiny ends for those who caused this terrible war.

Then silence, that strange, ghastly silence that follows the crash and roar of battle. A man moves up behind me—I jump at the sound of his voice, then realize how foolish I must appear—nerves. Then the people of the little town open their doors and peer through the narrow slit. As if released by some great spring, they suddenly descend in a rush and in a twinkling, the streets are literally filled with big and little, young and old, rich and poor—all in a state of insane joy that is beyond imagination. You're overwhelmed by their very physical efforts to bestow upon you their joy and happiness.

What a difficult thing to counter when suddenly, a shell comes screaming down to blast a gaping hole in someone's beloved home. Quickly you order all back inside and with the second shell landing even nearer, there comes a realization that even though we're there, the Hun is still nearby. The men deploy, and soon, in the distance, the air is filled with the rattle of machine guns, the crack of the rifles, and then the dull boom of the mortar that ends the whole thing. It all takes place in seconds, but in those brief spans of eternity, life is snuffed out forever—the rest of us struggle on.

In the night, the rumble of the guns and remains of his once proud *Wehrmacht* struggles through the blackness, seeking to escape the ever-closing iron ring that strangles him from this land of Normandy. Within a day, the battlefield is forty miles away. Such is this modern war.

We get on trucks, literally packed as tight as can be without actually crushing. Supplies must reach us from distant ports, so we double up. It's bitter cold, though yesterday was hot as an August day in Texas. The men are uncomfortable, but they bear it. As the convoy moves through the shattered towns and villages that mark the route of war, they soon lose some of their self-pity by the unforgettable sight of a city in ashes. Yet their peoples rejoicing and rendering a never-to-be-forgotten accolade to these who bring freedom, the basic of all life.

One's heart is troubled by this as little children vie with each other to press a flower in your hand as you slowly move along, saying in their broken English, "Thank you—*Vive les Americains!*" Old and young alike grasp your hand as if you were something holy and precious that must be touched, that in the years to come can mark an unforgettable experience. Yes, with it all is a soul-filling joy that comes from such expressions of appreciation. Long hidden bottles of wine, secretly cached apples, fruit and flowers are thrust upon you as they seek to shower their unbounded gratitude upon you. Still, on we go.

A chateau, once proud and gay, in the fashionable suburbs of their most famous city, surrounded by lovely trees and gardens once carefully tended and providing joy to one long since denied, this earthly treasure by the invader. The walls, crayoned with obscenity by some drunken Nazi bully who disported his animal passion in this, the home of someone else. The tapestries tattered and torn, the rugs covered with blotches of food and drink, furniture shattered and broken in mute testimonials to the vandals' ideals and insensibility. In the nearby grove of trees, we build our defenses for the night. In the distance, the majestic tower beckons to all to come to the city of cities. But even now, the Hun lurks in the inner recesses, shooting wildly and blindly. A patrol must go to assure the protection of the precious supply line just being established.

The night is dark as I travel along, never knowing what next will happen. Down this street, according to my route map—no, there's a roadblock. I back up. Psst! Zing! A shot whines by. I swing my jeep around and speed away. That's *not* the route. Now I'm in a forest, and suddenly, a shout: "Halt!" I don't know if it's friend or foe, but I stop. Sure enough, it's a *maquis* guarding a minefield hastily laid on this once beautiful avenue—now bespoiled [sic] by the wreckage of war.[6] I lose my way. Generally, a *gendarme* shows me the main road, and once more, I'm safe. Back to my bivouac at 5 a.m.—having seen Paris![7]

And then the rains came. Torrents descending to turn dust into mud and pools between the cobblestones, as we moved to the banks of the historic Marne. The pontoons rise and fall as we rumble across this once bitterly contested barrier of the last war. All goes well for some of us, as we quickly move into position along the hills overlooking Paris from the northeast.

But some of our group becomes separated. A column of fleeing Germans, racing from Paris, suddenly run right into a small group of my men. I get the word that they are about to be sur-rounded. With my tanks and a platoon, we race to the critical scene. We see the Jerries crouching behind a stone wall on the edge of the tiny village where my men are grimly holding on. My tanks begin firing—my riflemen spot a sniper. Soon, all our guns are lashing out at the threat. Chaos reigns as his returning fire showers us with whining steel.

We reach the town and move swiftly through to the other side, where the enemy has established himself. It's all or noth-ing, so I shot the works. Everything—medium, light tanks, ma-chine guns, rifles, tommy guns and grenades melted into one cre-scendo of thunderous din that spelled disaster to the enemy. How glad the men were to see us, and how relieved I was to find that only a precious few had suffered wounds. A parting volley as we moved out we dedicated to one of my brave sergeants that died there. Then back to our lines. Lifetimes are lived in such incidents as these.[8]

It is noon when we reach our objective for the day. Only a few hours before the enemy had departed a lovely chateau, formerly used as a staff headquarters for the Germans, so I move in. A charming young lady comes into the room I'm establishing as my C.P. [command post]. I introduce myself and she tells me her name. It seems the house belongs to her, and for the past four years, she has been living in the caretaker's cottage while the Prussian boots totally destroy the beautiful floors of her home. I accept her invi-tation to lunch. A simple meal, but delicious cannot do justice to describe it.

Her charm and beauty somehow throw me off my usual ur-bane stride, and I'm somewhat inhibited by my inability to ex-press myself in French. But she quickly puts me at ease, and soon, the words begin to fall in place. Her restrained joy and happiness was so evident as she told me how she has been there alone these past four years, living just for this day of days. Her mother and father were killed in an automobile accident six years ago, while her two brothers have been gone for four years, one having been killed in the war, while the other is a prisoner in Germany. Her two sisters are each alone with both their husbands, prisoners— they remaining in other parts of France where their homes were.

Such tragedy has left an unerasable [sic] imprint upon her, yet her charm and graciousness, as well as strength of character, are qualities that bespeak her wonderful self. Though in her thirties, she would easily pass for twenty-five, such is her beauty. I must confess that she has impressed me more deeply than anyone I've met abroad. To further add to my appreciation of her, the beautiful boxer bulldog she offered me was a gift that I felt was much too precious to endanger in this fast-moving war. If I survive, I shall return to see her, and my hope is to find her brother when I reach Germany.

If Roy doesn't show up soon, naturally I shall be here until I find him, if it takes the rest of my life. So it is that another will be made happier if I can succeed.

The hills of Soissons, Chateau-Thierry, and other never-to-be-forgotten battlefields of World War I have passed through my mind, as once more, the roar of the guns has filled the air over them and churned the soil into red-stained mud as the grim path is used once. We've moved on, on and on. I only wish I could remember all that I've seen these past eventful weeks, or recall these things that have occupied my every moment. Someday, I hope they will come back to me.

Now, as I sit high above the flat plains reaching into Belgium and I view the fields below from this ancient fortress that once deluded those who built it into thinking it the answer to defense, I pray that the end will swiftly come for, dear ones, I'm growing tired. Nevertheless, 'til it's over, I'm hoping God will grant me strength to see it through.

Know that I'm doing my best, though sometimes, that seems so limited. Your dear letters came today—as late as August 23rd, so I know that all are well. To Donna and Susanna, my heart is especially full, but for each of you, the rest is all devoted.

The first week in September began one of the most momentous weeks in the division's history, and G Company was in the midst of it. After the division's forward elements crossed the Belgian border on September 1, ULTRA intercepts confirmed that the remnants of the German Fifth Panzer and Seventh Armies might be trapped if the U.S. First Army turned northward and blocked the highways leading to Brussels through Tournai.

First Army estimated that twenty thousand Germans were still south of the Belgian border. U.S. First Army commander Courtney Hodges deployed VII Corps in rapid pursuit, with the 1st Division following Major General Maurice Rose's 3rd Armored Division in the direction of Mons. By September 2, Rose was on the outskirts of Mons, and the Big Red One suddenly met the brunt of enemy resistance below Maubeuge.

Unable to extract themselves from the Americans, the Germans were incapable of establishing a coordinated defense as Allied artillery and air pounded their retreating columns. The result, noted the division chief of staff, was "always the same—scattered units were bumping into us from the left at every crossroad and getting themselves killed or captured in droves."[9]

The 16th Infantry initially encountered resistance north of Maubeuge. They rapidly overcame this resistance, rounding up two hundred prisoners in the process. No sooner had they processed these prisoners than an enemy captive reported that the German 275th Infantry Division, now up to strength, was retreating eastward toward Belgium. If the Americans moved fast, they could bag the entire command. The ensuing battles constituted one of the most disastrous defeats in the *Wehrmacht*'s history.

The 16th Regiment's 2nd Battalion, now under temporary command of Major Ed Wozenski because Lieutenant Colonel Herbert Hicks was following an adjacent combat command, played a significant role in the engagements around Mons. At one point, Wozenski deployed his forces along a road on the edge of the Bois de Laniere forest. Dawson's mission was to clear the wooded area that was approximately one square mile, then advance east and join with the rest of the regiment on the main Mons road.

Mounting the lead tank, Dawson dispersed his command and entered the forest. He had not penetrated the woods more than a few hundred yards before he was engaged in a stiff firefight. No sooner had he done so than he was nearly shot by a sniper. Remaining characteristically calm under fire, he took his 45-caliber pistol and killed the enemy marksman.

Amid constant artillery and aerial bombardment, the Germans surrendered first in ones and twos, then in small groups, and finally in droves. By day's end, G Company had captured approximately 800 Germans, Dawson personally accounting for 37 of them. The roundup of enemy prisoners continued during the next three days as the 2nd Battalion remained in the woods for seventy-two hours, taking prisoners and evacuating enemy wounded to the rear. The total number of Germans taken during that period was 3,256—not bad for a few days' work. Casualties to Dawson's battalion were one man shot in the leg and two men wounded so slightly they were not even evacuated.[10]

By September 6, the 1st Division had netted 17,149 prisoners, including the commander of the 712th German Infantry Division and his entire staff, and had inflicted nearly 20,000 casualties.[11] The 1st Division's Report of Operations concisely summarized the extent of the German catastrophe: "Our infantry advance soon carried them against the whole length of the German columns which, thus caught on both flanks, were squeezed between the armor and infantry and raked by a murderous cross fire. Soon, every highway, road and country lane in the area was a mass of burning, wrecked vehicles. There seldom has been such a quick mass slaughter as this. The battle of the Falaise gap was several days in the developing, but the slaughter, decimation and dispersion of 20,000 to 30,000 Germans in the Maubeuge-Mons area took place within a few hours."[12] Division logisticians also noted that the fighting around Mons was the only action in the entire war in which the 1st Division consumed its entire allocation of small-arms ammunition.

On September 4, the division axis of advance shifted eastward via Charleroi, Namur, Huy, Liege, and Aachen. Again, the GIs of the Big Red One encountered a chaotic enemy situation, with the Germans scattered and in unpredictable small units. Initial resistance was light, and the division reached Charleroi in a single day. On September 11, the Fighting First liberated Liege, the largest city in its approach to the German border. Indian summer weather was now giving way to chilling temperatures and drizzly rain. Macadam roads, never intended for heavy military traffic, began to break down.

"No question about it," noted Colonel Stanhope Mason, General Clarence Huebner's chief of staff, "the heyday of sweeping across large segments of a heavily populated country was drawing to a close." Just two factors brightened the advance: the jubilation of the Belgians as town after town was reclaimed from the German occupiers, and the continual supply of accurate and timely information on where the Germans were and what they were doing.[13]

All in all, the extermination of the Mons pocket had been an exhilarating experience, and Dawson shared it with his family. On a more dismal note, he confessed that he was getting so tired that he was experiencing difficulty focusing on the task at hand. It was obvious that the captain was beginning to feel the strain, and the worst was yet to come.

Dawson to My Beloved Family

September 8, 1944

My last letter a few days ago was written in an ancient fortress high above the plains stretching into Belgium and located near the lovely city of Laon. Indeed, the recital of events can hardly do justice to everything that transpires in this swift-moving climax. The bewildering speed with which we maintain inexorable pressure upon the enemy is a military achievement without parallel, but if it means victory soon, then I only hope I can maintain the killing strain it creates upon me.

As I write this, I am deep in Belgium with only a few miles now before I will be in Germany. A brief few hours have elapsed since I was actually engaged with the enemy—yesterday noon—so I'll bring you down to date.

A few days ago, we were assigned an objective and were proceeding to it without any difficulty, when suddenly, an urgent call came from one of our units some five miles away to bring all possible support at once as they were overrun by a very large enemy force. Our air corps showed up about then and proceeded to wreak the most complete destruction I have ever seen on their guns and trucks. Then we moved in with our tanks and infantry.

I was given the mission of sweeping a rather large forest some mile square. I deployed my men on either side of a road, which bisected the woods and proceeded with my tanks, I being on the lead tank. I noticed a bit of movement in the thick woods just to my right, but thought it was one of my men. Suddenly, a couple of shots whined very close to my head, striking the tank and ricocheting away from me. I jumped off the tank and just as I did, another shot whizzed by me. Not more than twenty yards away, I saw the guy who was doing this poor job of marksmanship. Fortunately, my forty-five was in good order, and he was sent to permanent slumber without further delay.

By the time this took place, the entire woods seemed to come alive, and immediately, I was surrounded—by prisoners who came toward me crying, "*Kamerad! Kamerad!*" In less time that it takes to write this, I had captured thirty-seven *boche*. Meanwhile, my men were literally being overwhelmed by large numbers who were doing the same thing. Well, to make the story short, we finished sweeping through the woods, losing only three of our men and netting *800* prisoners. The total for the division ran into the thousands, so you can well understand what a great victory was achieved. We also captured a Major General, a Colonel, and many other officers. Thus the *Wehrmacht* is rapidly disintegrating.

But with all the rumors and reports, he still fights savagely and bitterly. I know it will end soon, but even so, I am growing *so tired*. God knows how I've stood it this long, yet still there is the old drive, drive, drive, putting one foot in front of the other. I'll continue somehow, but the old heart is beginning to slow a bit. Mayhap *this is* the real test now. Let's hope I measure up.

To my precious Donna, be assured that I shall seek Roy just as soon as I can, but at present, I am too deeply enmeshed in the front line to get to any sources of information. Keep the faith, darling, and know I adore you as no other in all this life. To each of you, a heart of devoted love.

Dawson's remark about physical exhaustion echoed similar sentiments by most combat infantrymen in World War II. Social historian Gerald Linderman describes the U.S. Army's policy governing relief from battle as a problem of increasing magnitude. For World War II, the army mobilized eighty-nine combat divisions, all of which saw extensive combat.[14]

With so slender a margin, the high command saw no option but to commit its divisions to combat indefinitely and to maintain their strength through a system of individual replacements, instead of a rotation of major units. Consequently, some divisions, including the Big Red One, remained in combat for months on end, until casualties so depleted its ranks that senior commanders had no option but to pull the division from the line. In the early stages of the war, most officers accepted the high command's rationale, but by 1944, those units that had been in the line continuously since the invasion began experiencing severe problems of motivation and combat fatigue.

In Sicily, one infantry scout in the 1st Infantry Division noted, "Men in our division gave up all hope of being relieved. They thought the army intended to keep them in action until everybody was killed." In March 1943, assistant division commander Teddy Roosevelt Jr. had written to his wife, "In this war, no units in the line get relief. We just go on and on."[15]

This was precisely what was occurring in G Company. Even their commander confessed he was getting so tired that "he could hardly think intelligently." Would his luck continue to hold? Would he survive the next engagement? He wasn't sure. Maybe it was time, he contemplated, that he "stop trying to win the war single-handedly." Dawson expressed his growing apprehension concerning his mental and physical health to his brother and family in early September.

Dawson to Dear L. B.[16]

September 8, 1944
Deep in Belgium

Even here, miles from famed "Easy Red Beach," the good old A.P.O. continues to operate, and your fine letters continue to boost my ebbing morale. I got to thinking the other day that maybe it is about time this old war-horse stopped trying to win the war single-handedly and take things a little easier. It has been my habit to be the lead person in all these fracases, and the luck that has been with me surely must be reaching the breaking point.

I was literally peppered the other day with shrapnel, five pieces ripping through my clothes, yet miraculously none penetrated this hunk of flesh that represents me. Now that I'm practically in Germany—the end of the journey—I would like to live to see the fruits of these efforts. But like a drunkard who craves just one more, I guess when tomorrow rolls around, and there's *boche* to be disposed of, I'll probably be in my usual spot.

Tonight, I am ensconced in a lovely old Belgian chateau with a charming family, who are semi-nobility. By that, I mean they are of the noblesse *Belgie,* but don't possess a title owing to the fact that when the *Vicomte* died, there was no son to wear the title, so the daughter assumed the estate, but could not claim the title. This is true of the Belgian aristocracy because, as you know, they are relatively a young nation as far as their independence is concerned, having been formerly under Holland and Spain. Their titles, however, are intricately involved with the French and Dutch, and these peoples' ancestors were some Flemish people, who, as I said, were unable to produce a son to assume the coveted title. . . .

Strangely enough, only the night before, the Germans occupied the same bed I have, and these people have greatly enjoyed the paradox of being host to two opposing groups within the same twenty-four hours. But so goes this swift moving war, and even now, I have a patrol searching some nearby woods for a German general, who is reported to be hiding there. There's not a whole lot of fight left in the majority of these *boche*, but still, there remains some who resist fiercely, the *SS* troops and elite Panzer elements continue the fight.

The other day, we smashed him terrifically when we surprised him by being at a place he thought was still his. I wrote the family about it and must refrain from elaborating in detail, but I can say that it won't take but about two or three more big losses like that to finish him for good.

Incidentally, I captured a beautiful Packard 1942 model coupe that is a dream. It's a special, which is their big job, and in pretty fair shape. Am having it restored to good condition and repaired as all the windows were blown out when one of my men tossed a hand grenade in and took care of the captain who was driving it. Will let you know more about it, though, when the war is over, and I can reclaim it. I feel sure that I shall be forced to remain over here for a while after it's all over, and if so, may get a chance to tour around a bit.

My brief glimpse of Paris in the middle of the night was not exactly the way I intend[ed] to see that certain city. However, my longing for home has assumed never-before-reached proportions, and I can assure you that this tired old man will welcome the all ashore signal from the P. of E. [port of embarkation].

It's cold as can be here, and ere too many more days pass, the weather will really start biting these bones of mine. If I can reach Goring first, I certainly plan to remove his fur coat and wear it myself. I have a beautiful pair of German fleece-lined flying boots as well as a fur lining for a vest. There is no doubt but his equipment is superb. That is true of his taste, as well, because I found a dozen bottles of Martell cognac, D.O.M. Benedictine and Yquem 1929 champagne that he had the misfortune not to consume before I swatted him into permanent oblivion. This by the way, is my first real "spoils of war."

Have had a letter from Mother saying a letter of mine was dramatized over the radio, and you received a war bond on my behalf. Guess I will hear from you anon, though. I'm beginning to wonder how keen the disappointment will be to all concerned when I return there and am shorn of this false halo of heroism. In truth, I'm a very violent, outspoken, profane, disillusioned bum that has seen too much of reality.

Maybe the Lord will help me get back on my feet, but right now, I'm so tired I can hardly think intelligently. Believe me, Bud,

I'm really looking forward to getting home and try to find some sanity. Probably be in Germany soon. Keep well and God bless.

Dawson to Dearest Family

September 12, 1944
Deep in Belgium

The cool weather now so in evidence presages a usual wail emanating from my bones, so naturally, I am looking with longing for the warmth of a nice, quiet home with a large fireplace. Of course, it is quite unpredictable even now as to when the end will come. One cannot measure success in battle until the final round has been fired. Here, as we are about to deal the last blow, I only wonder how long it will take to complete the knockout. Believe me, I can envision a lot of wonderful peace, and as it nears, I must temper my resolution to meet the final tests with a realization that I'm growing awfully weary and *must not* falter.

Well, there's little to say at present except that I'm hoping for some good letters real soon because there has been a considerable lapse the past week in the mail situation. That is easily understandable, but I'm somewhat petulant when they do not come regularly. Guess, though, school now beginning and election in the offing keep things at home rather interesting.

There still happens to be delicious joy over here as each town greets us with overwhelming gratitude. Though the people have suffered deeply, there is great evidence of an indomitable spirit pervading them, and their happiness now is something that can hardly be described.

Have been wondering if my D.S.C. has reached you.[17] I sent it by mail some weeks ago while still in Normandy. Let me know if and when it arrives. There are a couple more that should be forthcoming of somewhat lesser significance, though I don't know when I can take time off to have them awarded.

Well, that's all for now.

The Packard that G Company "liberated" was soon the object of much publicity in the 1st Division. With the speculation that the war was going to end that summer, Dawson and another officer had the local ordnance shop repair the car. With his new "command car" in tow, he toured the front until the daily *Stars and Stripes* ran a feature story on the Packard convertible.[18]

The column, titled "Used Car Bargain," noted that "while most front-line officers bounce along in a jeep or at the best, a captured German car, Captain Joseph Dawson, of Waco, Texas, tours his positions in his own 1942 Packard coupe." Though the reporter stated that Dawson had identified the civilian owner and acquired legal title to the car, no one from the lowest private to General Huebner believed that the transfer had been anything other than from the point of a rifle.

With so much adverse publicity and in obvious violation against army policy governing keeping souvenirs, Dawson concealed the car in a barn, where he intended to return as soon as the war was over. The damage, however, was already done. One of the Big Red One's heroes of Omaha Beach once again found himself the subject of an internal investigation by 1st Division headquarters, just as he had when he allegedly went AWOL from the hospital in England to return to his unit. The investigators soon discovered the Packard and confiscated the captain's prize war trophy just as the forward elements of the division reached the German frontier.

Within a few days, the 16th Regiment was once again on the move, though not as rapidly as before. By mid-September, however, gasoline supply, not enemy resistance, was hindering the Allied advance. As early as September 6, the 16th Regimental S-3 Report noted that combat efficiency was being undermined by low gasoline supply. Moreover, several tank tracks were sorely in need of replacement. Unless logistical needs were met, the regiment's tanks could go only ten more operational miles. The next day, the operations officer informed his higher headquarters that the gasoline supply was nearly exhausted. By the twelfth, First Army's advance had run its course.

As historian Cornelius Ryan noted, the truth was that the Germans were losing faster than the Allies could win.[19] The delay proved ominous for the 1st Infantry Division and the remainder of VII Corps. The Allies themselves were providing German Field Marshal Gerd von Rundstedt with the precious time he needed to stabilize the front. For the ordinary GI in the forward ranks of the Allied advance, the delay gave the Germans time to establish a coordinated defense, something they had not been able to do since July.

This "September miracle" would prove catastrophic, as Bradley's 12th Army Group approached Germany's western frontier. In the center of the 1st Division's advance lay the city of Aachen, located in a saucer-like depression, with hills and ridges surrounding it on all sides.

What G Company accomplished on D-Day and the advance into Belgium were "merely episodes in a long war," remembered Dawson as he reflected on his career fifty years later. The most brutal fighting the company encountered during the war occurred outside Aachen. The battles on D-Day and Aachen were distinctively different in scope and intensity. Dawson recalled, "D-Day was a few hours of combat under heavy fire, perhaps 8–10 hours. At Aachen, we were in combat for thirty-nine straight days. It was the most strenuous and challenging period of my command."

With a prewar population of 165,710, Aachen lacked any military significance other than as a hub of an elaborate road network and as the key to the second most heavily fortified portion of the West Wall.[20] Though Aachen was hardly a shrine to National Socialism on the scale of Munich or Nuremberg, the city nevertheless embodied a heritage precious to National Socialist ideology. Reputed to be the birthplace and burial site of Charlemagne and the capital of the Carolingian Empire, Aachen also represented the Holy Roman Empire, the First *Reich*.[21] As such, it held a special significance for Adolf Hitler, who ordered that Aachen be defended to the last man. The "eyes of Germany" are upon you, the *Führer* informed the city's defenders.

Despite increasing resistance, Hodges's First U.S. Army battered Germany's Western Wall in early September and pierced the huge tank traps, the so-called Dragon's Teeth, in front of Hitler's vaunted Siegfried Line.[22] Even though the wall was undermanned, it was still a formidable obstacle. It proved no match for the Allied onslaught, however. By mid-September, troops of the First Army encircled the ancient city. Taking an urban area the size of Aachen also presented tactical problems that the Americans had not encountered in the fighting from Normandy through the advance into Germany. There, they paused and prepared to meet the inevitable counterattacks. The brunt of several of these attacks was borne by the 16th Infantry Regiment—by G and I Companies, specifically—as they dug in on an 838-foot-high ridge running approximately 400 yards long at its highest point. Here Captain Joe Dawson would meet his greatest test of leadership.

8
Aachen

All that stood against the enemy was one lousy old GI company.

When the First Army attacked Aachen, Lieutenant General Courtney Hodges deployed his XIX Corps, commanded by Major General Charles Corlett, to attack from the north, while Major General J. Lawton Collins's VII Corps moved in from the south. Major General Leland S. Hobbs's 30th Division spearheaded Corlett's advance, which was directed to penetrate the west wall, north of Aachen, and then to turn south to the area of Wurselen, east of the city.

Meanwhile, the 1st Infantry Division conducted the main attack in VII Corps zone, with its 26th Infantry Regiment, whose mission it was to secure the city. General Charles Huebner envisioned that the 26th Infantry would conduct street-to-street fighting and that casualties would be high. To free the 26th from fear of an attack from its rear, Huebner directed the 16th and 18th Infantry Regiments to drive north from Eilendorf, penetrating the second band of the west wall at Verlautenheide, and to meet the XIX Corps in the vicinity of Wurselen. Such a maneuver would envelop the city and prevent reinforcements from reaching the German garrison.[1]

As the 16th Infantry moved to its defensive positions in mid-September, Dawson issued a classic attack order that directed G Company to conduct a non-illuminated night attack to seize and hold the high ground northeast of Eilendorf, then to clean out the pillboxes in their zone of action and to make contact with friendly units on their flanks. The company objective rested on a long, steep hill. Then Dawson told his platoon leaders how they were going to do it.

He directed the third platoon, with a section of light machine guns and one mortar squad attached, to advance from its present position as soon as possible and to proceed up the main road leading north from Eilendorf. When they reached the crossroads at the crest of the hill, Dawson told them "to stop, send out security, dig in, and attempt to maintain contact with the adjacent company." He then directed the first platoon to attack along the railroad, and upon reaching the tunnel, to turn left and attack north, along the ridge, eliminating any enemy from the woods and pillboxes. The specific objective for the platoon was to "clean the ridge, maintain contact with Company E on the right and with the third platoon on the left."

Dawson then ordered his second platoon to move by the most direct route to the ridge and "to establish contact with the third platoon on the left, and the first platoon on the right, and to prepare to defend towards the northeast." The company mortars were to remain in their current location by the company command post (CP) and to move up when summoned. "Are there any questions?" he asked. "If not, go back to your platoons and give them the dope I just gave you."[2]

Because it was dark and the platoon leaders knew approximately what type of terrain to expect, they did not make a detailed reconnaissance of the area to their front. The land was extremely rugged, with large boulders, a few quarries, some pits, and very little shrubbery. Preceded by scouts, G Company crossed the line of departure at 2300 hours and met minimal resistance. Although in preparation for this attack there had been no elaborate planning, it went off smoothly and efficiently.

By 0700 hours, September 16, the company reached its objective, and Dawson established his company's defense along the Verlautenheide ridge that covered a major avenue of approach from Cologne. The company dug in on the far side of a railroad embankment that divided the town of Eilendorf, on the outskirts of Aachen. There, they waited for the inevitable German counterattack.

Adjacent to G Company was I Company, commanded by Kimball Richmond, who like Dawson, was a veteran rifle company commander who had led his unit, with highest distinction, from Omaha Beach to the German border. Both commanders realized that the enemy would mount heavy attacks in their sector as soon as the Germans could muster sufficient combat power. The American commanders did not have to wait long, as the Germans struck immediately.

Unlike the offensive tactics that had characterized the American advance across the Low Countries, the order of the day in the 16th Infantry was now to defend. Defensive operations remained far more complex than originally envisioned by tactical planners. Stateside training and preinvasion maneuvers had always emphasized the attack, not the defense. With fuel running low and Allied logistical problems reaching catastrophic proportions, defensive operations now became a necessity, not to mention an undesirable change of pace.

Having chased the retreating Germans across France and Belgium, the 16th Regiment had fought some sharp engagements that had netted thousands of prisoners, but the key to that success had been the American ability to capitalize on its inherent mobility and firepower. Now in the defense, the GIs finally surrendered the initiative to the Germans, who could array their resources for a concentrated attack against a portion of the American line.

On the German frontier, the Big Red One encountered resistance of a character they had not previously experienced. Every inch of ground was bitterly contested; even the women and children were armed. To the commander of G Company, the Germans "had simply gone mad." "The [Germans] are bent on destroying themselves," he later reported. And Dawson favored accommodating them. Nazi fanaticism and resolution were exceeded only by what Dawson termed the "marvelous courage and irresistible force" of his own men.

From his command post in the cellar of a small house in Eilendorf, Dawson could look into Belgium and Holland, as well as Germany. What he saw startled him. In the distance, the enemy was assembling tanks and infantry and moving up in the woods about a thousand yards to the northeast and in an orchard to the southeast. Of greater significance was the enemy's massing of their artillery to soften the American defenses before their armor and infantry attacked. It was going to be a hell of a fight. The attack was not long in coming.

Two days after Dawson and Richmond initially fortified the ridge, two battalions from the enemy's 27th Regiment, 12th Infantry Division, attacked the 16th Regiment's forward positions. The enemy attack was the first major effort to drive off the 1st Division's threat to Aachen. The Germans struck first with artillery and mortars, and then they attacked in battalion strength at 0700. The 1st Division's after-action report characterized the German assault as "experienced, well-coordinated and powerful."[3]

The first platoon of G Company was hit especially hard. Dawson lost every man in the second squad. The intensity of the attack carried the attackers into the American lines, but the GIs held. At times, the enemy was so close that the GIs could hear them talking. The battle raged with an intensity that even eclipsed D-Day. At 1330, Lieutenant John D. Burbridge of La Grange, Georgia, led his platoon and physically drove the enemy back from where the sheer weight of their initial attack had carried them into the American lines.

Dawson recalled, "I lost men. They weren't wounded. They weren't taken prisoners. They were killed. But we piled up the Krauts, at least 70 of them, and after we counterattacked, there were over 200 bodies for eighteen of ours, spread over 400 yards."[4]

Amid constant shelling, the Germans renewed their assault, but the result was the same—massive enemy casualties and nothing gained. During the two-day struggle, Dawson lost 31 men and received only a single replacement. According to 16th Regimental records, G Company strength was down to 7 officers and 145 enlisted men.

The enemy suffered more severely, as bodies were stacked like a cord of wood in front of the company's position. Dawson's men didn't want the enemy dead moved. They could live with the stink because they didn't believe the Germans would attack over their own dead. They were mistaken.

Following their initial defense of the Verlautenheide ridge, Dawson improved his defensive position and then took time to write several letters to his sister and family to describe the previous days' action. His letters provided him a brief respite from the horrors associated from close combat, and relieved him, albeit temporarily, from the responsibilities of command.

Dawson's correspondence reflected his personal remorse that his sibling had still not received word about her missing husband and his own concern that his family misunderstood the carnage that had become his daily diet. His sister's loss mirrored his own feelings that as the battle increased in intensity and G Company soldiers became casualties, a member of his family also perished. War had taken on a new dimension that now dictated the utter extermination of the enemy. Then and only then would the war come to an end.

At times, Dawson reflected on his own good fortune, as well as that of his close friends, of staving off serious injury. A close call to Ed Wozenski prompted Dawson to contemplate divine intervention. Surely a "Divine Presence" hovered among them.

The subsequent letters reflected Dawson's increased shrillness and hatred toward the enemy. Whereas he treated the Italian adversaries he had fought in Africa and Sicily as contemptible subhumans, Dawson now equated the Germans with demons bent on their own self-destruction. So horrified by what he encountered, Dawson redirected his anger to Germany and its inhabitants once he crossed the border.

Dawson to My Darling, Precious Sister[5]

September 19, 1944
Germany

For the past several days, I have been so deeply involved in this present battle that I've been completely occupied with mere efforts of maintaining myself as best I could. The real concept cannot be revealed at the present time, but it will eventually be told, so you can know that this is the real McCoy.

Like some giant wounded beast with its life rapidly flowing from its body, the *Wehrmacht* is now making its final stand. At bay and facing the truth at last, one finds that the terrible impact is still present, and its bite is still sharp. When it's all over, I shall write of it in detail. Meanwhile, be assured that we are bitterly engaged and are doing our utmost to finish this long and hideous affair.

At the moment, there is an extremely heavy barrage that continues to shake the earth all around, but I thought perhaps this would relieve my tension a bit by inscribing a few lines to the dearest of all. Realizing full well the terrible impact of war in every sense, I can somehow get a little more understanding of how your emotions are torn at this time. The enigma of a person's MIA is always such a difficult thing to comprehend because it presents so many intangible hopes and possibilities. You probably seek to analyze the situation rationally by facing the worst and then compromising this whole scheme of thought and emotion by clinging to the hope that somehow it's not as bad as one would think, and that Roy is still alive and well, only a prisoner of war.

Particularly this is difficult on you, darling, because it is all wrapped up with one's deepest hopes and longings, yet tempered by the strong possibility that the worst may have to be faced. The days will undoubtedly drag out because time becomes oppressive when one's heart is so torn with uncertainty. The paradox of it all is the fact that there is so little one can do at the moment to relieve the burden for you.

There is a starkness of war that is so terrible that even I sometimes am shaken by it, though for over two years, I've callused [sic] my emotions with countless experiences that will never be recalled to memory if I can find power to erase them forever. Yet through these, I've found stability that has strengthened my resolve to finish off this task with cold dispatch. No longer can I face the enemy except with the knowledge that they must be exterminated. Though that may sound brutal beyond words, I find my men and comrades so precious, and find that all the crimes perpetrated by these criminals can no longer favor a lesser premise.

Now as the final phase unfolds, we find the bitterness of the struggle brings the whole thing into sharp reality with attrition ever present. There is no solace or comfort in this other than the fervent prayer that our enemies will feel the impact of it so deeply that never again will this means be sought to impose their will on the world. All of which is somehow small consolation to our own personal sorrows, but knowing you as I do, there is so very much that is in store for you in the future in precious little Susanna.[6] How I long to see her, though I'm afraid she will be quite a grown-up young lady before I am able to do so. Sitting here this after-noon, the battle rages with an intensity that even pales D-Day into just another skirmish. I've often wondered how I've managed so long in the midst of it all. Only yesterday, I was talking with my beloved comrade Ed Wozenski as the shells were beating a tattoo on the whole terrain, and we wondered how God had spared us so long. He left shortly, and in a few minutes, one landed right where he had been sitting not five minutes before. By some miracle, I was only slightly nicked in my forehead with a small piece of shrapnel.[7] One soon becomes philosophical about it all, though otherwise, I'd go mad. Perhaps the Lord will see me through, and that is what maintains me as I go.

I realize, dearest darling, that you, too, are leaning heavily on Him. Keep the chin up, for if I'm spared, you can know that I will find Roy if it's within human powers. My heart is so filled with tenderness that I'm at a loss to really confide to you my thoughts, yet with it comes the understanding I know you possess, so keep the faith.

Dawson to Dearest Ones

September 22, 1944
Germany

The battle continues to rage with terrific intensity, and now as the barrage from their big guns shake my position till it seems as if it were made of Jello, I cannot do much except remain defiladed [sic] as best I can, and hope the one with my name on it will pass on overhead. Believe me when I say that this present chapter is in-deed as rugged as I have yet encountered, and the severity of it all merely serves to add a few more gray hairs to my head and tauten [sic] the nerves a bit more.

Looking out over this terrain filled with the carnage of war and the destruction wrought by two armies locked in deadly com-bat, one envisions all sorts of happy days that will come when it's all over. In truth, we are all beginning to dream of an almost for-gotten Valhalla that once was home. How changed we all are, and undoubtedly, all our homes are different now after nearly three years of war. Well, it will someday end, and with it, I pray will bring everlasting peace. You mention reading an article by Chap-lain Burkhalter about D-Day. He was my battalion chaplain dur-ing those days and just prior to the invasion. Not a very effective person, but I guess he was sincere. Don't misunderstand this as-sertion, but there are really so few real people involved over here that one becomes somewhat scornful of the ineffectuals [sic]. That was his big drawback.

I trust all goes well there at home. . . . As for me, I'm OK, and the head does not offer any serious injury. God surely has walked with me, believe it when twenty-five pounds of steel and TNT explode only three feet away and all I get is a nick in the forehead and a headache!

I feel sure the pressures exerted on the enemy all along the front presages and end ere too long. Perhaps this year will finish it off, and so it may be that ere another year rolls by, I may be able to come home. That's my fervent hope; meantime, I must do the job here and see to it that it is completed. I've given up hope for any other philosophy.

Well, must go to work again.

Dawson to Dearest Sis

September 23, 1944
Germany

Doubtless, you will discern from the news accounts that all is not exactly a peaceful Saturday afternoon picnic over here, nor have I been in a position to add any footnotes to the historical record. You can appreciate the fact that my time has been spent rather fulsome of late, and when I'm not actually engaged in cal-isthenics, jumping and hitting the dirt while a shell explodes nearby, I am concerned with putting up as strong an argument as I can to persuade these people that they will see the eternal fires of Hades—but quickly—if they continue to resist. All of which is a round-about way of saying that we are engrossed in a little battle over here. Now that the month is just about passed, I am beginning to feel the forerunners of winter and ere too long, I'm afraid it is going to be quite cold. Already, the air has that crisp bite of fall, and I'm hoping that something final can be accomplished before winter descends. . . . But before things get too involved . . . I shall relate to you a little of what has transpired here.

Having chased his retreating armies across France and Belgium, we found some sharp but quickly ended engagements that netted much materiel as well as prisoners of war. A few of our men fell along the way, but the proportion was quite small in comparison to the devastation we wrought on him.[8] Then, one day, we suddenly found ourselves on his frontier. Things have been happening so thick and fast since then that I cannot recall dates at all. But to the point. Resistance of a character never before met was encountered, and every inch of ground we've been able to take has been bitterly contested. Their fanaticism and resolution have only been exceeded by the marvelous courage and irresistible force of our men. Here on the summits overlooking a very large city, we've managed to hang on to our positions though subjected to the most severe attacks I've ever known.

Every day has seen him try to throw us back, but somehow we've managed to hold him. To be truthful, it has been the supreme test for us, and the terrific losses he has suffered lay before us as mute evidence of his all-out efforts. They've penetrated a little only to find us with that little extra something and back he goes (or rather his shattered remnants).

The carnage has been frightful and recalls to mind some of the stories earlier in the war of his efforts in Russia. And his towns—subjected to our artillery and air before we enter—then his descending on us as we occupy them, leaves shattered walls of once lovely homes and rubble [and] death commingling in the scene of utter destruction. So goes the war. It's terrible beyond imagination, and only our grim resolve to end it as quickly as we can sustains us through these awful days.

I'm much better today, and now, six days after getting hit, my head is not buzzing or aching. It's fortunate that it was so slight, though, for a time, I feared I would have to be evacuated. But I've stayed by the job and will remain. Needless to say, I shall be a bit happy when the final round is over. . . . So it goes. I'm still in one piece, though I'm afraid I'm maturing rather rapidly. Thank God, though, I've still got my sense of humor.

It would take the Germans a mere two weeks to launch another serious assault. In the interim, Dawson was able to catch up on his correspondence because the weather was so cold and rainy, the only efforts the American soldiers could expend were occasional artillery barrages. Deeply ensconced in the midst of a cellar CP, surrounded by piles of sandbags, Dawson felt fairly safe from such abortive efforts to penetrate G Company's lines, but a direct hit on his CP resulted in his suffering a minor concussion.

As his company clerk later recalled, "We were in this house, the company CP, when an antitank shell was fired at the house. The captain was hit by debris from the brick building. It was a head and face wound." Dawson was immediately evacuated by one of his jeeps to battalion and regimental aid station, but he was back with the unit in just a few days.[9] Coupled with the laceration he received when Wozenski and he were discussing battle tactics, the concussion was enough to convince Dawson that there was no haven from the constant enemy bombardment.

What Dawson didn't realize—no one could have realized it—was that he was only in the first week of what would eventually be five and a half weeks of constant bombardment, sniper activity, and infantry attacks. For most veterans, the duration, not the intensity of combat, broke their spirit.

After one week on the line at Aachen, the soldiers of the 16th Regiment began experiencing combat fatigue. Major Eston T. White, the regimental operations officer, reported that on September 19, sixteen cases of battle fatigue had occurred in the previous twenty-four hours. Men were generally in need of rest and hot meals, neither of which was in ample supply.

Two days later, regimental commander Colonel Frederick W. Gibb informed General Huebner that combat efficiency was greatly reduced because of the large number of casualties, exposure, and the extended period of immediate contact with the enemy.[10] The worst fear was always artillery fire; there was literally no safe place on the battlefield in which to take cover—not his headquarters, not the ever-deepening foxholes.

Looking around the company, the commander noticed that GIs had that thousand-yard stare, a hollow-eyed, vacant look peculiar to men under extreme stress for days and nights on end. Every frontline infantryman experienced it, from the U.S. Marines on Pacific atolls to the riflemen arrayed along the Siegfried Line. At Peleliu, PFC E. B. Sledge, U.S. Marine Corps, almost broke under the strain. Putting his face in his hands to try to shut out reality, he began to sob uncontrollably. The harder he tried to stop, the worse it got. So sickened and revolted to see healthy young men get hurt and killed day after day, he became so terribly tired and so emotionally wrung out from being afraid that he seemed to have no reserve strength left.[11]

Every infantryman in G Company, including the company commander, would soon experience the same phenomenon. In the interim, Dawson discussed the company's successful defense against the initial German onslaught.

Dawson to Dearest Nonny[12]

September 28, 1944
Germany

Here I am in Germany—on the front line, as usual, have chased the Krauts from Tunisia through Sicily, France and Belgium. I marvel that I've lived through it, but so far, I've kept alive, though I received my third memento the other day, this time in the head. I'm still abed, but expect to be up and about in another week. Seems the Lord figures I'm too ornery to die right now, so He's prolonging the agony a while longer. I just hope He holds off till the end, plus six months, so I can get back to the good old USA for one more fling!

Here, in Germany, all hell is breaking loose as we close in on his final positions. This last phase is about as terrible as we have ever experienced, and it has only added to our realization of the necessity for ending this mess once and for all. Unquestionably, it is a war of attrition now, and I see little hope for the remnants of this once great nation. Nevertheless, I do not feel any pangs of remorse, and I share Sherman's viewpoint when I repeat his philosophy of war: "Make it so terrible and horrible that the people will never again choose this method of making their wants and desires public to the world!" His march through Georgia pales into insignificance compared to the devastation now being wrought on these towns and villages of Germany. I don't know when the end will come, but it cannot last much longer. . . .

Dawson to Dearest Dad

September 28, 1944
Germany

Here's a German handkerchief that a German colonel "gave" me when he surrendered his command post and all its fixtures to me a few days ago. I have his regimental sword, also, which I hope to send home as soon as practicable. Meantime, use this little memento as a gift of the *Reich*. You will note it is rather excellent material, which is true of about everything they have. It should be, after stealing from the world their most valuable assets for the last five years.

Dawson to Dearest Ones

September 30, 1944
Germany

How I wish it were possible to see you all. Maybe someday, that will be possible, and I truly hope it won't be too far distant. However, the present outlook is a little dim as to the possibility of the war ending soon. In truth, I feel it will continue into 1945, and then I guess I will have to stay for sometime even though hostilities will have ceased. But that may be the more pessimistic side, though I cannot see any other viewpoint at the present.

The Germans are indeed having a visitation of destruction never before equaled anywhere, yet one does not see any signs of a decrease in their desire to fight on. Indeed, one ponders his willingness to continue to lose men at an almost unbelievable rate. But then, one cannot understand why they started this mess, either, and I cannot find any reason why they should not suffer to the limit. Believe me, after seeing it in two continents and two islands, I feel there is some cold satisfaction to seeing them reap their desserts.

Well, the mortars are beginning to land and a few snipers are busy, so must close. Be assured I am OK and definitely improving in health.

As in the early days of America's involvement, far more unnerving to the American GIs in the foxholes were newspaper accounts that the people back home had grown tired of the war. With the election on the horizon, politicians began debating the merits of Roosevelt's policy of unconditional surrender. Some even attacked the commander-in-chief for not preparing the country adequately.

Such attitudes deeply affected Dawson, who wrote home to chastise the fainthearted minority that was raising its voice of dissent. What concerned Dawson most was the impression that various agencies in the United States were devoting too much energy to the post-war world, rather than pursuing the conflict of that moment. There was still a war to be fought, and his men were literally dying in the foxholes.

And contrary to press reports, every indication led Dawson to believe that German resistance was intensifying, not crumbling. The false optimism of the summer had yielded to the stark reality of the autumn. The war would carry on well into 1945 before every vestige of Nazi evil would be eradicated. How could the American public not realize it?

Dawson to My Dearest Family

October 3, 1944
Germany

Tonight, as the cold bites deep at us and the rain adds its discomfiture, I find that writing a few lines somewhat brings the old heart into even closer communion with you. Being the bulwark of strength that enables me to meet the tests that beset me, you really cannot know how deeply I love you and cherish your devotion to me. Truly, these tests have been many through the past two years, still I carry on in the knowledge that God and you are constantly with me. How I would have made it any other way is beyond possibility or even probability.

And for the past few weeks, the bitter struggle we've had here has been fraught with moments when I could only commit everything to His Will. Though I do not wish to appear to be one who runs to the Lord at every crisis, I do thank Him deep in my heart for this watch-care. Believe me, it's somewhat of a different prayer or worship that I offer when the very jaws of hell seem to be clenching, and I'm in the middle of them.

There are many hills and dominating ground here in Europe, upon which are located monuments to the Lord, and here in this war-ravaged sector, reposes on the landscape just such a feature. Two edifices are on this particular piece of ground, and amid the indescribable hell of battle stands this gigantic crucifix, immediately adjacent to a huge, massive, concrete pillbox.[13] From this commanding bit of ground, the enemy has waged his bitterest and deadliest destruction. The intensity of this cannot be overstated, and the fact that we have withstood his incessant rain of shellfire is really a story that will ever be an inspiration to me.

My men are absolutely without peer, and their courage and matchless fortitude in the face of unbelievable odds will truly stand out forever in my memory. They just cannot be touched when it comes to meeting the supreme test. May I know that with them breathes the God who guides their destiny. Somehow, I feel very close tonight to Him, and in the unfolding drama of life itself, I cannot help but feel that each one of us has been planted here on earth for just that specific mission that is in His program. And when the time comes to complete it, then the remainder carries on with the resolve to live up to those whom He claimed.

How odd I should think these thoughts when I possess such a deep, implacable hatred for the foe and get real satisfaction from their destruction. Yet this is based on a firm belief that they are definitely outside the ken of Christian understanding and my feeling that they are the devil itself reincarnated. What can one think after two long years of fighting them, seeing the results of their diabolical schemes and desires foisted on this world? The only sorrow that befalls me is when these precious men of mine are destroyed or maimed by their efforts. But with each successive casualty, I merely intensify my hatred for the whole dirty lot of them, and realize the utter necessity that they must be exterminated.

Can it be that the world refuses to recognize a cancer and refuses to operate? We pale at such terrifying statements, perhaps, but it's because America has never had her cities wiped out or its entire communities either murdered or borne into slavery. . . . Yet I've seen this a hundred times over. Your ordered sense of human behaviorism would revolt in unbelievable horror at countless sights or what this total war means and how cold, brutal and heinous it is . . . total victory will never be achieved until the USA convinces itself that it can be won only when we have destroyed every vestige of Nazism, and I feel that is a tall order that can only be accomplished with everyone there, sublimating their hopes for the future to the stern realities of the present.

It is all quite good and most commendable that we now have so many agencies devoting millions of man hours toward setting up agencies for the post-war and the peace that will be effected. Yet, how ironical to me, as I sit here midst an atmosphere that is charged with death, the one thing that is final to so many at the present. We all live in dreams, perhaps, dreams of a peace that will bring us back to all that we hold precious and dear in this world. Were it not for just these things to bolster us, we couldn't carry on with the tasks at hand.

Surely more would help the average American doughboy if he knew every American back home was thinking of winning the war first. Then evolve a peace because you will come to see in the future that those who are fighting the war will have many ideas as to just what sort of peace will be necessary, and how they will want it to be framed. The travesty of it all is the muddled political scene on the home front, coupled with the seeming false optimism that the war's over except for the shouting!

My thoughts are sobered by the knowledge that our military leaders are acutely aware of the situation, and their conduct of the war planning has been most gratifying because they realize the stern reality confronting us all and are dealing with it accordingly. But know, my beloved ones, that the tests of the past cannot match those now unfolding today and in the Gethsemane of the ensuing weeks.

Pray now as never before, because I will be able to carry on only through the strength that comes through God and you, who I devote my entire heart and soul.

The next day, a second German division attacked following two weeks of intense artillery bombardment. By that time, Dawson's and Richmond's men had already repulsed several attacks and endured five hundred shells per day from German 105s. Following yet another bombardment, "That other infantry division hit us. We had had constant shelling for eight hours, and we had had twelve direct hits on what was my command post because we were taking it from 270 degrees on the compass. When they stopped coming, we could count 350 that we ourselves had killed—not those killed by our artillery or planes, but just by one lousy little old GI company all by itself." Enemy casualties again littered the battlefield.

Nor were enemy attacks the only problem confronting Dawson. Since the weather had turned so disagreeable, Dawson had requested that his company be issued overcoats. He had submitted the request through proper military channels and had made more than one telephone call over the division field telephone net to various friends in the main CP, stressing his urgent need. The support network collapsed, and the troops on the frontline were literally freezing.

One evening after the company had repelled a particularly heavy attack, Dawson thought it would be a good time to call again and request the overcoats. Deeds of valor always pleased General Huebner, so when the division chief of staff heard Dawson's voice on the field phone, he waved a hand signal across the room to Huebner to listen in on the conversation. On the phone, Dawson was a bit "hot-under-the-collar" about not receiving the overcoats. At about the time the division commander picked up the conversation, Dawson told the chief of staff that if that "damned Santa Claus of a commanding general who had promised the overcoats didn't get off his duff and do something about it, he was going to march his entire company off the lines and leave a hole big enough for the whole German army to come through."[14] Naturally, Dawson didn't realize that the commanding general was listening, but the chief noticed a twinkle in the general's eye. The next day, overcoats had replaced ammunition when the trucks brought forward supplies.

Dawson to My Beloved Family

October 10, 1944
Germany

The old heart continues to pump, and the nerves are still intact, but the amazing thing to me is the marvelous resources vested within this human machinery that enables it to function, even though every hour seems interminable. Long, long ago I entered this land of horror, and even now, I question the fact that the dateline above is accurate. Can it be true that all these many days have passed, and still, I find my pen in hand and thoughts projected through this medium?

Each successive day, I've experienced the impact of total war and all its many faceted sides, yet I thank God for his constant watch-care, and still, I carry on. How odd that one measures life in terms of seconds, as we do here, when the ever-changing panorama of battle brings death and destruction within your own immediate sphere.

When the final page is written, I cannot say just what the reviewers will ascribe to this particular segment of the vast overall, but my own intimate relationship with the things transpiring has created a realization that no test yet demanded of us has required the measure of fortitude this one has. How I can describe it is when one has a pack placed on his back, then an extra pound is added each day until it seems the weight becomes unbearable, yet somehow the requirements of life enable—just one more! It's that indefinable something that makes us all wonder at the resources vested in us. Someday, I hope I shall have the privilege of revealing the true story of these who have measured up so nobly.

Though death has played an all-important part in this terrible drama, and the nausea of indescribable horror has constantly beset us, we've stood before the constant attacks of the enemy and sent him reeling each time he's sought to dislodge us. Often, I've marveled at what necessity will demand of me, and how I will meet these requirements. In my usual flippant manner, I've heretofore let the future take care of itself and adjusted the resources at hand to take care of the present.

Never before have I carried these personal expedients of the present in any direct relationship to the future. Now as life moves so swiftly, it still cannot be within my humble talents to envision far ahead, but I find myself envisioning things in a little different perspective than heretofore. It all adds up to the irrefutable fact that I'm getting older, I guess.

When the next day arrives, I seek to recall the events just passed, but believe it or not, there are so many things happening, one cannot remember much except that it was tough! With planes diving, bombing, strafing, artillery, mortars, tanks and the entire arsenal of land warfare descending all around, it is such utter chaos that you merely exist in a state of semi-consciousness as to the actual part you are playing in it all. Nerves no longer exist, and the peculiar part of that is oft times a shell lands ten feet away, yet you are not disturbed while another may explode a hundred yards away and the blast knocks you back like a punch on the jaw. So it goes.

Today is clear, and the devastation that is so complete as far as the eye can see is in sharp focus and reveals the terrific battle that rages. The paradox is that amid the diabolical horror of it all is the hill that has long been dubbed by my men—who named it first as they came up on it before any other units—with the Christ on Gethsemane. Now, this symbol is broken and shattered with only the broken stone, still recalling to all of us the once revered and sacred spot. The hill has the one characteristic, however, for it has been stained countless times with the blood of those who have laid their lives upon this altar in order to gain freedom for all.

The future indeed does not offer much assurance of bringing an early end to this mess. My personal observation from the tenacity of the enemy is the belief that he will fight 'til the bitter end, so gird yourselves for more sorrow and terrible suffering before the finale. We will continue in our way to carry out our responsibilities here, so know that the events to come may not be as optimistic as before thought would be the case. . . .

This is all for today, October 11, 1944, which you will recall when you receive this letter as one of marked significance.

On October 15, the enemy launched a final assault, this time spearheaded by the 3rd Panzer Grenadier Division.[15] Although VIII Corps had reported that the enemy division was moving north and could be expected in the Big Red One's sector at anytime, the first indications of the attack came around noon, when an enemy force infiltrated up the railroad draw and engaged G and I Companies with small arms fire. Approximately eight tanks supported the attack.

Again, the intensity of the attack carried the enemy into Dawson's lines, and again, Dawson called in final protective artillery fire within ten yards of his own CP. By 1300, the enemy had overrun a portion of G Company's lines, but the Germans were receiving heavy casualties from mass concentrations of mortar, artillery, and machine-gun fire.

How close was it? The *Regimental Journal* provides a clear picture of the intensity of the action. Here's a sample of what happened during a period of two hours.[16]

1210:S-3 (Wozenski) to 18th Infantry S-3: The right of G Company and I Company, an enemy attack. Wozenski says they have been using railroad draw as an approach.

1227:Second Battalion 2 to S-3: Our communication lines are out with G and I Companies. Situation serious. Considerable amount of small arms, mostly enemy.

1241:S-3 to F.A. Battalion S-3: I just got a report from the Second Battalion that G and I Companies are being overrun. They want fire immediately.

1242:Second Battalion C.O. to Lt. Kestlinger (liaison officer): We want air immediately . . . eight tanks with Infantry overrunning I and G Companies . . . they are hitting me hard. Get a Divarty (Division Artillery) shoot on the woods.

1242:S-3 to Division G-3: Infiltration around the right flank of
G company. Engaged in small arms fight. I Company is
being hit from the north in considerable strength. . . . We
want air out there immediately. Tanks are moving in on I
and G Companies.

1244:Major Rawie (artillery liaison officer) to F.A. Battalion S-
3: Priority mission for Divarty. G and I Companies are being overrun with tanks and infantry.

1258:Regt. C.O. to Second Battalion C.O.: What is the situation? Second Battalion C.O. We are out of communication
with Richmond and Dawson. A message came that G and
I Companies were being overrun. Situation critical. Wanted
artillery on Point 61 and woods in vicinity. A message just
came from Dawson. Situation very critical.

1310:S-3 to Second Battalion Executive Officer: Situation critical. If G and I Companies are knocked off, it will be difficult to regain it.

1336:G-3 to S-3: B Company of 18th ordered to Eilendorf to
be in support of you. The idea is to throw them in any gap
that occurs. No air yet. Artillery all firing now. 1st Battalion, 26th Infantry, less one company has been alerted,
and has one company of tanks with them. Keep us posted.

1346:G-3 to Lt. Kestlinger: Planes coming from 30th Division.
No bombs, but plenty of ammunition. Here is something
that just came in, apparently from forward Observer. Reports attack beaten off.

1414:G-3 to S-3: What is your situation now? (S-3) Considerable enemy tanks and half-tracks assembled at (gives coordinates). We put artillery in that area. . . . Infantry attacked I and G Companies. Seven tanks came in on G
Company. . . . Had a fire fight. We put plenty of artillery in
on the attack. We got a report that G and I Companies
were overrun. The situation is clearing some.

1417:Second Battalion S-3 to S-3: I Company situation under
control at the moment, but the enemy close in strength. G
Company situation still tense, especially on the left. . . .
We would like some more air.

In the midst of the assault, the commander of the 16th Regiment's
second battalion, who had commanded so gallantly since D-Day,
cracked under pressure. The battalion staff officers were virtually

zombies without direction; consequently, Colonel Frederick W. Gibb, the regimental commander, had to take drastic action. On the recommendation of several junior officers, Gibb relieved the battalion commander that afternoon. Until a replacement was named, it fell to Major Ed Wozenski and the frontline commanders to coordinate the defense.[17]

Once again, officers like Joe Dawson, Karl Wolf, and Kimball Richmond met the challenge. Massing tremendous amounts of artillery fire to offset the German numerical advantage, the commanders withstood the assault. Then, the heavens cleared, and P-47s came to the rescue, targeting enemy armor and troop concentrations. By 1500, the enemy tanks withdrew, and mass concentrations of mortar, artillery, and machine-gun fire repulsed the infantry. At 1614, the German penetration had been sealed, and the situation restored.

Evening brought no respite, with the enemy attempting to infiltrate Dawson's lines under cover of darkness. At approximately 1040, G Company's commander reported to regiment that the critical area to his front was an orchard where the Germans were now attacking with fresh troops. A German tank platoon took the company under direct fire, but the Americans resisted valiantly until a company from the 26th Regiment moved forward to support them. In the meantime, Dawson, now commanding a task force of infantry and armor, moved his own armor forward and engaged the enemy. The Germans temporarily withdrew, but they maintained a steady fire on Dawson's position.

Shortly after four o'clock on the morning of October 16, the enemy attacked again, this time in company strength. Quickly overrunning two squads, they poured through the gap in Dawson's lines. Within seconds, the enemy was among the foxholes, and their tanks were within twenty-five yards of the company's main defensive line.

Soon thereafter, a second German company and three tanks struck I Company as well. The situation was as critical as the preceding day, and Dawson reported to the 16th Regimental headquarters that he was unsure whether he could hold off another attack. The men were worn out, yet Dawson's infantry again proved equal to the occasion. With armor support, he counterattacked and regained a lost pillbox, then destroyed the enemy tanks in G Company's sector. In the process, his men killed seventeen Germans and then another eight in a subsequent attack. It had been a brutal two-day fight in which Dawson's nerves were strained, but not broken.

What was it like in the forward foxholes of G Company? Decaying enemy bodies littered the battlefield to Dawson's front. It was gruesome to see the stages of decay proceed from killed, to bloated, to maggot-infested and rotting, to partially exposed bones—like some biological clock marking the inexorable passage of time. Added to the awful stench of the dead of both sides was the repulsive odor from thousands of rotting, discarded rations and human excrement everywhere. It remained virtually impossible to practice even the simplest field sanitation in the forward positions.

Field sanitation during combat was usually the responsibility of the individual soldier, but in G Company, it was impossible to leave the safety of the foxhole because of the constant artillery bombardment. Consequently, a soldier typically defecated in an empty grenade canister or ration can, threw it out of his hole, and scooped dirt over it the next day if he was not under heavy enemy fire.[18]

Throughout it all, G Company held its position in the face of overwhelming enemy numbers. Why had the troop succeeded? There were certainly many other companies that had compiled an equally impressive combat record. Too humble to credit himself for G Company's success, Dawson turned to the junior leaders.

In the commander's words,

> The real leaders in G Company were the sergeants, the squad leaders. Real success rested almost exclusively with the squad leaders. Due to the casualties suffered by the junior officers since D-Day, many newly arrived platoon leaders were not well equipped for the task at hand. The officers did not have time to mature, since they were thrown into battle during the later stages of the war. The spirit of the army was centered in the noncommissioned officer corps. The best platoon leaders earned their commissions in the field, having emerged from the unit. They seized the initiative and exerted the requirements of leadership.[19]

That was only part of the story, however. On October 16, the day after the initial onslaught, a number of correspondents were at the front, seeking a full explanation of just what had taken place and what the situation was at the moment. All of the correspondents were newspaper or radio reporters who wanted to get the scoop on what was then the biggest story of the war. They included Bill White of the Associated Press; Drew Middleton of the *New York Times;* Jack Frankish of the United Press; Bill Heinz of the *New York Sun;* Bunny Austin of an outfit in Australia; and George Hicks and Gordon Fraser of the NBC Blue Radio Network.[20]

The newsmen were aghast at Dawson's appearance. The six-foot-two-inch captain was so thin, his uniform hung loosely on him. He had lost twenty-five pounds in the previous five weeks. Heinz described him as having a "bony face and large ears and very brown eyes, long straight black hair. His nose didn't stick out from his face, but ran straight along, down through the middle."[21]

The real reason for the American success lay in Dawson's own words—courage and determination. Speaking to war correspondent Heinz after five weeks in the line, the beleaguered commander reflected on the loneliness of leaders who must make the crucial decisions in war. Heinz particularly wanted to know how Dawson had held it together against so many determined assaults. For several days, the correspondents remained at the company CP, observing Dawson, talking to soldiers, and visiting the GIs in their foxholes.

Scattered around Dawson's basement CP was a table with maps and magazines. On another table against the far wall, dance music was emanating from a small shiny radio. Next to the radio were two field phones—black phones resting on tan leather cases. They connected the captain to his platoons out in the mud less than a hundred yards away, and with the 16th Regimental CP in the rear. Beside the phones, radio, and maps were one candle and one small kerosene lamp for illumination.[22] It was not much light, noted Gordon Fraser, but it was enough so they could see each other's faces.

As the correspondents gathered around the table in a semicircle, Dawson asked, "Do you know why we have this cellar here? You know why this candle burns here? It's because of those guys out there, and I don't have to tell you what they've got. It's mud. It's deep in the ground, and the water seeps in. It's horrible. It stinks. It's got lice in it. It's cold and it's exposed. Out there on this ridge, starting fifty yards from here, there are kids who have nothing, except wet and cold and shelling and misery and the Germans coming at them, and they're dying."[23]

Before long, Bill Heinz got the commander to elaborate. And when Dawson spoke, he gave the correspondent the most vivid portrayal of a rifle company commander in combat in the European theater. "Nobody will ever know what this has been like up here. You aren't big enough to tell them, and I'm not big enough to tell them, and nobody can tell them," Dawson said.

Heinz promised to do his best and asked Dawson to address the strain of sending American boys to die. Dawson responded, "I had a kid come up and say, 'I can't take it anymore.' What could I do? If I lose you, I lose a squad. If I lose a squad, I lose a platoon. If I lose a platoon, we lose this ridge, and we're not gonna lose this ridge. So I grab him by the shirt, and I say, 'You will, you will. There ain't any going back from this hill except the dead.' Then I turn him around, and he goes out, and I watch, and a mortar comes in, and he's dead."

He continued,

> I've lost 112 out of 136, but we took your goddamn ridge and we're holding it . . . we came up here and we died. We died right here, because they'll never be another G Company like this one. Never. . . . How do you think I feel when I tell them there is no coming off the hill? They come in and say . . . 'I can't stand it any longer. I can't. I can't' . . . and I take them by the shirt and say, "You will . . . you will . . . you've got to stand it in spite of yourself.' And what do they do? They go back up there and die.

Another time, two dirty and unshaven GIs—Sergeant William Cuff from Girardville, Pennsylvania, and PFC James Mullen of Pittsburgh—reported to the CP. "Sergeant Cuff, I'm sending you both to Paris for a six-day furlough," Dawson announced as the two men stood, holding their helmets in their hands, in the middle of the room. "Thank you, Captain," Cuff replied, and Mullen said the same thing. "Well, you had better like it, and you better stay out of trouble. Please, for me, stay out of trouble, and if you get in trouble, find a hole and crawl into it. But have a good time, and bless your hearts." The two GIs then turned around and walked out, and Cuff's rifle, which was slung over his shoulder, banged on the door as it shut behind them.

Why had they been selected, inquired Heinz? "Two of the best boys I've got," the captain replied. "I've said right along that when I got a chance to send somebody back, they'd be the first. Wire boys, they've had to run new lines every day because the old ones were chopped up. One day, they laid heavy wire for 200 yards, and by the time Cuff got to the end and worked back, the wire was cut in three places by shell fire."

Pausing for a moment, Dawson continued, "Another time, they put a phone up to one of my machine guns, and by the time Cuff got back to tell me to try the phone, the machine gun had been blown up. So I have been thinking for a long time that they would be the first to have some fun when I could send somebody back." The next morning, a lieutenant came in and informed Dawson, "Captain," he said, "Cuff and Mullen say they don't want to go."

217

"All right," Dawson sighed, "Get two other guys—if you can."[24]

Dawson also informed Heinz that he had men who had been wounded in mid-September and had returned because they were concerned for their buddies if G Company remained on the ridge. Just as Dawson had done after he was hit on D-Day, they went AWOL from the field hospital and returned to their platoons. Dawson couldn't explain it. What made men want to return to this inferno? It was absolutely crazy.

"Somehow they get out of those hospitals, and the first thing I know, they show up again here, and they're grinning from ear to ear." Left unsaid was the camaraderie that existed among the fighting men of Dawson's Company G, a closeness that compelled soldiers to repeatedly risk their lives for their buddies on the front line.

Heinz and Dawson covered a wide range of topics, including the almost unbearable burden of commanding GIs in combat. How did Dawson do it? "I have got to answer those guys because I wear the bars. I've got the responsibility, and I don't know whether I'm big enough for the job. But I can't break now. I've taken this for thirty-nine days, and I'm in the middle of the Siegfried Line, and you want to know what I think? I think it stinks."

Then Captain Joe Dawson put his head in his hands and one of the toughest fighting commanders in the Big Red One broke down and cried. There was not a sound in the room. Heinz remembered that nobody even moved, and it must have been about fifteen seconds before the captain raised his head and did a peculiar thing. Without looking at anybody, he said, "Shut up! Shut up, I want to hear this. It's the 'Bell Song' from *Lakme*." The radio was clear and the soprano's voice was soft, and so was the string accompaniment. "No," Dawson said, "Not Puccini. Not Puccini, but I can't remember the name of the guy."

By September 17, the German attack had spent its force. Huebner quickly demanded the city's surrender, and effective resistance ceased on the twenty-first, just before the 1st Division launched a final assault on the four-story bunker housing *Oberst* Gerhard Wilck, the commandant of the garrison of Aachen. *Time* magazine reported that two U.S. sergeants who had been taken prisoner carried the surrender flag.

The German commandant initially refused to surrender unconditionally out of fear of Nazi retaliation against his family, but the Americans insisted, and so Wilck wrote another draft that said: "Aachen's defending German garrison ran out of food and ammunition. I am forced to give up my command and surrender Aachen unconditionally, with all its stores, to the commanding officer of the victorious Americans."[25]

With Wilck's capitulation, the Battle of Aachen was history. The Americans had paid a stiff price: the 30th Division suffered 3,100 casualties, the 1st Division a comparable number in proportion to the number of troops engaged. Over the course of thirty-nine days, Dawson's G Company, minus attachments, suffered 11 killed in action, 33 wounded, and 4 missing, from an average daily strength of approximately 6 officers and 140 enlisted men.[26]

In his conversations with World War II veterans, historian Stephen Ambrose remarked that one night in a foxhole in Belgium or Germany was memorable, but ten, twenty, thirty nights was hell. Thirty-nine nights was worse than hell. And yet for thirty-nine days in the fall of 1944, the men of G Company, under the inspirational leadership of the son of a Waco preacher, fought and died in their foxholes along what entered 1st Infantry Division lore as "Dawson's Ridge."

When they write the history of these campaigns, Heinz reported, "They will tell you that this ridge was the key to Aachen. This is where three German divisions tried to crack through the shell we had thrown out beyond Aachen while we cleaned up the city." By battle's end, Aachen remained secure.

With the battle won, Dawson's initial thoughts were of home and family. Two weeks after G Company was pulled from the line, he wrote his grandfather to express his pride, as well as to inform him that he had reached the end of his tether. Five months of combat had taken its toll.

Dawson to My Dear Grandfather

October 28, 1944

The strangeness of life ever brings unusual situations and circumstances to mind, whenever I set [sic] down and start to write a letter. At the present moment, I am most comfortably ensconced in a concrete fortification that still has the blood of men smeared within its interior. The good part about it, however, is that it was Germans who suffered and not my boys. It's just another segment of the Siegfried Line, and right now, things are simply perfect. Not one enemy shell has landed near me for three hours, so after the constant hell of weeks past, this is something of a record.

Grandfather, you have so many children who have measured up to life's tests, so much more so than I, yet I want you to know that here, in faraway Germany, I fought a never-to-be-forgotten battle and denied the enemy three times. The press has dubbed the spot "Dawson Ridge," and yet I feel it should be known as hallowed ground for those who died there. The horror and ghastly side of life and death was encountered by all of us, so rather than your name and mine, posterity should know it as another tribute to the blessed men who lost their all on the spot.

My nerves are somewhat shattered as a result of such constant pressure these past bitter months, yet my faith remains unshaken, and God has always answered my prayers for strength. You who have seen life for many years know wherein I say that these bitter tragic months of terrible war leave one morally as well as physically exhausted. Yet the heritage that came to me through you, Dad and Mother will never falter, I promise you. Only through this innate strength that has been given me by my forebears has enabled me to stand up. I'm deeply proud of you and Dad, and know that I shall ever seek to carry out the tasks of life, honorably and without discredit to you.

In this terrible war, life is short and very futile, yet I pray each day to God that I shall have the privilege of seeing my loved ones once more. If this cannot be, I just want you to know that I love you with a tenderness and devotion that can never be expressed in words. It's just the intangible quality that has given me the courage to meet life. God bless you, Grandfather, and know my heart is ever there, and someday, I hope we will be together once more.

For its role in the defense of the city during the final attack, G and I Companies, 16th Infantry Regiment, received the Presidential Unit Citation. The citation read in part:

> During the period 15–17 October 1944, companies "G" and "I," 16th Infantry, lodged in captured fortifications along the outskirts of Eilendorf, Germany, were charged with defending a ridge overlooking the commanding approaches to Aachen. . . . For three days, the strength, courage and determination of two infantry companies stood between elements of the German army and a serious breakthrough of the First Infantry Division's foothold on German soil. In this seventy-two-hour battle, the defenders faced at different times, three battalions of enemy troops and approximately twenty-five tanks, sus-

taining thirty-seven major casualties against an estimated 300 for the enemy. The magnificent heroism, combat proficiency and brilliant achievements of Companies G and I, 16th Infantry, helped pave the way for the eventual capture of Aachen.[27]

The official army history did G Company one better. Noting the futility of the *3rd Panzer Grenadier Division*'s constant attacks, the record demonstrated that the enemy division had lost approximately one-third of its combat effectives. The men of the 16th Infantry could attest to these losses, for in front of G Company alone were 250 dead, "a figure," the division operations officer noted, was "unprecedented in the Division's history."

That went a long way toward explaining why the *3rd Panzer Grenadier Division* never again came close to breaking the Big Red One's defensive arc. Quite simply, the Germans had lost their chance to break through the ever-tightening encirclement, thwarted by a lone rifle company that would not recognize when it was beaten.[28]

Recognition of his command constituted Dawson's proudest professional achievement, far more significant in his eyes than any personal honors he had received at the hands of the supreme commander. Eisenhower also nominated the Big Red One to receive the Distinguished Unit Citation, stating that the fighting surrounding Aachen was the outstanding operation of the 1st Infantry Division in the European theater. That was the big picture. On the front line, all that had stood against German success was what Dawson termed "just one lousy little old G.I. company"—one lousy company and the indomitable spirit of its commander.

Dawson remained immensely proud of his company's achievement to his dying day. In his eyes, they had measured up in the most critical combat yet experienced on the European continent. Was there anything he would have done differently if he had it to do all over again? He didn't think so.

"I tried to do the best I knew how. That was always the hallmark of my character. I took seriously my role as a leader of men with the total responsibility resting on me. I felt keenly that any deviation, on or off duty, would have been detrimental."

He had seen a number of officers who faltered in discharging their duties, men who failed to measure up, whether through lack of initiative or lack of awareness of responsibility. "I felt a sense of personal responsibility for my men. I was where the buck stopped. If I made the right decision, we'd make it. No game in life is more deadly, more absolute, than war. Always present is the necessity of measuring up to responsibility, when you have men's lives in the palm of your hand. You must make the right decision. Far too many battle wounds were the result of negligence."[29] And on the Verlautenheide ridge, Dawson consistently made the correct decisions.

Dawson also took immense pride in a letter he received from his forward observer, who was convalescing in a field hospital. Written on the final day of the German offensive, the officer placed G Company's achievement in perspective.

Lawrence Johnson to Joe Dawson[30]

October 17, 1944

I am enclosing a few clippings in which I thought you might be interested. It was published in the *Daily Express* on Tuesday, October 17, 1944.

You and G Company certainly have been covering yourselves with glory. They can always count on the 2nd Battalion when the going gets really tough.

I have often thought about you—wondering whether the Jerries ever got a direct hit on that CP of yours, which they shelled so much—they sure tried hard enough. I seem to get hit every time the going gets rough. I guess I just can't take it.

I certainly hope you . . . and all the rest of them are OK. Give my best to them all.

Take care of yourself and congratulations on one hell of a swell job. One day, I'll be saying, "I was once the FO for Dawson of Dawson Ridge!"

P.S. How did Verlautenheide look after all that artillery we poured on it?

During the final week of October, Captain Joe Dawson relinquished command of G Company and was evacuated from the front. After five months of commanding soldiers in combat, he was mentally and physically exhausted. Combat fatigue had finally extracted its toll. The constant pounding from the previous thirty-nine days had not only shattered his nerves, but had also left him a physical wreck. What Dawson needed was a respite from the front line. He hoped that a few months of peace would restore some vim to his fighting spirit.

Other unit commanders experienced similar problems. After two weeks of hellish fighting in the Hurtgen Forest, Captain George Wilson of F Company, 22nd Infantry, had to fight with all he had to keep from going to pieces. He had seen so many others go, he knew he was on the "black edges." After nearly fifteen days of brutally inhuman fighting in those damned woods, he confessed that he, too, had reached his breaking point.

On one day alone, he lost three of four company officers, all his medics, all his noncoms, and 90 of 140 riflemen. The toughest thing for Wilson that terrible day was to hear stricken men all over a slope of a hill crying out for a medic who was no longer there. During the peak of the shelling, the lieutenant leading his left platoon simply went berserk and had to be sent to the rear. Replacing him with a new officer, Wilson ordered him to attack an adjacent hill. The lieutenant immediately began to cry, and he sobbed that he couldn't do it. Coming in fresh and going out onto that hill looked to him like an execution.

That was life on the front line as U.S. Army soldiers invaded Germany. The ordeal was beyond human comprehension, and Wilson could not understand how anyone, including himself, survived. Throughout the battle he had barely maintained his composure.[31] Wilson, like Dawson, had simply reached the limit of his physical and emotional endurance.

Thirty days of continuous combat on Peleliu also left Private First Class Sledge an emotional wreck. Speaking only from a personal perspective and making no generalizations, Sledge could just as well have been describing Dawson's experience at Aachen as he was his own. What those thirty days of severe, unrelenting inhuman emotional and physical stress revealed to Sledge were proof that: he could trust and depend completely on the marine on each side of him and on his leadership; his men could use their weapons and equipment efficiently under severe stress; and the critical factor in combat is duration of the combat rather than the severity.[32]

Reporter Ernie Pyle had also reached his personal limit, which he expressed in his final column from Europe on September 5. Asked why he was leaving, Pyle replied, "I'm leaving for one reason only— because I have just got to stop. 'I've had it,' as they say in the army. I have had all I can take for a while. . . . I've been twenty-nine months overseas since this war started; have written around 700,000 words about it; have totaled nearly a year in the front lines. I do hate terribly to leave right now, but I have given out. I've been immersed in it too long. My spirit is wobbly, and my mind is confused. The hurt has finally become too great."[33] All of a sudden, it seemed to Pyle that if he heard one more shot or saw one more dead man, he "would go off his nut. And if I had to write one more column, I'd collapse. So I'm on my way."

Like Pyle, Dawson had spent twenty-eight months overseas. Moreover, he had been in constant combat for six weeks. Noted historian Ambrose, it was a wonder that more commanders didn't break under the stress of combat considering the additional burden placed upon them of making decisions constantly, under pressure, when they had been deprived of sleep and adequate food.[34] That was true in Dawson's case. Having lost twenty-five pounds while defending the ridge, the commander needed time to rest and recuperate for the trials that lay ahead.

9
Return to Europe

*Though I know war in all its bitterest forms, I found even my
jaded senses shocked at this house of horror.*

Following a brief visit to Paris and London, Dawson returned to
the United States, where he prepared to assume new duties with
the Office of Strategic Services (OSS). He was surprised at his
welcome in Washington: nearly every senior officer paid tribute to
the "hero of Dawson's Ridge." Gordon Fraser's graphic broadcasts
and Bill Heinz's scintillating columns depicting the defense of the
Verlautenheide ridge had made G Company's former commander a
national hero.

Granted a generous leave before reporting for his next overseas
assignment, Dawson returned to Waco to see his parents. A few days
later, he checked in to McCloskey General Hospital, where he enjoyed
a private room. While he regained his strength, he contemplated his
next duty assignment, which he anticipated being in the Pacific Theater. Life at McCloskey was a far cry from the front, and in the evenings, his mind returned to his beloved company.

Dawson to Colonel Fred W. Gibb[1]

November 25, 1944

As this is the first letter I have sought to write since my return
home, you will understand the circumstances under which I am
doing it. But I felt that my first letter should be inscribed to you for
a number of reasons—most of all, the fact that I was unable to
come by the CP and personally tell you goodbye. That, in itself,
was keenly felt by me, and one of my greatest regrets in leaving.
But when the wheels of administration began to move, I could do
[little] on my own, and as a consequence, was hurried about thither
and yon until I finally reached Washington.

So it has been, and only the assurance that when our respective tasks are finished and the situation allows, I want to make a
date with you, and we will explore the past together over a con-
genial bottle of Scotch and plot the destinies of the future.

I will only briefly comment on the mechanics of returning home by reviewing a few of my experiences. Upon leaving the 1st Division, I went to Paris with Ken Downs and spent four days there awaiting orders to be cut, which called for air transportation to Washington. Naturally, I wasn't idle during that period and was able to see much of Paris; even though it was done mostly at night. . . . I left Paris by plane and then stayed in London until I could secure overseas passage, which took another four days. Aside from going on a party with the boys who sank the *Tirpitz*, the stay was uneventful. They were swell, and I got the first hand report from Wing Commander Tate, who led the mission. All were most keen on our doings there in Germany, so in truth, it was a sort of mutual admiration society.

The only other thing of interest to relate about the trip was the fact that I virtually flew the Atlantic twice before I finally got home. My plane was originally scheduled to go by way of the Azores, and we started in that direction. When we almost reached this point, the weather took a sudden turn for the worse and closed in, necessitating us to return to Pristwick. All told, this little jaunt consumed about 12 hours.

Well, we struck out again that afternoon, this time by way of Iceland and Newfoundland. This time, we were successful and come right along all the way to Washington without incident and most comfortably. It's really amazing when you realize how air travel has reduced the time and space factor. The future indeed will dwarf it even more.

I reported to General Donovan upon arrival in Washington, and he was most gracious in his reception.[2] In fact, I was somewhat embarrassed by the hospitable manner in which everyone greeted me. It seems that the damn radio and press alike had played up my small participation in the action there at Aachen to a rather alarming degree. As a consequence, the publicity had colored the facts a bit. Nevertheless, the General was most solicitous for my welfare, and granted me a most liberal leave in order to visit my family and regain my strength.

You, of course, are more keenly aware of the need for the latter than most people. And as this hospital is only a few miles from home, I requested admittance just as soon as I had spent a few days with my family. Here, they are giving me a complete checkup and stuffing vitamins, glucose pills and God-knows-what into me in order to bring my weight up. Nothing is bothering me, and I have nice private room without the noise and bother of a ward. And everyone is most helpful in trying to fix me up as quickly as possible. So with no visitors, plenty of food and sleep, I hope to be "in the pink" by Christmas.

I am not sure just when I will leave for China, but if the body responds to all the treatment, and I get back in shape, it will probably mean sometime around the 1st of February. As to the assignment, it sounds most interesting as it will involve a command and test not only my abilities, both mental and physical, but also my ingenuity and resourcefulness.

It *will not* be a seat-warming job, nor will it be a non-combatant job. So whatever the thing brings forth, you can know that I shall be doing my best to live up to all of you who are carrying on over there. In truth, it will probably be hell in more ways than one, and the living conditions will undoubtedly be bad, still if it's a job worth doing, it will be worth every bit of effort I can put forth to see it done well. I shall keep you posted as time passes.

I cannot write what's in my heart when I think about old "G" Company, but I can say to you that it was a privilege and honor that will ever remain as the outstanding event of my life to have commanded the outfit. Measured in terms of the scroll of war, our little group never once faltered or failed to accomplish the mission, though the cost was sometimes great. Their noble spirit and indomitable will were ever present, and their unsurpassed courage was something out of another world. I'm deeply proud of them, Colonel, and pray God will see them through the remainder of this war. I know they are in good hands in John Finke, and I shall closely follow them in the days to come.[3] They made a home for me in that company, and I shall never forget them for it. Then the old 16th Infantry is *the* regiment of the world. Someday, when the war is over, we will truly have much to be proud of, but somehow my deepest satisfaction is in the knowledge that I served with the finest of them all.

May you ever know that my sincerest best wishes go with you wherever your destiny leads you, and my earnest prayers for your welfare will be offered each day.

On January 1, 1945, Dawson returned to Washington for reassignment to the Foreign Service. He was not at all displeased to discover that instead of being transferred to the Pacific, OSS had reassigned him for extended service in Europe.

The tone of his letters changed considerably from the previous autumn, when his primary concern had been the lives of the men entrusted to his care. Early in 1945 he wrote of visiting historical sites, the changing weather, and his improving health. At times, he drifted to memories of combat, but Dawson realized that aside from an occasional visit to the front, his combat days were probably over, at least in the short term.

January also brought a much-deserved promotion to the rank of major, and in that capacity, Dawson began his service with the OSS.[4] A final physical checkup at McCloskey General Hospital cleared him for overseas duty. By February, he was in London for unspecified duties.

Dawson to My Dear Family

February 17, 1945
London

Once more, I am over here, but this time, with slightly different status as well as feelings. Nevertheless, we will see how things work out. The trip was all right and rather uneventful. No ill effects, though somewhat of an ordeal from the weather standpoint. But it's quite pleasant here in London, and not at all cold.

Will secure a billet here tomorrow if I can locate one, so will let you know the outcome on completion of the deal. Everyone most gracious and have enjoyed their reception very much. Feel sure I shall be able to dispose of my work here with much more effectiveness than had I gone the other way.

Will write in greater detail tomorrow concerning certain other matters that relate to the senior members of the family—meantime, be assured I am well, reasonably happy and in good fettle.

Dawson to My Dearest Ones

February 22, 1945
London

The wonderful weather here the past week has been most acceptable to all concerned, even though I contracted a cold earlier in the week. However, it has now disappeared, and I am feeling grand. I started to write last night, but made the mistake of trying to do it propped up in bed—sure enough, I dropped off to sleep and as a consequence, virtually slept the clock around.

This is a most gratifying sign to me, as it is the first time in months that such a thing has been possible. As I told you at home, this insomnia or catnap type of sleep has haunted me ever since Aachen, and I'm hoping the spell has been broken. Living on a high tension with lots on my mind has been anything but conducive to an eight-hour unbroken sleep. Let's hope for the best. . . . .

There has been little to report insofar as my sojourn here in London is concerned. I've been busy acquainting myself with the demands of the new work, and in my odd moments, have sought to answer all the mass of back correspondence. This has indeed been a rather big job in itself, and I trust you will receive favorable repercussions from them. . . .

I hope all are well there at home. I have asked Donna to write me all the pertinent information relative to Roy that may be checked in France.[5] I shall be there sometime and will find out everything I possibly can. As this is about all that can now be done, I so hope her period of readjustment will not be too trying. . . . My tenderest love to each of you. I know you will be thinking of me as I of you.

Dawson to My Dear Family

February 25, 1945
Somewhere in France

The letterhead will reveal the presence now being far removed from the London fog. Here, the beautiful sunshine and bracing crisp air collaborate to give one a sense of well-being, though far away from home. Indeed, I found a great sense of satisfaction to once more be near the fighting front, though not *too* near. However, in the distance, the sound of the artillery can be plainly heard.

I was in Paris only briefly, so was unable to do much aside from purely business. . . . I spent a most interesting afternoon in Strasbourg, where I strolled around the town and visited the various points of interest. The dominant edifice is the magnificent cathedral, which is regarded as one of the finest in the world. It is fifteenth century, and has one of the most magnificent spires I have ever seen. The ravages of war have fallen upon the city rather severely, and even this fine structure has had the mark of war upon it. All the windows are either destroyed or removed, and the interior is not open to the public. But the exterior is really lovely, being deep, rich rose-colored sandstone . . . with innumerable figures.

The other portions of the city have much of interest, both from an aesthetic as well as historical standpoint. In company with a French friend of mine who knew the city well, we went down to what is known as the old part of the city, which still has the walls around it. It dates back to the fourteenth century, the very spot bespoke a wealth of lore, and one's imagination could run wild. It was truly a most profitable afternoon, and I enjoyed myself immensely.

Well, with March just around the corner, I feel sure that the warm weather will be here soon. At the present moment, it is quite lovely, and though there is a snap in the air, it is not uncomfortable and indeed quite acceptable. I had feared a rather bitter cold and snow to greet me, but it seems this has long since gone. It is quite agreeable, particularly when one thinks of the lads up in the foxholes. As for me, I am most comfortably set up and have no cause for complaint. . . . So be assured I shall weather the remainder of these days (I hope) in comfortable surroundings. . . .

Dawson to My Dear Family

February 28, 1945
Deep in France

Surely the fortunes of war have provided me a liberal education, and what with all the past scenes I've witnessed and the places I've visited, I find a distinct pleasure in having the opportunity to add another section of this continent to my long list. And as the weather has been very mild and pleasant, I've found travel a real pleasure and have enjoyed myself to the utmost, particularly in view of the fact that I am not exposed to the rigors of combat in its fiercest way. The compensations have indeed been generous, and my good fortune, both in the past and present, has made me realize how well life has treated me.

My health is almost unbelievable, as I have been eating more than I can ever remember, and when ten o'clock comes, I am usually deep in sleep. This, too, has been most gratifying, for aside from an occasional nightmare, I virtually sleep the clock around. Fortunately, fresh eggs are to be found in plentiful numbers, so I manage a most formidable breakfast . . . so if I can continue in my present state, I feel sure I will soon be an applicant for the "circus fat boy" assignment.

The news today is most heartening, as I learn that the old 1st Army is moving once more. Surely, no other group of men has contributed more to the success of this war than has my old organization. I so hope I will be able to see them before too many weeks pass, and nothing would give me more pleasure than to follow them into the heart of Germany. . . .

Today is a beautiful one, with the air clear and the sun beaming down gloriously. The cloudless sky augurs well for operations in the air, and hence the war can be accelerated toward conclusion. . . . Though the tragedy of it all mars the beauty somewhat, I still feel that in bringing it to an end as soon as possible, we will be much better off.

One thing that does amuse me, however, is the way all the little nations are climbing aboard the bandwagon, as today marks the end of the time allowed by the Yalta Conference to join the United Nations. If only Tierra del Fuego would declare war, I think that would complete the group.

But the serious side does enable one to enjoy a feeling that the majority of the world is in accord with the precepts we base our actions upon. I do find the report Mr. Churchill made to Parliament yesterday most comprehensive, yet there is an underlying attitude of subservience to the dominant role that Russia took in the discussions. Of course, I cannot but feel the Polish problem will cause many headaches in the future, still, I am not sufficiently informed on the political trade-outs to make any clear or accurate surmise on the matter. There is much comment in the British papers about this question, and several strong editorials have appeared denouncing the decision and showing how far from the Atlantic Charter the matter has strayed. Yet it seems that we will see as an outgrowth of Yalta an arbitrary attitude adopted by the big three in fashioning the peace.

One cannot develop any positive understanding of the real American thought on this problem because in Washington, there did not appear to be any well-defined sentiment in regard to the majority of the nation, but that may have been due, at the time of my departure, to the rather limited amount of information released up to that time as to the decisions reached. I shall watch with great interest the coming San Francisco conference, and if you go to it, Dad, I would like very much to know your reactions and just how broad the American representation will be. There is, of course, a feeling of hurt on the part of France for her exclusion from Yalta and the De Gaulle-Roosevelt incident, but this seems a bit elementary to me, so cannot feel too concerned about it.

Well, this is about all I can report on the close of February. Just know I am quite well and happy, and hope that ere too many more months elapse, I will be returning to America.

With the war winding down to a successful conclusion, Major Dawson returned briefly to the front in the 36th Division's sector. To his relief, association with combat soldiers produced pleasant memories of the camaraderie that exists only among frontline units. It was like "old home week," as he described in his next letter to his family. The three months' rest had obviously done some good.

Dawson to My Dear Family

March 3, 1945
France

I spent a very interesting day yesterday, as I visited the front in company with an old friend of mine who was formerly in the regiment with me and who now is in command of a regiment of the 36th Division. The front was comparatively quiet with no big events taking place in the particular sector we visited, though we were accorded a brief, but rather severe, barrage of mortars and light artillery.

It seemed very much like old home week for me, and I was comforted at my nervous reaction to it. In fact, the strange part of it all was the fact that I almost relished it, and it really gave me a measure of pleasure. So there appears to have been little permanent disorders for the old trials and experiences. In fact, I think I was the calmest of the lot, but then that is because of my long rest. . . .

There is really little I can say of any noteworthiness [sic] as I am in the throes of work that is slightly different than any I had been engaged in before. . . . Also, there is not the strict responsibility that I formerly had, so the old heart and mind are not strained as much as before. Do try and keep me informed, though when I finally receive the mail, I will, I trust, have an abundance.

In March, as the Allied armies raced across Germany's west wall and prepared to bridge the Rhine, Dawson witnessed his initial glimpse of a Nazi concentration camp. The experience repulsed the affable

Texan and convinced him that all of the bloodletting had not been in vain. He had never observed such ghastly horror at the hands of human beings.

Dawson to My Dear Bee

March 9, 1945
France

In the last installment, I think I closed rather abruptly due to a journey impending. Now that I am back again, I shall try and relate some of the observations, though I warn you at the outset that one requires a strong stomach to read these lines, much less see the things described in their actual physical being.

I was told by some French friends that there existed in this general region one of the Nazi concentration camps, and though it was now in the hands of the French, it was almost impossible to gain admittance because it is now being used by them as an internment camp for internees and collaborators. However, being curious, I decided to take a chance of at least seeing the exterior, and so in company with a fellow officer, we started forth.

The day was cold and murky with a fine, misty rain falling, making visibility virtually zero. Yet as we journeyed down the valley road, the sun would strive to break through the heavy overcast, meeting with no success other than allowing an occasional interior when the atmosphere would assume a silvery brilliance that caused one to feel a strange sense of unreality. In the distance, one could hear the dull boom of the big guns as they pounded their missiles to and fro on the battle lines. 'Twas a gloomy, ghostly day, filled with all these atmospheric elements to form a perfect background for the horrible sight we were to witness.

For several miles, we traveled through a broad valley, the fields newly turned and a meandering narrow stream paralleling the roadway reminded one of the startling contrast that nature affords in the changing vistas of a few miles. For this setting was soon lost as we turned south into the mountains and began to climb the low-lying foothills leading to the higher peaks in the distance.

Through small communities and villages, consisting of a few homes and the always dominating, lofty spire of an ancient church, the road wound around through the hills in ever-increasing gradients. And as we neared the higher peaks, one could sight an occasional blanket of snow on steep, fir-studded crests, and too, the cold became more intense as the elevation increased. For ever an hour, we traveled through such a landscape, then dipping sharply into a long, narrow valley, the fields interlaced with narrow drainage ditches leading into the large stream flowing down its center, like a great artery fed by countless veins, we rounded a sharp turn and suddenly entered our destination.

Upon arrival there, however, we learned that the camp was actually located on the top of the mountain, overlooking the village, so upon ascertaining the route, there we proceeded. As we began the steep, circuitous climb, we stopped to pick up a young French soldier who was walking to the very place we were going. The road was amazingly smooth and of excellent surface as well as a masterpiece of highway engineering.

I ruefully remarked that I presumed the camp prisoners had been made to create this road, whereupon the Frenchman told us that such was the case as he had been a former internee there. He told us his story as we climbed ever upward into the mists and clouds that soon became so dense, one could see only a few hundred yards. It seems that his home was only a few miles from the camp, and being suspected of membership in the *Maquis*, he was seized by the Germans and made to work in the construction of the camp. For several months, he was forced to break rock in the quarry, along with many others—Polish, Russians, Czechs, Slavs, Belgians, French and Norwegians.

Arising at 4 a.m., they were marched from their makeshift shelters to the quarry, where they toiled 'til 10 p.m. Finally, in desperation, he and two Russians made a break and successfully escaped. They made their way through Germany and eventually reached Russia, where they joined up with the Russian counterpart of the *Maquis* and fought the hated enemy. In two years, he was wounded five times as he worked with this organization, which operated inside the German lines and German-held territory. Then, when the news of the American liberation of his homeland reached him, he made his way once more across the breadth of Germany, back to his home. *Now he is one of the guards.* As most of the guards are of similar background, I am confident that the prisoners now held are being watched very carefully.

We finally reached the entrance to the camp after a climb of over 4,000 feet. There, high in the mountainside, inaccessible and removed from all civilization, lies *Stalag IX*. We left our car at the base of the camp and proceeded on foot up to the main HQ, which is located about 1,000 feet above the entrance. The snow was well over a foot in depth, and the thick, forbidding atmosphere gave one a sense of uneasiness.

I asked the guard to direct me to the commandant, and after a brief interrogation as to who I was, he led me into a well-built, nicely furnished and comfortably warmed house, and into the quarters of this officer. I introduced myself and told him that I had heard of this establishment and was keenly desirous of seeing it. He told me that it was absolutely prohibited to all visitors, except those who possessed official passes, and these could be secured only through highest official French Army channels.

I showed my disappointment and expressed my ignorance of this formality, as I had come a great distance to see the place. Too, I was departing from this general area very soon, and therefore would be unable to make application through the proper channels. I also told him that my interest was more than mere curiosity, as I had been in most intimate contact with the Germans for several years, and related a brief history of my combat experiences in Africa, Sicily, France and Germany.

He showed great interest in me after this, and graciously said that in view of these circumstances, he was willing to make an exception. And further, as my French is not too good, he would have the camp doctor act as a guide for me, as the medic could speak English. I thanked him profusely for his generosity and offered him a cigarette while we waited for an orderly to take us to the doctor. He expressed his appreciation of American cigarettes, and as I had several packs with me, I gave him three, whereupon I rose 1,000 percent in his estimation.

In a few moments, the orderly appeared, and we followed him up the mountainside to a building marked "*Infirmerie.*" I digress here a moment to say that the side of the mountain was very steep, so in constructing the camp, the Germans cut this into a series of terraces, upon which were built the various barracks and other buildings used in the operation of the camp. One could ascend from the bottom to the top on either winding paths or concrete steps. Reaching the *Infirmerie*, we stood inside the hallway while the orderly searched for the doctor.

While awaiting his coming, a door opened and a very attractive girl came out of one of the rooms and in perfect English, inquired of us if we were waiting for someone. Though startled by this bit of English, I replied that we were waiting for the doctor. I then asked how she had learned to speak English so well, whereupon she replied that she had lived in New Jersey for ten years, from the age of six to sixteen, and knew much about America. This gave me much to think about, but soon after this brief exchange, the young doctor arrived.

He was only twenty-six and a very exuberant personality, apparently overjoyed at the opportunity to show us around and to practice his English. Though far from perfect, it was much more understandable than my French, as he told us about his college days in Portsmouth, England, and that he had studied languages. He proudly asserted that he could carry on a fair conversation in English, German, Polish, Russian, and of course, French. Indeed, he required this attribute, as there were many holdovers in the camp that were of these nationalities.

Now, this building was situated with two or three others in what can be termed the outer portion of the camp, and it was here that the SS guards and camp operators lived, as well as where they were cared for medically—Naturally none of the prisoners enjoyed any medical treatment, as you will see as I continue. They were well-constructed, comfortably furnished and attractively decorated, and divided into rooms equipped with lavatory, water-closet and good substantial furniture. Also reposing in each room was the picture of *Der Fuhrer*, as well as countless pictures of nude females assuming various poses. This, however, is universal in every previously occupied German billet I have seen, so it was not unusual. So it was, that we began our inspection with the knowledge that the Germans were very well housed in this tragic spot.

From these buildings, we made our way to the entrance of the inner camp, wherein lies the story. Surrounded with an electrically-charged, fifteen-foot barbed wire fence, guarded at each corner with a towered cupola, fitted with powerful searchlights and containing guards armed with machine guns and automatic rifles, one felt the utter futility that must have gripped those who entered this gruesome spot. A word to the guard and we passed through a small gate, only wide enough to admit one person, and we proceeded down the roadway a few hundred yards to a spot that our guide informed us as being the center of this portion of the camp.

Though the immediate buildings were visible to us, owing to the thick, murky fog, one could discern that each was uniform

236

to the other—simply four walls with a roof—to house these nameless souls. We were told that the capacity of the camp was set up to handle three thousand people, but during the last year, the Germans often had double that number squeezed into the narrow confines. Just to the left of where we were standing were located two gallows—one smaller than the other—one for men and one for women. Like evil reminders of the bestiality of man, these two structures stood silhouetted in the gloom as silent witnesses of criminal atrocity. Here, he said, were murdered the Poles, Russians and Czechs.

We passed these and descended four terraces, barracks on either side, 'til we came to a building somewhat removed from the rest of the camp. Here was the workshop of these fiends who fostered this Hell Hole. We went around to the rear of this building on a path that led to a descending stone stairway that opened into a tiny concrete room, about twelve feet square, situated underneath the center of the structure. Here, the SS guard stood with pistol in hand, and as the victim started down the steps, he shot him in the back of his head. Then, as the body pitched forward into the room, another guard rolled the body over to the side where a stretcher-like lift was constructed, and just above, on the next floor, the body was removed from this elevator and placed on another flat, iron stretcher and with this, by means of long, iron handles, was shoved into the boiler-like oven of cremation.

The terrible thing to me was the fact that in the door to this oven was a glass aperture, through which these sadists could gloat, as the body slowly dissolved to ashes. Often, they didn't even bother to kill them first, but placed them in while still alive! On the evil day of September 23, 1944, one German SS Master Sergeant stood at the head of the steps and shot ninety-six men and women before he finally went mad. Two days later, he too, was shot.

All these scenes were visible to the poor, helpless creatures, as they stood in line, awaiting their turn. Though every effort was made to keep the victims silent, their screams resounded throughout the countryside and were heard several miles away by the natives. God knows what horror that day must have wrought. Only French and Belgians were accorded this method of destruction.

In a room adjacent to the crematorium were found clay urns and metal urns and small fireproof discs that were numbered.

In typical German fashion, letters were sent to relatives, stating their loved one had died, and for the sum of one hundred marks, they could receive the ashes in a nice clay urn—and for 250 marks, they could have a very nice metal container!

On down the hall, where bodies were laid when business was too great, rooms for those who awaited the basest of all rooms, the vivisection chamber, where in the interest of "science," these devil-spawned fiends committed acts beyond description! This is no untruth, for the records are intact, for the Germans left in such a hurry, they didn't have time to dispose of them.

We went out of this part of the building and around to the front or forward part, where were located the torture rooms. A small, eight-foot square room with steel bars suspended parallel to the ceiling, with iron hooks on them. In the left hand corner, a five- or six-inch air vent, through which hot air was emitted into the room on the naked bodies of humans, suspended head down from the ceiling. Of course, it was very bad if one of the victims died during this treatment, and some thoughtless guards were shot when such a thing occurred.

As they were revived, they were taken then to the whipping room, where, on a table with wrists clamped to the legs of the table, they were beaten into insensibility. They were rendered conscious by being placed in alternating iced cold water and very hot water. The doctor stated that one survived only a single experience like this in few instances. Of course, if he did, it was merely repeated!

Fortunately, my time was about up, and rather than continue any further, I expressed the fact that I had to start back to my station. But as we were going out, he pointed to the high fence that encircles the camp and related how a young Russian prisoner had escaped from the camp last summer by pole-vaulting over the fence with the aid of a pole he had secreted in the camp. Of course, he didn't get very far, because in addition to the immediate guards and defenses, the Nazis had dogs and men patrolling several miles on all sides of the camp.

He was caught soon after this miraculous feat and returned to the post commander. This cruel beast made quite a lot over the Russian, and with much palaver, praised the victim's daring, as well as physical prowess. He then told him that he, too, was a sportsman, and if the Russian cared to try it again, he would allow him to do so and if successful, would grant him his freedom.

Sure enough, the prisoner vaulted over the fence, but like all Germans, the commander had placed two guards at nearby points—and without notifying them of his bargain with the Russian. He was shot as he landed!

The one thing that is comforting to me is a complete roster of all those formerly connected with this camp is on record, and eventually, justice will be meted out to them. The records reveal over 15,000 people were murdered in this camp! And when we realize that this was actually one of the smaller ones, it is not difficult to recognize the terrible, horrible, hideous magnitude of the scale these creatures have tortured and murdered. I can only say that there will be many repercussions in the years to come!

So ends this story. It's one of the unforgettable experiences I've ever had, and perhaps more gory than one would care to envisage, but it gives you an idea of what has been going on over here in a forceful manner few things could equal. Though I know war in all its bitterest forms, I found even my jaded senses shocked at this House of Horror. So in case you have anyone say these are old wives tales, just show them this letter—that should convince them. Promise you I won't be quite so curious next time!

Shortly before the end of the European war, Dawson left Paris and drove to the border of Germany and Czechoslovakia to see his battle comrades in G Company. En route, he passed through the village of Dachau, where again he witnessed what he later termed, "a monument to man's inhumanity to man." The unspeakable stench of death, the terrifying walking skeletons, the ground strewn with the remains of the dead burned into his brain, never to be forgotten.

Nothing he had experienced in three years of combat surpassed the horror of the extermination camps. Both of the camps he had visited provided vivid reminders that "uncontrolled hate, hatred, evil hate" could reduce rational people to beasts. Dachau, particularly, illustrated the most hideous expression of hate to befall mankind.[6]

Dawson to My Dear Family

April 5, 1945
Paris

Just a few lines to say I am well and now back from the front. The news gives you the picture of events quite clearly, and it is now approaching the final round. I can begin to feel a great deal of optimism after visiting the front from the south to the north, and everywhere, I find things going well. I am now stationed here so will give you the rear echelon version as I continue my residence. So far it's been pleasant, though frankly, I miss the close and intimate friendships that I formed when I was up front.

Inasmuch as I have been touring so much, I am just now receiving my mail for the past six weeks. It's good to know that all of you are well. The latest document is from Donna, with the letter enclosure from the captain concerning Roy. I am planning to go up there in the next few days if I can secure transportation. This is the critical item at the moment, but I'm trying to pass some wires to get a jeep. In all events, I'll get up there.

Easter Sunday was lovely here in Paris, and I must confess a twang in the heart because of my feelings that day. I arose early that morning and took the subway *to Notre Dame*, where sunrise services were held. Indeed, it was a most significant affair, and I felt much the better for it. Though, my dear ones, my attendance is rather irregular, I still hold firm to my basic faith that is inherent within my heart. So don't worry about that.

The lovely ceremony, Monday, when the French Army was reconstituted by De Gaulle, was most impressive in the *Place de la Concorde,* as was the relighting of the *Arc de Triumphe* [sic] Sunday night. Though they have suffered defeat in the past, and much apathy is demonstrated toward their present status, the French state manages to "put up a front" that is really amazing at times. Needless to say, it will prove most interesting in the next few months at the elections, when they decide what sort of France is to their desires in the years to come.

I'm as glad Matt got to come home for a brief spell. Apparently, Beatrice just missed him when she was at St. Augustine, for she called him at the hospital only to learn he had come to Texas. Too bad, however I hope he will follow through on my recommendations to try and improve his lot.

I'm scratching this note just before I go out to Versailles, so forgive the brevity. Will do better when time permits.

One month after he wrote his final letter, the Allies celebrated V-E Day. The greatest war in history was over. No longer assigned to deploy in the Pacific, Joe Dawson was going home.

Epilogue

I will not be there as Joe Dawson. I am a symbol of all those veterans.

Like millions of other veterans, Joe Dawson returned home from the war and began a new career as far removed from the battle field as possible. In Dawson's case, home was his beloved Corpus Christi, Texas. He did his best to put the horrors of war behind him, seldom talking about the war except when former G Company soldiers visited their old company commander.

He officially retired from the U.S. Army in 1946, but he remained active in the Army Reserve. He was appointed commander of the 2nd Battalion, 142nd Infantry Regiment of the 35th Division, holding the rank of lieutenant colonel before resigning his commission in 1948.

Having already received his college degree in 1933, Dawson did not take advantage of the GI Bill. Rather, he returned to Ren-War Oil Company as the assistant to the CEO from 1945 to 1951, when he resigned to become an independent oil operator.

In October 1945, he met vivacious Melba Bruno, whom he married the following February. Together, they raised two daughters. The family moved from Corpus Christi to Denver, Colorado, in 1953, where they lived until 1963, at which time they returned to Texas. Corpus Christi became the home base for Dawson Oil. Joe Dawson managed his enterprise until the final months of his life. According to his daughter, Dawson Oil remained a profitable enterprise due in no small part to her father's reputation as a "classic wildcatter and a hell of a geologist."

The former commanding officer of G Company also channeled his energies toward civil service in his adopted community of Corpus Christi. The list seemed endless. Dawson served on the City Council from 1947 to 1949, and later as chairman of the Civil Service Commission. In addition, he was a member of the City Arts Commission, the chairman of the Corpus Christi Red Cross, the chairman of the Corpus Christi Heart Association, and president of the Reserve Officers Association of Corpus Christi. Later, he served as vice chairman of the University of Corpus Christi, and remained in the forefront of the

241

city's effort to obtain Ward Island for the university, when it moved from Beeville, Texas. The school is now Texas A&M University–Corpus Christi. In short, Dawson led a full life, devoted to professional pursuits and service to the city of Corpus Christi.

When Congress decided to commemorate the fiftieth anniversary of World War II, a special committee decided that the capstone event would occur in Normandy, France, on June 6, 1994. Politicians and veterans from eighteen nations would participate in the ceremonies marking what historian Stephen Ambrose called "the climactic battle of World War II."

Retired Major General Albert H. Smith Jr., himself a veteran of Omaha Beach, was serving as an unpaid consultant to the secretary of the army. When asked to suggest a nominee who could introduce the president of the United States, he immediately replied, "Joseph T. Dawson, hero of Omaha Beach, is your man." Smith's recommendation was readily accepted.[1]

Not surprisingly Dawson was humbled, and once again he feared that he might not measure up to the task at hand. Cancer had already begun exacting its deadly toll. In and out of sessions of chemotherapy, he had had a hard year in 1993. Would he be able to make the trip? How should he introduce the commander-in-chief? He decided to accept the invitation and go to Normandy, but not for himself. As he told his community, "I will not be there as Joe Dawson. I am a symbol of all those veterans."

For the next several months, Dawson worked feverishly on his remarks, and in June 1994, he traveled to Normandy, accompanied by his wife, Melba, and daughter Roslyn. At 1700 hours, fifty years after that pivotal day on Omaha Beach, President Bill Clinton arrived at the Normandy American Cemetery near Colleville-sur-Mer.

Gathered before him were more than 6,000 veterans from the Allied nations who prosecuted the war. Also present were 9,386 American dead, arrayed in row upon row in the cemetery, as well as the names of 1,557 servicemen and women missing in action in the region but whose remains had not been recovered or positively identified. Walter Cronkite, who had accompanied President Dwight D. Eisenhower to Normandy on the twentieth anniversary, spoke first. Shortly thereafter, the chairman of the Joint Chiefs of Staff introduced Captain Joe Dawson.

Prior to introducing President Clinton, Dawson paid homage to the participants, living and dead, who so nobly advanced the Allied cause. "Today," he said, "this battlefield has been transformed into a sanctuary that will stand forever for those who gave their lives for our country. Where in all the world can one find a more fitting tribute than the magnificent bronze 'Spirit of Freedom' figure that immortalizes forever the men of D-Day? I cannot tell you what it means to me to stand on this spot."[2] With tears in his eyes, Dawson remembered the carnage and the sacrifice of American boys on the beaches below. Returning to the scene of that most special of all days, he said:

> In the face of crisis, men rise above themselves to accomplish great things. Here, on this hallowed ground, is where the battle was joined. What better examples of courage and bravery were ever displayed than by the men of the assault elements of the 16th Infantry Regiment of the 1st Division, and the men of the 116th Infantry Regiment of the 29th Division, who were our comrades here on Omaha Beach, June the sixth, 1944.
>
> I cannot tell you what it means to me to stand on this spot, where the path we took led us to where we are today. Where we landed, at 0700 on the beach below, was total chaos. Men lay dead or dying, and the equipment and wreckage of battle was choking the shoreline. I recall how I was overwhelmed with a feeling of anger and hate, and I knew we had to get to the enemy before we were destroyed.
>
> Suddenly, I saw a path, blocked with obstacles and obviously mined, leading toward the crest of this bluff that dominated the beach. Upon clearing the minefield, we swiftly moved to engage the enemy entrenched here on the crest. By sheer luck, or perhaps by fate, we found the opening that became the first penetration of the enemy. The path that we cleared became the route for our comrades to follow and was the only exit off the beach until later that day.
>
> We are here to recognize and pay homage to those who shaped the course of history. Only one who holds the highest office in the land can express to the world the pride and gratitude of our nation to you, the men of D-Day.
>
> And so, on behalf of the soldiers of my company and all other army warriors who stormed these beaches and bluffs; and on behalf of our Navy, Coast Guard and Air Force comrades who fought with us and for us on D-Day fifty years ago; and, finally, on behalf of all men and women who served their country in World War II, it is my special privilege and great honor to present the President of the United States.[3]

President William Jefferson Clinton then rose to address the gathering. His first words were, "Mr. Dawson, you did your men proud today." And proud Dawson was, just as he had taken immense pride in what G Company had accomplished on that beach fifty years earlier.

Nineteen ninety-four also brought one final tribute by a grateful U.S. Army to the former infantry commander. In late summer, the Officer Candidate School at Fort Benning, Georgia, inducted Joe Dawson into the OCS Hall of Fame. It had been fifty-two years since Dawson had graduated from the course that launched his military career. Present at the ceremony was the secretary of defense, who read remarks drafted by Maj. Gen. Albert Smith. The secretary described the carnage of Omaha, and noted that the tangle of beach obstructions delayed, damaged, or destroyed many of the landing craft, while continuous heavy fire from blockhouses, bunkers, trenches, and machine-gun nests claimed a devastating toll on the troops who landed in the first wave.

Perhaps 50 percent of the soldiers of the assault infantry companies were casualties within minutes of debarking into chest-deep water. There was one notable, important exception. With luck, a good beach landing, and—most importantly—courageous, battle-hardened leadership, G Company, 2nd Battalion, 16th Infantry, penetrated German defenses in the Easy Red sector. Led by Dawson, the company fought its way to the top of the bluffs, eliminating enemy machine gunners and riflemen blocking the route inland.

It was a familiar story, but Dawson once again shed tears at the memories of so many brave veterans who remained on the beach. As he had done at the ceremony in June, he accepted the induction to the Hall of Fame with his characteristic humility.[4]

In the final years of his life, Joe Dawson dedicated himself to civic affairs. And Corpus Christi remembered its favorite son. On Sunday, September 14, 1997, the Corpus Christi Independent School District dedicated the Joseph T. Dawson Elementary School in his honor. Not surprising, the school adopted the name "Dawson's Patriots" to honor its namesake. The school selected red, white, and blue as its official colors, and "Where Stars Earn Their Stripes" as its motto.

Fifty-three years to the day that he directed G Company to entrench on the ridge that forever bears his name, he sat silently as speaker after speaker paid tribute to Captain Joe Dawson. Once again, Dawson was humbled by the experience. And once again, Dawson spoke eloquently, reminding the audience that teachers "challenge the mind, fix the hopes and dreams of lives yet to unfold. We entrust our greatest treasures to them, and I know these treasures are in safe and caring hands." The remarks were typically Dawson—no mention of personal achievement, just a dedication to make the school a hallmark of educational excellence.

"I don't deserve it," he remarked, "but it's very sweet. I love this city, and I've loved everybody in it. I'm deeply proud that they see fit to do it. That's the thing that makes it so tremendously moving to me is the fact that I'll be a part of the heritage of this city. I appreciate it more than I can say."

On November 28, 1998, Joseph Turner Dawson died from complications of cancer in the city that he loved. On December 12, the family held a memorial service in his honor in the sanctuary of the First Baptist Church, Corpus Christi. In attendance were old friends and comrades, as well as soldiers from the 1st Infantry Division. The congregation joined in and sang the "Battle Hymn of the Republic," a song that would have thrilled the captain.

Mourners then heard a grandson trumpet "Taps," the warrior's farewell to a fallen comrade. Somewhere in the distance, across the decades and on a ridge outside Aachen, seven rifles simultaneously cracked; their echo reverberating beyond the hills and among the tombstones on the bluff overlooking Omaha Beach. Then all was still. Captain Joe Dawson had finally come home and joined his beloved company in eternal rest.

Postscript

I first met Joe Dawson in June 1998. We had corresponded for four years, but had never seemed to be able to get together. I wanted the captain to come to West Point to address the Corps of Cadets on leadership under fire. He was quite naturally willing to come, but he was always too ill to travel. "No problem," I said, "I'll come to Corpus Christi."

Then in mid-May 1998, I received a phone call late one evening. "I've lost my beloved Melba, and I don't know if I can go on. Will you come to Texas and see me?" I tried to reassure him, but my words proved inadequate, as would any words on such an occasion. I flew to Corpus Christi and went outside to hail a cab. Sure enough, there was Joe. We spent two days together discussing leadership and what qualities make a successful commander.

He gave me his wartime letters, upon which I commented that a constant theme appeared to be "measuring up." I inquired as to what he meant by that term and he responded, "I was not even aware of that. It was certainly an unconscious thought. What I was asking myself was, 'Do I measure up to my own standard?' I have always set high goals. If I measured up to them, I'm over the hill."

When he was finished, I felt I had a pretty good grasp of the warrior ethos from Dawson's perspective. Yet, I wanted to know more about Joe Dawson, the man, so I asked him to reconcile Captain Dawson of the Big Red One with the kindly gentleman sitting across from me in his office.

"You have to understand this," he told me, "Joe Dawson, the soldier, is not Joe Dawson, the man. If I couldn't learn to make that separation, I'd have gone crazy by now. Battle is battle. When someone is trying to kill you, you don't think about one being more dangerous than another. North Africa and Sicily had prepared me for command. D-Day was just a job to me."[5]

I then asked a final question: "How would you like to be remembered?"

"As a leader," he responded without a moment's hesitation. And that's how I remember Joe Dawson—a leader who measured up to the crucible of combat at Omaha Beach and Dawson's Ridge, and who always found time for his friends and his community.

Notes

Chapter 1

1. See Christopher Gabel, *The U.S. Army GHQ Maneuvers of 1941* (Washington, D.C.: Center of Military History, 1991), 18, for a synopsis of the mobilization training program (MTP).
2. By the content, Dawson wrote this letter on May 16 or 17, 1941.
3. Kitchen Police, one of the more onerous duties in which every soldier participates.
4. Noncommissioned officers, the traditional backbone of the Army.
5. Probably May 21.
6. Private First Class, the rank immediately below that of the lowest grade noncommissioned officer.
7. Charles A. Lindbergh, the famous aviator, was an avowed non-interventionist.
8. Marshall was an exception to the West Point clique that dominated the Army's senior command. A 1901 graduate of the Virginia Military Institute, he entered military service in 1902. Following a stellar career in World War I, he served as General of the Armies John J. Pershing's military aide immediately after the war. Subsequent service as Assistant Commandant of the Infantry School and his work with the Civilian Conservation Corps marked Marshall as one of the most brilliant and politically astute officers in the Army. He was promoted to Brigadier General in 1936, served as Deputy Army chief of staff for two years, and assumed his duties as Army chief of staff on September 1, 1939, the day Hitler invaded Poland.
9. As quoted in Peter Mansoor, *The GI Offensive in Europe: The Triumph of American Infantry Divisions, 1941–1945* (Lawrence: University Press of Kansas), 19.
10. Letter, General Lesley McNair to all Army commanders, September 8, 1941, subject: Complaints from Soldiers, as quoted in Kent Roberts Greenfield and Robert R. Palmer, *Origins of the Army Ground Forces: GHQ, United States Army, 1940–42* (Washington, D.C.: Government Printing Office, 1946), 47.
11. McNair was a 1904 graduate of the U.S. Military Academy. An artilleryman who served with Pershing on the Mexican border and on his GHQ staff in World War I, he was appointed by Marshall as chief of staff of GHQ, with primary responsibility for training every American soldier in the U.S. Army in World War II. As commander of Army Ground Forces, he designed the Texas-Louisiana maneuvers of August–September 1941.
12. Gabel, *The GHQ Maneuvers*, 193.
13. In his memoirs, Bradley listed the founding of the Fort Benning OCS as his greatest contribution to the mobilization effort. The school eventually produced thousands of junior officers who filled the infantry ranks in Europe and the Pacific. Omar Bradley and Clay Blair, *A General's Life* (New York: Simon & Schuster, 1983, 97.

14. See Robert R. Palmer et al., *The Army Ground Forces: The Procurement and Training of Ground Combat Troops* (Washington, D.C.: Government Printing Office, 1948), 328–29, for selection criteria.
15. Dawson is referring to the low pay that characterized the American military establishment.
16. As the American army rapidly expanded, many senior officers in reserve units lacked sufficient training in basic infantry skills. Consequently, Army chief of staff Marshall insisted that officers attend a refresher course to acquaint themselves with current doctrine.
17. Palmer, *The Procurement and Training of Ground Combat Forces*, 108.
18. Ibid., 109, 344–45.
19. The 1st Infantry Division achieved a number of firsts in World War I—first to arrive in France; first to see action at the front; first to fire at the enemy and to suffer casualties; and first to be cited in general orders. See Office of the Theater Historian European Theater, *Order of Battle United States Army World War II, ETO, Divisions* (Paris: HQ: United States Forces European Theater, 1945), 1.
20. Then as now, Texas A&M University at College Station, Texas, was one of the premier ROTC institutions in the country.
21. Peter R. Mansoor, *The GI Offensive in Europe*, 52.
22. Field Marshal Sir John Dill was former Chief of the Imperial Staff for the British Army. Assigned to Washington in late 1941, he was Winston Churchill's personal military representative in the American capital and the British officer whom Marshall most admired. When Dill died in 1944, Marshall obtained congressional authorization for Dill to be interred at Arlington National Cemetery, the only foreigner so honored.
23. As quoted in Larry I. Bland and Sharon Ritenour Stevens, ed., *The Papers of George C. Marshall*, III (Baltimore: The Johns Hopkins Press, 1991), 286.
24. A member of the Officers' Reserve Corps, Roosevelt returned to active duty in April 1941 as the colonel commanding the Twenty-Sixth Infantry Regiment of the First Division. Recommended for promotion to brigadier general by General Lesley J. McNair, his nomination was approved by Marshall and forwarded to President Roosevelt, who in turn submitted the proposed promotion list to the Senate for approval on December 15, 1941.
25. Rick Atkinson, *An Army at Dawn* (New York: Henry Holt, 2002), 82.
26. Letter, Marshall to Allen, dated June 5, 1942, as quoted in Bland and Stevens, *The Papers of GCM*, II, 224.
27. Letter, Marshall to Allen, dated July 30, 1942, Ibid., 286.
28. Stanhope Brasfield Mason, *Reminiscences and Anecdotes of World War II*, unpublished manuscript dated 1988, 2, on file at the Robert R. McCormick Research Center, Cantigny.
29. Division G-3 is the Assistant Chief of Staff for Operations at the Division or higher level of command.
30. See "The Story of the Embarkation of the 1st Infantry Division" in file folder N-6172, Combined Arms Research Library; Fort Leavenworth, Kansas. Hereafter cited as CARL.
31. The 16th Regiment's Second Battalion had deployed to England the first week of July and moved to Tidworth Barracks to prepare a camp for the remainder of the regiment.
32. Sailing aboard the *Queen Mary* were 671 officers, thirty-six warrant officers,

14,321 enlisted men and four civilians. Of the personnel aboard ship, all but one officer, twelve enlisted men and four civilians belonged to the 1st Infantry Division.

Chapter 2

1. Mansoor, *The GI Offensive in Europe*, 53.
2. Dwight D. Eisenhower, *Crusade in Europe* (New York: Doubleday & Company, 1948), 53.
3. Eisenhower arrived in England on June 24 and assumed command of the European Theater of Operations, United States Army (ETOUSA), which then comprised of only the United Kingdom and Iceland. His command consisted of 55,390 officers and men. Accompanying Eisenhower was Major General Mark Clark, who initially served as commander of II (US) Corps, to which the 1st Division was eventually assigned.
4. Eisenhower to Marshall, August 9, 1942, as quoted in Alfred D. Chandler Jr. et al., *The Papers of Dwight David Eisenhower, The War Years*, I (Baltimore: The Johns Hopkins Press, 1970), 453. Hereafter cited as *The Papers of DDE*. Eisenhower directed General Clark to relinquish command of II Corps and to serve as his deputy in charge of planning. Ike's new command for TORCH was activated on September 12, 1942, as Allied Force Headquarters, though the headquarters had existed as soon as the Combined Chiefs of Staff approved its creation on August 24.
5. Memorandum, TORCH Operation, G-3 Report, dated November 24, 1942; R-11272, CARL.
6. The vast majority of the soldiers in the 1st Infantry Division were from the Atlantic seaboard, with a disproportionate number from New York, New Jersey, and Pennsylvania. Only later in the war when individual replacements arrived to offset casualties did the 1st Division acquire a truly national flavor.
7. On August 19, 1942, a combined British-Canadian force, accompanied by fifty U.S. Rangers, landed on the coast of France at the port city of Dieppe. The raid was the brainchild of Lord Louis Mountbatten's Combined Operations headquarters and was designed to test amphibious tactics and techniques in a large-scale operation. The raid was an unmitigated tactical disaster, costing the Allies 3,600 casualties of 6,100 men engaged. On the strategic level, however, the Dieppe raid provided invaluable experience in the planning and execution of amphibious operations.
8. Wife of Brigadier General Teddy Roosevelt Jr., assistant commanding general of the 1st Infantry Division.
9. Great Britain's Royal Air Force
10. Dawson was referring to the Battle of Britain in August-September 1940, when the RAF alone stood against Hitler's *Luftwaffe* and prevented a German invasion of England.
11. V-mail was an acronym for victory mail. In addition to regular mail that arrived to and from England by ship or plane, army postal authorities requested that at least two of every three letters be sent by V-mail, a process by which letters were photocopied and reproduced on reels, which were then sent to the States where the process was reversed. V-mail saved a considerable amount of valuable space, and could not be lost even if the plane carrying the shipment crashed. The mail could easily be re-filmed and sent again. Officers routinely censored

all mail from the enlisted men to prevent the disclosure of any information that might be useful to the enemy. See *The Stars and Stripes*, June 4, 1943. All *The Stars and Stripes* columns are from the London Edition unless otherwise noted.

12. Nelson was the greatest sailor in the history of the Royal Navy. His victory over the combined French-Spanish fleet at Trafalgar in 1805 confirmed England's superiority of the seas. Field Marshal Sir Archibald Wavell was a British Army officer who served as Commander-in-Chief Middle East Command during part of the Western Desert Campaigns and was later Viceroy of India.

13. Dawson acted as his own censor.

14. Eisenhower to Marshall, October 20, 1942, quoted in *The Papers of DDE*, I, 626–27.

Chapter 3

1. For the Army's official history of the Mediterranean Theater of Operations, see George F. Howe, *Northwest Africa: Seizing the Initiative in the West* (Washington, D.C.: Government Printing Office, 1985).

2. As quoted in H. R. Knickerbocker et al., *Danger Forward: The Story of the First Division in World War II* (Washington, D.C.: Society of the First Division, 1947), 34.

3. See Terry Allen's *Combat Operations of the 1st Infantry Division During World War II*, a factual summary of the Division's combat operations in North Africa and Sicily, 7. Hereafter cited as *Combat Operations of the BRO*.

4. Dawson interview conducted by Lieutenant Colonel John Votaw, April 16, 1991, 10–11, on file at the McCormick Research Center.

5. Battle casualties sustained by the 1st Division from November 8–11 were eighty-five killed, 221 wounded, and seven missing. Total casualties sustained by the Allied Forces in the Algerian-French Moroccan Campaign during the same period were 530 killed, 887 wounded, and fifty-two missing. Howe, *Northwest Africa*, 173.

6. Dawson would have to wait until August 1943, about ten more months, to receive command of a rifle company.

7. As quoted in Martin Blumenson, *The Patton Papers, 1940–1945*, 144. Patton and Allen had long been friends dating to the days when both played polo. Patton and Allen were among fifty-two colonels nominated by President Roosevelt for promotion to the grade of Brigadier General. The Senate confirmed both promotions on October 1, 1940, prompting Patton to write, "The Army has certainly gone to hell when both of us are made [promoted]. I guess we must be in for some serious fighting and we are the ones who can lead the way to hell with[out] too much thinking." Blumenson, *The Patton Papers*, 13.

8. Military lingo for the "nuthouse."

9. Major Gaskell was an officer serving on the 1st Division staff.

10. *Generaloberst* Juergen von Arnim commanded the Fifth Panzer Army in Tunisia. He arrived in Tunis on December 8, 1942, and assumed command the following day. The Axis strategy was to operate as aggressively in Tunisia as resources permitted, and then deliver to von Arnim enough forces and logistical support to strike boldly into French North Africa. Howe, *Northwest Africa*, 326. Rommel was now concentrated in Tripoli, repeatedly urging a fighting withdrawal to Tunis.

11. Eisenhower reported to the Combined Chiefs of Staff that losses were approximately one hundred medium tanks, thirty field guns, and 260 vehicles. See

Eisenhower to CCS and British Chiefs of Staff, Cable 2160, dated February 21, 1943. Chandler, *The Papers of DDE*, II, 973.

12. In assessing Fredendall's leadership in the battle, Eisenhower informed Marshall that the II Corps commander was "tops" in every aspect of generalship except one thing. He had difficulty picking good men and, even worse, in getting the best from his subordinates; in other words, in handling personnel. After Ike relieved him on March 5, Fredendall returned to the United States "without prejudice" and became deputy commander of the Second Army at Memphis, Tenn. In June 1943, he assumed command of the Second Army.

13. Shorty was Joe's older brother Leighton. Leighton was also known as L. B.

14. Alexander assumed command of 18th Army Group on February 20, 1943, consisting of the Allied First Army and the British Eighth Army. In reorganizing Allied ground forces, he concurred with Ike's suggestion that the 1st Infantry Division be reassembled as quickly as possible and permitted to function as a separate entity. Elements of the Big Red One had been on loan to the French XIX Corps.

15. See Howe, *Northwest Africa*, 543, 563 and Chandler, *The Papers of DDE*, II, 1013.

16. Atkinson, *An Army at Dawn*, 438

17. Rommel departed Africa on March 9, never to return. He repeatedly lobbied Hitler to evacuate North Africa, as continued resistance was futile in the wake of increasing Allied reinforcements. Such efforts proved futile as the *Fuhrer* remained determined to defend the African continent until the last man.

18. This is the battle of El Guettar immortalized in the movie starring George C. Scott.

19. Allen, *Combat Operations of the BRO*, 25

20. As quoted in David Nichols, ed., *Ernie's War: The Best of Ernie Pyle's World War II Dispatches* (New York: Simon & Schuster), 104.

21. Eisenhower's and the soldier's letter are quoted in Atkinson's *An Army at Dawn*, 443–44.

22. II Corps now operated as a separate autonomous command responsible to Alexander. The troop list included the 1st, 9th, and 34th Infantry Divisions and the 1st Armored Division.

23. Official casualties for the U.S. forces in the Tunisian campaign from November 12, 1942, to May 13, 1943, were 18,221, including 2,715 killed, 8,978 wounded, and 6,528 missing. 1st Infantry Division casualties totaled 3,916, of whom 634 were killed, 2,585 were wounded, and 697 were missing. Overall Allied casualties numbered 70,341. Howe, *Northwest Africa*, 675.

24. On December 6, 1915, *Punch* published anonymously a poem entitled "In Flanders Fields." Written by a Canadian medical officer, John McCrae, during the Second Battle of Ypres, it became the most famous poem of World War I.

25. Dawson was referring to the battle at Kasserine Pass.

26. General Hideki Tojo was Japan's political and military leader during the greater part of World War II, as prime minister from 1941–44, and as army minister from 1940–44; Benito Mussolini the dictator of Fascist Italy. The name of the inventor of Spam is fortunately lost to history.

27. Back home referred to Oran, where the 1st Division closed on May 19, 1943, and immediately began preparations for the invasion of Sicily.

28. Captain Alex Schenck, a friend of the Dawsons, was an officer from Waco, Texas.

29. Mason, *Reminiscences and Anecdotes of World War II*, 2.
30. As quoted in Jeffers, *Theodore Roosevelt Jr.,* p 224.
31. Dawson interview by John Votaw, April 16, 1991.
32. As quoted by Lieutenant Colonel Derrill M. Daniel, "Landings at Oran, Gela and Omaha Beaches: An Infantry Battalion Commander's Observations, N-16759-3, 11, CARL.
33. Harmon's observations are found his "Notes on Combat Experience During the Tunisian and African Campaigns," undated, 10–11. Copy in possession of the author and on file at the Military History Institute, Carlisle Barracks, Pa.
34. 1st Infantry Division Report of Operations, 15 January to 8 April 1943, dated 17 April 1943 in Historical Documents World War II, 1st Inf Div-Invasion of North Africa and Campaign in Tunis, 16–17, in Microfilm Box 318, Item 15121, Combined Arms Research Library (CARL) Fort Leavenworth, Kansas.

Chapter 4

1. Albert Garland and Howard McGaw Smyth, *Sicily and the Surrender of Italy* (Washington, D.C.: Government Printing Office, 1963), 11.
2. Ibid., 52–53.
3. Major General Troy H. Middleton, who had been the youngest regimental commander in the American Army in World War I, commanded the 45th Infantry Division; Major General Hugh J. Gaffey, Patton's former chief of staff in II Corps, commanded the 2nd Armored Division; and Major General Manton S. Eddy, who had fought brilliantly in North Africa in the fight to seize Hill 609, commanded the follow-up 9th Division. Two other commanders, Major General Lucian Truscott of the 3rd Infantry Division and Matthew Ridgway of the 82nd Airborne Division, were rapidly emerging as superb commanders, though only Truscott had commanded a division in combat, having assumed command of the 3rd Division on March 8, 1943.
4. In early April, *Time* magazine quoted a remark attributed to Patton, disparaging American soldiers. Allen took Patton to task for the alleged comment, prompting Patton to write a "Dear Terry" letter on May 1, in which he excused Allen's confrontation by assuming that he must have been "very tired" to believe that he [Patton] would ever make such a remark about the American GI. Blumenson, *The Patton Papers, 1940–1945*, 249, 251.
5. "Terry Allen and the First Division in North Africa and Sicily," author unknown. Original document is in the Terry Allen Papers, "1st Div & 104th Div. Plus Miscellaneous" box, Military History Institute, Carlisle Barracks, Pa.
6. Major General Paul Conrath commanded the Hermann Goering Division. In anticipation of the invasion, he had assembled the division in the vicinity of Caltagirone, roughly twenty-five miles from the disembarkation beaches of the two U.S. divisions. Thus, he was in a perfect location to counterattack.
7. As quoted in Garland and Smyth, *Sicily and the Surrender of Italy,* 174.
8. See Atkinson, *An Army at Dawn*, 518–19, for a discussion of Allen's encounter with Eisenhower and Bradley following the attack.
9. Blumenson, *Patton Papers*, 263, 271–72.
10. Gerald F. Linderman, *The World Within War* (New York: The Free Press, 1997), 118.
11. Bradley gives his account of the battle of Troina and his subsequent decision to relieve Allen in Bradley, *A General's Life*, 210–11.

12. As quoted in John W. Baumgartner et al., *The 16th Infantry Regiment 1861–1946* (Du Quoin, Illinois: Cricket Press,1999) , 59.

13. Allen, *Combat Operations of the Big Red One*, 43.

14. Bradley, *A General's Life*, 195.

15. Replacing Roosevelt was Brigadier General Willard G. Wyman.

16. Letter, Allen to Major General Harold K. Johnson, May 11, 1962; as cited in "A Summary of the El Guettar Offensive During the North African Campaign with special reference to The Offensive Drive & Night Attacks," N-3901.3, CARL. See also N-3901.5, "A Summary of the Sicily Campaign with special reference to The Continued Offensive & Night Attacks," CARL.

17. Omar Bradley, *A Soldier's Story* (New York: Henry Holt & Company, 1951), 154–55.

18. As quoted in Atkinson, *An Army at Dawn*, 520.

19. Bradley, *A General's Life*, 171

20. As reported in Mason, *Reminiscences and Anecdotes of World War II*, 91.

21. Blumenson, *The Patton Papers 1940–45*, 303. Eisenhower was quite cognizant of the perception that Allen had been relieved for inefficiency. In a brief reply to a letter from Allen, Ike wrote, "I am certain that after you have had your well-deserved rest from the battlefront, your experience and courage will command your assignment to equally if not more important duty." Chandler, *The Papers of DDE*, III, 1597. Allen later returned to the European Theater and commanded the 104th Infantry "Timberwolf" Division with his customary efficiency. Teddy Roosevelt Jr., was initially assigned to Allied Army Group Command and later returned to duty with the 4th Infantry Division for the invasion of Normandy. He was awarded the Congressional Medal of Honor for heroism at Utah Beach on D-Day, and later suffered a fatal heart attack on the eve of assuming command of the 90th Infantry Division in July 1944.

22. Letter, Quentin Reynolds to Mrs. Terry Allen, June 20, 1944, Terry de la Mesa Allen Papers, USAMHI, Carlisle Barracks, Pennsylvania. Quoted in Mansoor, *The GI Offensive in Europe*, 53.

23. Major General Clarence Huebner enlisted in the army in 1910 and was commissioned in the infantry in 1916. A veteran of the 1st Infantry Division, he served in the Big Red One in every rank from Private to Colonel. During World War I, he was a company commander and served at Luneville, Beaumont, Cantigny, and in the Aisne-Marne. He was twice wounded and received the DSC with cluster, the DSM, and Silver Star. Huebner also served several tours on the General Staff and was known as a strict disciplinarian, exactly the type of officer Bradley wanted to bring the 1st Division back into line.

24. Dawson is referring to the Battle of Troina. Casualties had been severe enough that following the battle, Bradley passed Manton S. Eddy's 9th Division through the 1st Division, thus terminating the Big Red One's combat tour in the Mediterranean Theater.

25. As quoted in Mansoor, *The GI Offensive in Europe*, 106.

26. Charles MacDonald, *Company Commander* (Washington: Infantry Journal Press, 1947), 6, 153.

27. Greenfield et al., *The Organization of Ground Combat Troops*, 300–301.

28. Major General Terry Allen received the Distinguished Service Medal for commanding the Big Red One in the campaign of North Africa. Rather than receiving the Congressional Medal of Honor for Sicily, he received another command, which he led with distinction in the Rhine campaign of 1945.

29. Dawson's two brothers.
30. Garland and Smyth, *Sicily and the Surrender of Italy*, 417 and Knickerbocker et al. *The Story of the First Division*, 147
31. During the first week of September, Pyle left Sicily and flew to the United States via North Africa for a short vacation. As he informed his readers, he was "just too tired in the head." He had been too close to the war for too long. Rather than "writing unconscious distortions and unwarranted pessimisms when you get too tired," he decided that a leave of absence would rekindle his spirits. He didn't stay long. In late November 1943, he was again on the job, this time in Italy where he remained until May 1944.

Chapter 5

1. Bradley, *A Soldier's Story*, 236–37. In the original American plan, two infantry divisions, the 29th and the 4th, were selected to spearhead the invasion. Unfortunately, neither had combat experience, and Bradley found that worrisome. Consequently, he substituted the Big Red One for the Omaha assault, and placed the 29th Division under General Huebner's operational control for D-Day only. He then added Teddy Roosevelt Jr., to the 4th Division in the hope that his presence with the assaulting forces would be an inspiration.
2. Eisenhower to Marshall, February 9, 1944, quoted in Chandler, *The Papers of DDE*, IV, 1716.
3. Throughout the war, particularly in the early stages, the government pursued an active policy of censoring mail to ensure military secrets were not inadvertently disclosed to the enemy. The transfer of the 1st Infantry Division from the Mediterranean to England for the forthcoming invasion was a significant piece of information.
4. Dawson was referring to Syracuse, the scene of the climactic campaign in the Peloponnesian War (431–404 B.C.) between Athens and the allies of Sparta.
5. Doc was a family friend who lived in Texas.
6. *Time* correspondent John Hersey accompanied Wozenski in the attack on one of the hills outside Nicosia in the early days of the Sicilian campaign. He featured Wozenski in an article entitled, "The Hills of Nicosia," in the August 9, 1943, issue. *Time*'s cover story was devoted to General Terry Allen of the Big Red One.
7. Donna was Joe's youngest sister. She married Roy Booch and gave birth to a daughter in the spring of 1944. Joe was determined to meet his brother-in-law in England, but he was unable to establish contact with Roy, who was a bombardier-navigator in the Eighth Air Force.
8. See *First United States Army Report of Operations 20 October 1943–1 August 1944*, undated, 18–20, for a summary of First Army Training directives. Report was unclassified on June 23, 1945.
9. Interview with the author. Dawson shared similar perspectives in an oral interview conducted by John Votaw, the director of the First Infantry Museum at Cantigny, Ill., on April 16, 1991.
10. As quoted in Nigel Hamilton, *Monty: Master of the Battlefield* (New York: McGraw Hill, 1983), 509.
11. History of Co. E, 2nd Battalion, 16th Infantry Regiment in 301-Inf (16) 9-0.1, Historical Records of the First Infantry Division, NA RG 319.
12. Ike discusses the importance of morale in *Crusade in Europe*, 238.
13. Linderman, *The War Within War*, 330.

14. Ambrose notes there were thousands of ordinary criminals in the ETO. Many were caught and tried by courts-martial and sentenced to the stockade, or, in cases of severe crimes, sentenced to death by firing squad. Sixty-five soldiers were ordered shot, but Eisenhower commuted sixteen to life imprisonment. Only one deserter, Private Eddie Slovik, went through the entire process from confession to court-martial to sentence to execution by firing squad. See Stephen E. Ambrose, *Citizen Soldiers* (New York: Simon & Schuster, 1997), 342–43.
15. Anti-aircraft fire.
16. Dawson celebrated his thirtieth birthday on March 20.
17. Exercise TIGER resulted in one of the greatest tragedies of the war, when two German E-boat flotillas attacked one of the convoys, sinking two LSTs and damaging a third. About 700 men lost their lives in an event that remained classified for several decades after the war.
18. Gordon A. Harrison, *Cross-Channel Attack* (Washington, D.C.: Government Printing Office, 1950), 270.
19. Derrill M. Daniel, "Landings at Oran, Gela and Omaha Beaches," 21–22, N-16759-3, CARL.
20. Harrison, *Cross-Channel Attack*, 270. See also Eisenhower, *Crusade in Europe*, 238.

Chapter 6

1. See Baumgartner, *The 16th Infantry 1861–1946*, 74–77, for the 16th Regiment's plan for the invasion. See also the 16th Combat Team, Invasion of France, S-3 Combat Report, 6, Historical Documents of World War II, 1st Infantry Division-Northern France Campaign, Microfilm Box 401, CARL. Hereafter cited as S-3 Combat Report.
2. As quoted in Nichols, *Ernie's War*, 276.
3. Company clerk Larry Krumanocker compiled the assault rosters that are on file at the Robert R. McCormick Research Center.
4. Dawson's records do not indicate Lange's first name.
5. History of Company G, 16th Infantry, from 6 June–7 June 1944, dated June 15, 1944, in Historical Records of the First Infantry Division and its Organic Elements, National Archives, RG 319.
6. Wozenski compiled a "chronological listing of events, action and circumstances surrounding the landing of E Company" immediately after the battle. Copy is in 16th Infantry Regimental Reports, Box 147, reel 3.24, 301-INF (16)- 1.6, RG 319, McCormick Research Center. See also S-3 Combat Report, 1–3, CARL.
7. For the best account of Dawson on D-Day, see Stephen E. Ambrose, *D-Day: The Climatic Battle* (New York: Simon & Schuster, 1994), 355–57.
8. The survivors of G Company were interviewed on August 22, 1944, at Ferte la Mace. Copy of the interview is in 16th Infantry Regimental Reports, Box 147, RG 319.
9. Monthly strength figures for Company G are on file in Box 147, Reel 3.24, 301-INF (16)-1.6. RG 319. Microfilm is on file at the McCormick Research Center.
10. See Dawson's oral history at the Eisenhower Center in New Orleans.
11. Tatara received the Silver Star with cluster for his heroism on D-Day. He had received his first Silver Star in Sicily and later earned the Distinguished Service Cross in the fighting around Aachen. Peszek also received the Silver Star, but was later killed in action.

12. Spaulding received the Distinguished Service Cross for heroism in action.

13. Veterans generally disagree as to which company-size unit was first to reach the summit of the bluffs overlooking Easy Red. Not surprisingly, there is considerable speculation within the 1st Division as to who deserves the honor of first reaching the summit, and many of Dawson's contemporaries credit their own units with this distinction. Historian Ambrose states categorically that Dawson's Company G was the first. This is not to say that other officers did not reach the summit prior to Dawson, but Dawson was able to bring the majority of his command to the summit and then deploy for subsequent operations.

14. In the Navy's defense, they were operating under orders to fire on Colleville at H + 60 minutes, or as soon thereafter as visibility permitted.

15. By D + 1, the entire 16th RCT was ashore, but losses had been horrendous. The regiment had suffered 971 casualties, including thirty-six officers and 935 enlisted men. G Company casualties ranged from forty-nine to sixty-three, depending on the source.

16. Phil Caputo, *A Rumor of War* (New York: Ballantine Books, 1977), 127.

17. MacDonald discusses similar perceptions and fears in *Company Commander*, 49.

18. Correspondent Don Whitehead of the Associated Press was first to write Dawson's story, which later appeared in Washington's *The Evening Star*, July 12, 1944, B-8.

19. Dawson was referring to his wounds sustained at Colleville-sur-Mer.

20. Dawson's reference to the Germans.

21. Quoted in Nichols, *Ernie's War*, 277-79.

22. Dawson's escapade of going AWOL to return to G Company captured more publicity than he cared to have. An all-points-bulletin for his arrest was posted in England, but his reemergence in Normandy led to dropping all charges against him.

23. See Ambrose's *Citizen Soldiers*, 311-30, for numerous tributes by American GIs to the medics, nurses, and doctors of the European Theater.

24. As quoted in Tobin, *Ernie Pyle's War*, 185.

25. *First U.S. Army Report of Operation*, 121-22.

26. As quoted in Nichols, *Ernie's War*, 293.

27. As quoted in Baumgartner, *16th Infantry Regiment*, 119.

28. Ernie Pyle remained America's most beloved war correspondent. He covered the First Infantry Division in North Africa, Sicily, and Normandy. It was Pyle who "discovered" Omar Bradley and labeled him the "GI's General." At Bradley's insistence, Pyle returned home in September 1944, suffering from battle fatigue. The war, however, was never far from his mind. He participated in the invasion of Okinawa on April 1, 1945, and was killed in action in the assault of Ie Shima. The inscription on his marker in the 77th Division's cemetery read: "At this spot, the 77th Infantry Division lost a buddy, Ernie Pyle, 18 April 1945." He is now interred in the National Cemetery of the Pacific in the Punchbowl outside Honolulu, Hawaii.

29. The American VII Corps under Major General J. Lawton Collins severed the Cotentin peninsula on June 18, and reached the outskirts of Cherbourg on the 20th. Following a week of intense fighting, the German garrison capitulated on June 27. Prior to surrendering, the garrison damaged the port facilities so badly that it took the engineers six weeks to repair the port. In the interim, Allied supplies came across the beaches and through the Mulberry artificial harbor at

Arromanches. The American Mulberry at Omaha Beach was destroyed by the Channel storm during the third week of June.

30. In addition to Dawson, the DSC awardees included Brigadier General Willard Wyman, Colonel George Taylor, Lieutenant Colonel Herbert Hicks, Major Charles Tetgmeyer, Captains Kimball Richmond, Thomas Marendino, and Victor Briggs, and Lieutenants Carl Giles and John Spaulding, 1st Sergeant Lawrence Fitzsimmons, Staff Sergeants Curtis Colwell, Philip Clark, David Radford, James Wells, and Kenneth Peterson, Tech Sergeants Raymond Strojny and Philip Streczyk, Sergeants Richard Gallagher and John Griffin, T/4 Stanley Appleby, and Private First Class Peter Cavaliere. Colonel William Waters and Master Sergeant Chester Demich received the Legion of Merit. See *The Stars and Stripes,* July 5, 1944, 1, 4.

31. Copy of the citation is in Joseph T. Dawson World War II Letters, on file at the McCormick Research Center.

32. A copy of the War Department Distinguished Unit Citation is in Box 147, reel 3.24, 301-INF (16)-1.6 Historical Records of the 1st Infantry Division on file at the McCormick Research Center. Regimental citations seldom listed subordinate units by name, but Dawson's company had opened the breach.

33. In the days of the Roman Empire, the Praetorian Guard was a select military command charged with protecting the emperor. Its commander reported directly to the emperor for orders and was not responsible to any other political or military official.

34. As reported by Associated Press correspondent Don Whitehead in "Normandy: As I Saw It" in H. R. Knickerbocker et al., Danger Forward, 217–19. Story also appeared in the July 5, 1944, edition of *The Stars and Stripes.* See also ETO, Press Release Number 1969, dated July 4, 1944.

35. The "highest command" refers to Ike.

36. Jones had fought at Guadalcanal and understood war from the ground up. His later works included *The Thin Red Line, WWII, The Pistol, Whistle,* and *From Here to Eternity.* Jones's description is quoted in Linderman, *The World Within War,* 252.

37. Karas received a battlefield commission in North Africa and earned the DSC at Gela, Sicily. He was wounded in action outside Colleville-sur-Mer when a German machine pistol bullet shattered his helmet visor, sending a small fragment into his eye.

38. Lieutenant Kenneth Bleau also received the Purple Heart as results of wounds incurred on July 13. He was later killed in action by friendly fire on August 1, 1944, outside St. Lo. Baldridge received the Bronze Star Medal for actions on D-Day.

39. Earlier in the day, Dawson received word of the attempted assassination of Hitler by a group of German officers. The plot failed and a number of senior commanders, including Field Marshal Erwin Rommel, were killed or forced to commit suicide.

40. *The Stars and Stripes* (London), August 28; September 4; September 7, 1944.

41. By all accounts, Wozenski was one of the 1st Infantry Division's most outstanding rifle company commanders. At the end of the war, he was a Lieutenant Colonel, commanding the Third Battalion, 16th Infantry Regiment. His numerous decorations included the DSC with cluster, and Silver Star with cluster. Stanley Karas was Dawson's company executive officer.

Chapter 7

1. Charles MacDonald, *The Siegfried Line Campaign* (Washington, D.C.: Government Printing Office, 1984), 6–7.
2. Roy was the husband of Dawson's sister, Donna. He was shot down over the Continent and officially missing in action since July 8.
3. Paris was liberated on August 25.
4. Pyle's columns appeared in *The Stars and Stripes,* August 31 and September 1, 1944.
5. For gallantry in action at Ile-de-France on August 28, Dawson received the Silver Star. See HQ, 1st Infantry Division, General Orders No. 139, dated December 6, 1944.
6. A maquis is a member of the French Resistance.
7. This was Dawson's initial visit to the City of Light. Despite his close call with the sentry, he was determined to return to Paris under more favorable circumstances.
8. This is the incident that Sergeant Ed Tatara, who exploded the bangalore torpedo under the wire at Omaha Beach, said confirmed Dawson's status as an exceptional company commander. When Tatara's platoon was pinned down by enemy fire, the platoon sergeant told his platoon leader to call the company commander for assistance. Dawson arrived with two tanks and rescued the platoon.
9. Mason, *Reminiscences and Anecdotes of World War II,* 206.
10. Headquarters, 1st Infantry Division, "The Mons Pocket," R-3901.2, 1–5, CARL.
11. Colonel S. L. A. Marshall, the SHAEF Theater Historian, recommended that the 1st Division be awarded a Distinguished Unit Citation for its victory at the Mons pocket. Eisenhower disagreed, stating that although the Supreme Commander thought the operations were commendable, he did not feel that they met the criteria for a Distinguished Unit Citation.
12. As quoted in G-3 Report of Operations, dated October 5, 1944, 56, in Historical Documents World War II, 1st Infantry Division-Northern France Campaign, Microfilm Box 401, Item 1951, CARL.
13. Mason, *Reminiscences and Anecdotes of World War II,* 207–8.
14. The number of divisions mobilized for World War II and the number that saw combat is not only subject to speculation, but it is an accountant's nightmare. According to retired Army Colonel William T. Bowers, there were actually ninety-one—ninety-two if the Philippine Division is counted, although it went out of business in early 1942 with the fall of the Philippine Islands—divisions mobilized for war, although only eighty-nine were maintained at combat strength in 1945. The 2nd Cavalry Division was inactivated twice, the last time in the period February–May 1944. See the Army's official history written by Robert R. Palmer, Bell I. Wiley, and William R. Keast, *The Procurement and Training of Ground Combat Troops* (Washington, D.C.: Government Printing Office, 1948), 489–93, for a list of World War II divisions, minus the Philippine Division, with their dates of activation. This table lists ninety-one units activated with the 2nd Cavalry counted twice. The author's figures indicate that eighty-nine divisions saw combat in World War II, ninety if the Philippine Division is included, a figure echoed by Peter Mansoor, *The GI Offensive in Europe,* 10.
15. Linderman, *The World Within War,* 44–46.
16. Leighton Dawson, Joe's older brother.

17. Dawson's DSC is now in the possession of his daughter, Roslyn.
18. *The Stars and Stripes*, Continental (Paris) Edition, November 15, 1944.
19. Cornelius Ryan, *A Bridge Too Far* (New York: Simon and Schuster, 1974), 59.
20. The strongest portion of the line was the segment along the Saar River, between the Moselle and the Rhine. This area was in Patton's Third Army zone and the scene of some of the bitterest fighting of the European war.
21. MacDonald, *The Siegfried Line Campaign*, 29.
22. By summer 1944, the West Wall was as much of an illusion as Hitler's Atlantic Wall. Construction had begun in 1936, after Hitler had sent German troops into the demilitarized Rhineland. Work began in earnest two years later, but after four years of neglect, it was something of a Potemkin village. See MacDonald, *The Siegfried Line Campaign*, 30–31.

Chapter 8

1. Russell F. Weigley gives a detailed analysis of the Allied plan of attack in *Eisenhower's Lieutenants* (Bloomington, Indiana: Indiana University Press, 1981), 356–59.
2. A copy of Dawson's attack order is on file at the McCormick Research Center.
3. Headquarters, 1st Infantry Division, "Report of Breaching the Siegfried Line and the Capture of Aachen," dated November 7, 1944; R-3901.1, 4, CARL.
4. Reporter W. C. Heinz of the *New York Sun* recorded the saga of Dawson's company in a series of stories that appeared in the Fort Worth *Star-Telegram*. Copies of the October 22, 23, and 31 reports are on file at the McCormick Research Center.
5. Dawson was writing to his sister, Donna, who still hoped to receive definitive word on her husband's whereabouts.
6. Susanna was Roy and Donna's daughter.
7. This was Dawson's second wound, the first having occurred on D-Day.
8. Dawson's casualties in the advance to the German frontier were relatively light. Casualties in August numbered two killed and nine wounded. During the initial German attack against the ridge, however, he lost seventeen men killed and wounded, roughly 10 percent of his total force, according to G Company strength reports.
9. Telephone interview with Lieutenant Eugene A. Day, conducted by Andrew Woods, April 30, 1999. Transcript on file at the McCormick Research Center. Day was Dawson's executive officer at Aachen. During Dawson's brief absence at the aid station, Day assumed command of the company. He was later awarded the Silver Star for action at Aachen on September 17.
10. Memorandum from Headquarters 16th Infantry, Subject: Historical Records, dated October 3, 1944; 3 in Historical Documents of World War II, Microfilm Box 401, 1st Infantry Division—Northern France Campaign, Item 1951, CARL.
11. E. B. Sledge, *With the Old Breed at Peleliu and Okinawa* (New York: Oxford University Press, 1981), 125.
12. An acquaintance Dawson knew prior to his deployment overseas in August 1942.
13. What became known as Crucifix Hill was approximately 1,000 yards from the ridge where G and I Companies were entrenched. If "Dawson's Ridge" reflected the heroism of the 16th Infantry Regiment, Crucifix Hill emerged as one of the sterling examples of the courage of Dawson's sister regiment, the 18th Infantry.

14. Mason, *Reminiscences and Anecdotes of World War II*, 228–29.
15. Both Dawson and correspondent W. C. Heinz identify this unit as the 3rd SS Panzer Grenadier Division. The official U.S. Army history of the Siegfried Line Campaign written by Charles MacDonald, however, states that the enemy unit was the "3rd Panzer Grenadier Division."
16. As quoted in Baumgartner, *16th Infantry Regiment*, 165–72.
17. In November, Lieutenant Colonel Walter H. Grant assumed command of the 2nd Battalion.
18. Sledge, *With the Old Breed*, 143.
19. Interview with the author, June 4, 1998.
20. Transcripts of Gordon Fraser's radio broadcasts are on file at the McCormick Research Center.
21. W. C. Heinz later published his columns on Joe Dawson in *When We Were One: Stories of World War II* (Massachusetts: Da Capo Press, 2002), 33–51. Citations here are from the initial newspaper accounts. Following the war, Dawson and Heinz exchanged occasional telephone calls and correspondence until Dawson's death in 1998.
22. Ambrose, *Citizen Soldiers*, 149–53.
23. Twenty years after the war, Heinz returned to Eilendorf and found Dawson's command post. He spoke to the owner of the house and reminisced about the week he spent in her basement. Heinz's reminiscences are featured in the *Saturday Evening Post*, December 12, 1964. Quotes by Dawson come from either Heinz's or Fraser's accounts of the action on Dawson's Ridge.
24. Cuff survived the war, but Mullen was later killed in action.
25. As quoted in "Battle of Germany (West)," *Time*, October 30, 1944, 23.
26. Company casualty reports as reflected in the 16th Regimental returns are far lower than what Dawson himself remembered, because Dawson included all units attached to his command, whereas the regimental records referred only to those soldiers assigned to G Company.
27. Copy of the complete citation is in Baumgartner, *16th Infantry*, 174–75.
28. MacDonald, *The Siegfried Line Campaign*, 293. MacDonald incorrectly lists Dawson as a battalion commander with the rank of Lieutenant Colonel.
29. Interview with the author, June 4, 1998.
30. Lieutenant Johnson was Dawson's artillery forward observer. He was evacuated for wounds early in the battle, but followed G Company's progress by the newspapers.
31. George Wilson, *If You Survive* (Canada: Ivy Books, 1987), 168, 173.
32. Sledge, *With the Old Breed*, 157.
33. As quoted in Nichols, *Ernie's War*, 357.
34. Stephen Ambrose, *Band of Brothers* (New York: Simon & Schuster, 1992), 206.

Chapter 9

1. Gibb had succeeded Colonel George Taylor as the 16th Regiment's commanding officer on July 19, 1944, when Taylor was promoted to Assistant Commanding General of the 4th Infantry Division. Taylor later returned to the 1st Division as its Assistant Commanding General in October 1944. Gibb had previously served as G-3 of the 1st Infantry Division.
2. William J. Donovan was chief of the Office of Strategic Services, the forerunner of the Central Intelligence Agency. Created by executive order 9182 on June 13, 1942,

the OSS was responsible for covert propaganda, foreign intelligence and unorthodox warfare. Over the course of the war, Donovon built an organization of more than 30,000 men and women. They operated under "the direction and supervision of the Joint Chiefs of Staff to collect and analyze information, and to plan and operate special services taken to enforce our will upon the enemy by means other than military action."

3. Captain John Finke had previously commanded F Company, 16th Infantry, at Omaha Beach. Like Dawson, he was one of the premier combat commanders in the 1st Infantry Division.

4. Though he received a subsequent promotion in the Reserves, Dawson always remained the "Captain," a rank that he associated with service with G Company.

5. Locating his sister's husband became an obsession to Dawson, but it was two months before he could obtain any definitive information. The search for Roy had a tragic conclusion. It became Dawson's unenviable task to escort Roy's remains back to the United States.

6. In an address commemorating Armed Forces Day on May 19, 1995, Dawson discussed his experience at Dachau. He compared the expression of mindless hate to the Oklahoma City bombing that had occurred during the previous month, in which hundreds were killed or permanently maimed.

Epilogue

1. As quoted in Smith's eulogy for the Joseph T. Dawson Memorial Service, December 12, 1998.

2. Yale Youngblood, "D-Day Revisited," *The Baylor Line*, Fall 1994, 49.

3. An autographed copy of Dawson's remarks is on file at the McCormick Research Center.

4. Draft introductory remarks are located with the 3rd Battalion, 11th Infantry, Officer Candidate School at Fort Benning. Dawson's folder includes unit citations, personal records, and photographs. His induction number to the OCS Hall of Fame is 1664.

5. Interview with the author, May 31, 1998.

Selected Bibliography

Primary Sources

Combined Arms Research Library, Fort Leavenworth, Kansas
Historical Documents, World War II, 1st Infantry Division (Microfilm), Boxes 318, 401
N 3901.3 Summary of the El Guettar Offensive (Mar 20–Apr 6, 1943)
N 3901.4-2 Summary of the Final Drive on Tunis
N 3901.5 Summary of the Sicily Campaign
N 6172 The Story of the Embarkation of the 1st Infantry Division
N 7371 Alert Order #1, March 27, 1944
N 12030 After-Action Report, G-4 Section, 1st Infantry Division, June 1944–May 1945
N 16759-3 Landings at Oran, Gela and Omaha Beaches
R 3901.1 & 2 Breaching the Siegfried Line and the Capture of Aachen—1st Infantry Division
R 11272 TORCH Operation-G-3 Report

National Archives of the United States, Washington, D.C.
Records Group 319, Historical Records of the First Infantry Division and Its Organic Elements, World War II 1940–1945; from the Collection of World War II Organization and Operational Records Assembled by the Army Adjutant General's Office
Records Group 407, Army Adjutant General Decimal File 1940–45

Robert R. McCormick Research Center, 1st Infantry Division Museum, Cantigny, Illinois
Dawson, Joseph T., World War II Letters
Mason, Stanhope Brasfield, Reminiscences and Anecdotes of World War II

United States Military Academy, West Point, New York
Allen, Terry. Combat Operations of the First Infantry Division in World War II, undated.
First United States Army, Report of Operations 20 October 1943–1 August 1944; 1 August 1944–22 February 1945.

History of the Office of Censorship. University Publications of America microfilm. Reels 1–3.

Office of the Theater Historian, Order of Battle of the United States Army World War II: European Theater of Operations, Divisions. Paris, France, 1945.

Published Primary Sources

Bland, Larry I., and Sharon Ritenour Stevens, eds. *The Papers of George Catlett Marshall.* Baltimore: The Johns Hopkins Press, 1991.

Bradley, Omar. *A Soldier's Story.* New York: Henry Holt & Company, 1951.

Bradley, Omar, and Clair Blair. *A General's Life.* New York: Simon & Schuster, 1983.

Chandler, Alfred D., Jr., et al., eds. *The Papers of Dwight D. Eisenhower: The War Years.* Baltimore: The Johns Hopkins Press, 1970.

Eisenhower, Dwight D. *Crusade in Europe.* New York: Doubleday & Company, 1948.

MacDonald, Charles B. *Company Commander.* Washington: Infantry Journal Press, 1947.

Sledge, E. B. *With the Old Breed at Peleliu and Okinawa.* New York: Oxford University Press, 1981.

Wilson, George. *If You Survive.* New York: Ivy Books, 1987.

Secondary Sources

Ambrose, Stephen E. *Band of Brothers.* New York: Simon & Schuster, 1992.

——. *Citizen Soldiers.* New York: Simon & Schuster, 1997.

——. *D-Day: The Climatic Battle.* New York: Simon & Schuster, 1994.

Atkinson, Rick. *An Army at Dawn: The War in North Africa, 1942–1943.* New York: Henry Holt and Company, 2002.

Baumgartner, John W. et al. *The 16th Infantry 1861–1946.* Du Quoin, Illinois: Cricket Press, 1999.

Blumenson, Martin. *The Patton Papers, 1940–1945.* Boston: Houghton Mifflin Company, 1974.

Caputo, Phil. *A Rumor of War.* New York: Ballantine, 1977.

Gabel, Christopher. *The U.S. Army GHQ Maneuvers of 1941.* Washington, D.C.: Center of Military History, 1991.

Garland, Albert, and Howard McGaw Smyth. *Sicily and the Surrender of Italy.* Washington, D.C.: Government Printing Office, 1963.

Greenfield, Kent Roberts, and Robert R. Palmer. *Origins of the Army Ground Forces: General Headquarters United States Army, 1940–42.* Washington, D.C.: Government Printing Office, 1947.

Hamilton, Nigel. *Monty: Master of the Battlefield.* New York: McGraw Hill, 1983.

Harrison, Gordon A. *Cross-Channel Attack.* Washington, D.C.: Government Printing Office, 1984.

Hastings, Max. *Overlord: D-Day, June 6, 1944.* New York: Simon & Schuster, 1984.

Heinz, W. C. "After Twenty Years: The GI's War Fades Away." *Saturday Evening Post,* December 12, 1964. 22–40.

———. *When We Were One: Stories of World War II.* Massachusetts: Da Capo Press, 2002.

Howe, George F. *Northwest Africa: Seizing the Initiative in the West.* Washington, D.C.: Government Printing Office, 1985.

Jeffers, H. Paul. *Theodore Roosevelt, Jr.: The Life of a War Hero.* Novato, CA: Presidio Press, 2002.

Knickerbocker, H. R. et al. *Danger Forward: The Story of the First Division in World War II.* Washington, D.C.: Society of the First Division, 1947.

Linderman, Gerald F. *The World Within War.* New York: The Free Press, 1997.

MacDonald, Charles. *The Siegfried Line Campaign.* Washington, D.C.: Government Printing Office, 1984.

Mansoor, Peter R. *The GI Offensive in Europe: The Triumph of American Infantry Divisions, 1941–1945.* Lawrence: University Press of Kansas, 1999.

Nichols, David, ed. *Ernie's War: The Best of Ernie Pyle's World War II Dispatches.* New York: Simon & Schuster, 1986.

Palmer, Robert R. et al. *The Procurement and Training of Ground Combat Troops.* Washington, D.C.: Government Printing Office, 1948.

Ryan, Cornelius. *A Bridge Too Far.* New York: Simon & Schuster, 1974.

Tobin, James. *Ernie Pyle's War: America's Eyewitness to World War II.* New York: The Free Press, 1997.

Weigley, Russell F. *Eisenhower's Lieutenants.* Bloomington: Indiana University Press, 1981.

Youngblood, Yale. "D-Day Revisited." *The Baylor Line,* Fall 1994. 46–48.

Index

Leeds, Ray, 43
Leigh, Vivian, 35–36, 38
Licata, 90
Liege, 188
Linderman, Gerald, 96, 190
London, 29, 34–36, 125–26, 132–33, 137–38, 228–29
Longest Day, The (film), 169
Luftwaffe, 75, 94

MacDonald, Charles, 109
mail service, 37, 57, 59, 110, 249n11, 254n3
Malojoa, 28
Maquis, 234
Marbeuge-Liege-Aachen axis, 178
Marendino, Thomas, 257n30
Mareth Line, 69, 73
Marshall, George: and Allen, 24, 26–27; at Camp Blanding, 23; career of, 247n8; and decision to invade Sicily, 89; and Dill, 248n22; maneuvers of, 12; in Operation TORCH, 30; and promotion of Theodore Roosevelt, Jr., 248n24; responses to complaints, 7, 8; on selection of troops for D-Day, 119; on training of officers, 248n16
Marshall, S. L. A., 258n11
Mason, Stanhope Brasfield, 39, 86, 188
Matthews, Colonel, 102
Maubeuge, 178, 187–90
McCloskey General Hospital, 225–28
McNair, Lesley, 8, 9, 174, 247n11, 248n24
Messina, 102, 114
Metz-Kaiserslautern gap, 178
Middleton, Drew, 126, 215
Middleton, Troy, 102, 252n3
Mitchell, Arthur, 25
mobilization training program (MTP), 1
Mons, 187–90
Montague, Lieutenant, 102
Montgomery, Bernard L., 50, 69, 90, 102, 126
MOSSTROOPER, 48
Mountbatten, Lord Louis, 249n7
Mt. Etna, 110–11
Mullen, James, 217
Mussolini, Benito, 79–80, 97, 100

Nazi defeat, 173–74
Nelson, Lord, 38, 250n12
Nevada, 145
news media, 75–76, 84, 154, 162, 171, 206–7, 215–18
Niscemi, 95, 96, 115, 123
Normandy, 145–77; fiftieth anniversary of invasion, 242–45. *See also* D-Day; Omaha Beach
North Africa, 50–88; conclusion of campaign in, 74, 82–87; description of, 55–56, 60–61, 66; embarkation for, 49; preparation for landing in, 41. *See also* Operation TORCH; Tunisia

Office of Strategic Services (OSS), 225, 227–28
Omaha Beach: Americans landed on, 152; description of landing on, 147–49, 170; exercises for landing on, 137; schedule for landing on, 144–45; securing of, 158. *See also* D-Day; Normandy
Operation COBRA, 174–75
Operation HUSKY, 89–91, 102, 114–15. *See also* Sicily
Operation OVERLORD, 140, 146, 157–58
Operation TORCH, 29–30, 50–55. *See also* North Africa
Oran, 30, 50–52, 55–56, 85–86

Packard convertible, 192–94
Palermo, 97, 99
Panzer Division, 10th, 69
Panzer Grenadier Division, 3rd, 212–14, 221, 260n15
Paris, 180, 181, 184, 192, 226, 229–30, 240
Parris, John, 174
Patton, George: on 1st Division's attitude, 86; alleged disparaging remark of, 252n4; and Allen, 24, 95, 104–5, 250n7, 252n4; command of II U.S. Corps, 62; on entry into war, 56; in Operation COBRA, 175; in Operation HUSKY, 90, 114; in Operation TORCH, 50, 68–69; at Palermo, 97; and Ponte Olivo attack, 95

About the Author

Colonel Cole C. Kingseed, U.S. Army (Ret.) is a thirty-year Army veteran who commanded infantry units at the platoon, company, and battalion level. His last military assignment was chief of Military History at the U.S. Military Academy at West Point. A 1971 graduate of the University of Dayton, Ohio, Kingseed graduated from U.S. Naval War College in 1992 and holds a Ph.D. in history from The Ohio State University. He is the author of *Eisenhower and the Suez Crisis of 1956* and *The American Civil War* and is an assistant editor of the five-volume *The Encyclopedia of World War II*. Now retired from active military service, he is founder and president of Brecourt Leadership Experience, Inc., a leadership consulting firm that conducts leadership seminars at Gettysburg and Normandy.